12.95

TELLING GOD'S STORY

This book presents narrative theology as radically orthodox. It is orthodox because in the tradition of all those who maintain the priority of the story of Jesus, as it is sacramentally performed in the Church; and radical because it eschews all modern attempts to found Christian faith on some other story, such as that of reason, critical history or human consciousness. Acknowledging the indeterminacy and textuality of human existence, *Telling God's Story* presents the Christian life as a truly postmodern venture: the groundless enactment of God's 'future now'.

In the epilogue this book focuses on the Eucahrist as the sacramental site in which the story and body of Christ consumes and is consumed. Through this bodily telling and consumption the Church is enabled to receive again God's gift of return and to be the telling of God's story, once more.

John eats the book (Revelation 10.9–10); early fourteenth-century manuscript in the Cloisters Collection of the Metropolitan Museum of Art, New York (MS 68.174, fo. 16v).

TELLING GOD'S STORY

Bible, Church and Narrative Theology

GERARD LOUGHLIN

Senior Lecturer in Religious Studies
University of Newcastle upon Tyne

PUBLISHED BY THE PRESS SYNDICATE OF THE UNIVERSITY OF CAMBRIDGE
The Pitt Building, Trumpington Street, Cambridge, United Kingdom

CAMBRIDGE UNIVERSITY PRESS
The Edinburgh Building, Cambridge CB2 2RU, UK http://www.cup.cam.ac.uk
40 West 20th Street, New York, NY 10011–4211, USA http://www.cup.org
10 Stamford Road, Oakleigh, Melbourne 3166, Australia
Ruiz de Alarcón 13, 28014 Madrid, Spain

First published 1996
First paperback edition 1999

Printed in the United Kingdom at the University Press, Cambridge

A catalogue record for this book is available from the British Library

Library of Congress Cataloguing in Publication data
Loughlin, Gerard.
Telling God's story: Bible, church and narrative theology /
Gerard Loughlin.
p. cm.
Includes bibliographical references and index.
ISBN 0 521 43285 5 (hardback)
1. Storytelling – Religious aspects – Christianity. 2. Lindbeck,
George A. 3. Frei, Hans W. 4. Bible – Use. 5. Church. 6. Lord's
Supper. I. Title.
BT83.78.L.68 1996
230–dc20 96–13490 CIP

ISBN 0 521 43285 5 hardback
ISBN 0 521 66515 9 paperback

WD/CP

For my parents
Vincent and Frances

See, the home of God is among mortals.
Revelation 21.3

Contents

Preface

Fifteen years ago George Stroup wrote an impressive book on *The Promise of Narrative Theology*.[1] It sought to introduce and consolidate a way of doing theology that had emerged during the previous ten years. It also sought to suggest that narrative theology was not just another fad, soon to pass away as some predicted. It has not passed away. But perhaps it should have done so? Stanley Hauerwas – often cited as a narrative theologian – has written that 'one can be told once too often that "God made man because he loves stories."'[2] Hauerwas is concerned that narrative should not be thought a general theological category dominating all others, for 'Jesus is prior to story'.[3]

The present book seeks neither to make good on Stroup's promise nor to announce the passing of a theological fashion. This is because it understands narrative theology as one thematic among many, which at best emphasises what is presupposed in all theology. Not all theology need make the emphasis, but all theology should presuppose what a narrative

All biblical quotations are from the New Revised Standard Version of the Bible – *The New Oxford Annotated Bible*, edited by Bruce M. Metzger and Roland E. Murphy (New York: Oxford University Press, 1991).

1 George W. Stroup, *The Promise of Narrative Theology* (London: SCM Press [1981] 1984).

2 Stanley Hauerwas, 'The Church as God's new language', in *Scriptural Authority and Narrative Interpretation*, edited by Garret Green (Philadelphia: Fortress Press, 1987), pp. 179–98 (p. 188). Hauerwas is quoting Elie Wiesel, *The Gates of the Forest*, translated by Frances Frenaye (New York: Holt, Rinehart and Winston, 1966), p. xii.

3 Hauerwas, 'The Church as God's new language', p. 190.

theology emphasises: the priority of the story of Jesus Christ. Hauerwas continues his comment on the priority of Jesus by noting that 'Jesus' life and resurrection can be displayed only narratively'. He thus acknowledges an intimate connection between person and story; so intimate that it goes beyond prioritising one over the other. It is the *story of Jesus* that is prior to any narrative category or other conceptuality. Whatever the interest of some narrative theologians, the theology of the present book is a modest affair: it has no designs on theology in general. It merely seeks to remember that theology is the discipline of a practice which is first and last the following of a story: the life, death and resurrection of Jesus Christ.

Any theology that remembers the story is in part narrative or narrativist in character. Thus there are many theologies not usually so considered that are narrativist in this sense. While Hans Frei and behind him Karl Barth are obvious narrativist theologians, they stand in an ancient tradition that includes Augustine and Thomas Aquinas.[4] It is not possible to read either of the saints without becoming aware of how profoundly their theologies are written between the lines of Scripture and upon the story it tells. Thinking Augustine and Aquinas narrativist theologians can appear surprising only because not every writing or discourse that passes for theology remembers the story, or does so only at the last. If narrativist theology has a polemic – a design on other ways of doing theology – it is that theology has no foundation other than the community that tells the story by which it is told.

The prologue to the book (chapter 1) introduces the problematic of doing theology in the context of postmodernism, the late twentieth-century culture of the West that thinks itself at

[4] The present book is really no more than scribbling between the lines of Frei's essays, which are themselves written upon the pages of Barth's tomes. There is little mention of Karl Barth in the present book, as also of J. G. Hamann. Yet in another writing of the book they would be everywhere evident. See further George Hunsinger, *How to Read Karl Barth: The Shape of His Theology* (New York: Oxford University Press, 1991) and Isaiah Berlin, *The Magus of the North: J. G. Hamann and the Origins of Modern Irrationalism* (London: John Murray, 1993).

the end of history: the closure of the book. It distinguishes two forms of theological response to such a culture, nihilist textualism and orthodox narrativism. The chapters that follow are exercises in the latter.

The first part of the book (chapters 2 and 3) explores the idea of narrativist theology in the work of Hans Frei and George Lindbeck. It shows how the distinction between narrative and story (worked out through consideration of Gérard Genette's narratology) enables one to read the Bible as a single story that finds its focus in Jesus Christ. The larger argument moves from the idea of the Bible as consuming text to the consumption of the biblical text in the practice of the Church, establishing the mutual constitution of book and community as the context in which Jesus Christ makes himself known and available for faith.

The second part of the book (chapters 4 and 5) attends further to the intimacy of text and people in the Church's use of Scripture, defending the inspiration, historicity and truth of the biblical story as it is performed in the life of the Church. In the third part of the book (chapters 6 and 7) a number of dogmatic themes – Trinity, resurrection and salvation – are linked to the preceding chapters as examples of how a narrativist theology enfolds and unfolds doctrine within the telling of God's story. They are only examples or linkages and others could, perhaps should, have been made.[5] Christology is a submerged theme of these chapters.

The epilogue to the book (chapter 8) serves to focus its central themes in the Church's celebration of the Eucharist: the meal in which the one and the many are united, the Body and the Word with the bodies and words of the enstoried Church. The great theme of eucharistic theology – that the Eucharist makes the Church by which it is made – is paralleled in the teaching of narrativist theology: the

[5] In a longer study I would have indicated possible linkages between the Church's story and that of other religious traditions. See further J. A. DiNoia OP, *The Diversity of Religions: A Christian Perspective* (Washington DC: Catholic University of America Press, 1992) and Gavin D'Costa, 'Revelation and revelations: discerning God in other religions', *Modern Theology*, 10 (1994), 165–83.

scriptural story makes the Church by which it is made in the telling of the story.[6] But the two themes are closer yet, for the Eucharist is the telling of the story that is at the same time the telling of the Church as the very Body of Christ. Thus the epilogue is concerned with the question of transubstantiation – the mystery of the crucified and risen Christ in the gathered community – and concludes with the picture of John eating the book[7] as a figure for narrativist theology.

Some parts of the present book have appeared in other places, either orally or written, though all have been reshaped by their new context. Chapter 1 was 'At the end of the world: postmodernism and theology', in *Different Gospels*, second revised edition, edited by Andrew Walker (London: SPCK, 1993). Some parts of chapter 4 were given in a seminar paper at the Durham conference on Interpretation and Belief in 1989, subsequently published as 'Making it plain: Austin Farrer and the inspiration of Scripture', in *Hermeneutics, the Bible and Literary Criticism*, edited by Ann Loades and Michael McLain (London: Macmillan, 1992); while other parts of chapter 4 were given in a paper to the George Shrut Conference on Letterality and Literality (Sedh Boker, Israel 1993), subsequently appearing as 'Using Scripture: community and letterality', in *Words Remembered, Texts Renewed: Essays in Honour of John F. A. Sawyer*, edited by Jon Davies, Graham Harvey and Wilfred G. E. Watson (Sheffield: Sheffield Academic Press, 1995) and as 'Following to the letter: the literal use of Scripture', *Theology and Literature*, (1995). Parts of chapter 5 were given in papers to the Christian Philosophy Conference (Allen Hall, London 1994) and to the seminar of the Durham Centre for Theological Research (1994), as well as in a public lecture in the series 'The Word and the Spirit', organised by Terry Wright at the University of Newcastle upon Tyne in 1994. Other parts of chapter 5 were given in a seminar paper

6 See further Paul McPartlan, *The Eucharist Makes the Church: Henri de Lubac and John Zizioulas in Dialogue* (Edinburgh: T. and T. Clark, 1993).

7 Revelation 10.9–10.

at the Durham conference on the Rebirth of Tragedy in 1990. Parts of chapter 6 were given in a paper to the Trinity Seminar convened by Colin Gunton at the conference of the Society for the Study of Theology in Cambridge 1991, and published as 'Writing the Trinity', *Theology*, 97 (1994), 82–89; while parts of chapter 7 were given in seminar papers at the Society for the Study of Theology's annual conferences at Leeds in 1988 and at Soesterberg in the Netherlands in 1992, and in a paper to the Cumbria Theological Society in 1995. Parts of chapter 8 were given in papers to the British Sociological Association Conference on Religion and Postmodernity at Bristol in 1993 and to the Sacramental Spirituality Seminar convened by Ann Loades and David Brown at the Durham Centre for Theological Research in 1993.

Theologians are symbiotic parasites, living off others' toil. I could not have written the present book without the nourishment of many other labourers. The University of Newcastle upon Tyne provided both technical support and sabbatical leave for the writing of the book, and my colleagues in the Department of Religious Studies supported me throughout, in particular John Sawyer and Jon Davies. Among my many theological hosts, I recognise the work of five as particularly nourishing: Stanley Hauerwas, Nicholas Lash, John Milbank, Kenneth Surin and Rowan Williams. My book is unimaginable without theirs. However, the theologian with whom I have most often dined, who has been my most constant critic, is Gavin D'Costa. Finally I must thank George Newlands who first suggested that I might write a book on narrative theology, and Alex Wright, my editor at Cambridge University Press, who took up the suggestion and without whose encouragement, perseverance and patience – together with the finessing of Christine Salazar – this book would be not only unimaginable but unproduced. It need hardly be said that whatever is wholesome in this book derives from the sustenance of these others.

Preface to the paperback edition

All books are of their time, and three years ago this book imagined the culture of its production as a time of ending, without a future. To such a culture it sought to repeat the Christian story of a true *telos* that brings not closure, but an infinite prospect: temporality construed as the gift of eternity. Appearing again – in a corrected and more accessible form, in what is being called the 'millennium year' – it is hoped that the story of our giftedness, and of the God who comes in and as gift, will still be found relevant and appropriate to the times.

No doubt if the book were being written today, I would attempt greater clarity and say some things differently and others newly. An indication of these potential changes can be found in my essay in *The Cambridge Companion to Christian Doctrine*, edited by Colin E. Gunton (Cambridge University Press 1997). In particular, the essay offers a supplementary account of how Christian understanding of the Bible and tradition changed in the modern period, and outlines the nature of authoritative scriptural performance in the Church. It may clarify, if not alter, the concerns of those readers who have found – or still and will find – the book's ecclesiology either too open or too oppressive, too liberal or too limiting of developments in the telling of God's story.

A book changes as its readers change, as it is encountered in different ecclesial and life stories. While some found *Telling God's Story* clearly Protestant, others found it deeply Catholic. I thought it was Ecumenical, as did some readers. Perhaps it therefore answers not so much to a particular church story, as to an imaginary one; the story that all our church narratives are trying to tell. Readers are invited to take from it what they will, to make their own linkages, for their own telling of the story.

Gerard Loughlin
Epiphany 1999

Prologue
At the end of the book

The sky vanished like a scroll rolling itself up.
Revelation 6.14

CHAPTER I

Future now

Human beings are calendrical animals. They are always noting changes, marking time. As they grow and mature, age and decay, so they mark bodily transitions from infancy through childhood to adolescence, from youth to middle and then old age. These changes are noted with all manner of festivities, with rituals and ceremonies, with tests and sacrifices; with routines, repetitions and returns. By means of the calendar differences and changes are rendered significant and safe, or as safe as they can be. The day still passes into night, the summer into winter, the child into youth: the human animal still has to leave the safety of the garden. But it knows what is coming, it knows what repeats and returns, and what doesn't. It can prepare.

Calendars come to an end and have to be remade. Seven days to the week, twelve months to the year, ten years to the decade, ten decades to the century, ten centuries to the millennium; and then some more? Each time human beings pass from one calendar to another – from the long days of childhood to the ever shorter days of winter, from one year to the next – they become anxious and fretful. Is there a day after tomorrow? The time before the calendar ends is one of anticipation and sometimes dread, for at that time, time itself trembles: on the threshold it begins to fall apart. Humans are once more safe only when the calendar has been remade and time has been re-established.

The endings of years, centuries and millennia are such times. For perhaps this time the calendar will not be remade, or remade so differently that it will mark not the return of time, but the beginning of something altogether different, a new sort of time – beyond time. At the end of an age certainties collapse and differences abound. It is as if time stops and there is no more sequence and progress, only multiplicity without procession or order.

The close of our century is potent with the sense of ending. The grand narratives human beings used to tell themselves – about how tomorrow would not only follow today but be better than anything that had gone before – have become incredible. The idea of human progress has suffered one set-back too many. It is as if history had used up time and we are now counting the days on the world's last calendar. In a sense the eschaton has already arrived, it has already been realised: and this realisation, a *delighted* realisation, is postmodernism.[1]

The above is an attempt to sketch the cultural space of postmodernism. In likening it to millennial fears, to the terror of unmarked time when all is permitted, I want to suggest not so much a new period in world history as history's cessation. For postmodernism does not seem to be a new epoch. Older forms of social, political and economic organisation still persist, along with the cultural ideals and values of earlier ages. The world is still dominated by capitalism, even if now entered upon a third phase of multinational marketing.[2] Equally there is still a place for so-called traditional and Victorian values, even if only as pastiche of their former selves (as in Thatcherism).[3] Postmodernism is not the dawning of a new age, but of a day without a tomorrow, a time without a future.

[1] What's in a hyphen? Margaret A. Rose, in *Parody: Ancient, Modern, and Post-Modern*, Literature, Culture, Theory 5 (Cambridge: Cambridge University Press, 1993), notes that the word 'postmodern' has most often been used by deconstructionists, while 'post-modern' is used by Charles Jencks and others, and is 'also the more correct form of English' (p. 195 n. 1). I adopt the less 'correct form'.

[2] See Ernst Mandel, *Late Capitalism* (London: Verso, 1978).

[3] I use 'pastiche' in Fredric Jameson's sense of blank or blind parody: 'the wearing of a stylistic mask, speech in a dead language: . . . parody that has lost its sense of humour'. ('Postmodernism and consumer society', in *Postmodern Culture*, edited by Hal Foster (London: Pluto Press, 1985), pp. 111–25 (p. 114).) For a critical discussion of Jameson's use see Margaret A. Rose, *Parody*, pp. 220–4. For Thatcherism see Nicholas Boyle, 'Understanding Thatcherism', *New Blackfriars*, 69 (1988), 307–24.

Postmodernism is the idea that the once hoped-for future of the human race has arrived.[4] It is not a new age because the ages have come to an end, and now everything that once was is to be recuperated and used – as we like – in our fashioning. There is a vast proliferation in all areas of life, but without direction, for without a future there can be no direction or point to our endeavours. We are not governed but managed, and efficiency is our watchword. But we no longer know why or care. For some this is wonderful; for others it is more terrible than anything imagined by the Seer of Patmos.

Postmodernism is a complex cultural phenomenon arising in capitalist societies of the late twentieth century. It takes many forms. One of the most noticeable is the postmodern style of building; indeed postmodernism was famously announced by Charles Jencks in *The Language of Post-Modern Architecture* (1977).[5] In buildings it is a sort of eclecticism, the marriage of earlier idioms with modern techniques: pilasters and architraves upon steel frame constructions. (It can be distinguished from deconstructive architecture which seeks to destabilize its form, inhabitants and environment.)[6] Postmodernism is the economics of the consumer market applied to all areas of human life. There is nothing that cannot be bought and sold: health, education, ideas, blood, bodies, babies. Postmodernism is a fashioning of commodities – of films, food and clothes, and of people (who no longer have

4 Though he does not describe his narrative as postmodern, this is the tale told in Francis Fukuyama's *The End of History and the Last Man* (London: Hamish Hamilton, 1992). It is a 'final' metanarrative for the legitimation of Western capitalist hegemony. Remarkable for what it effectively manages to ignore about the late twentieth century – not least the West's construction of a free-market arms economy – it announces the arrival of 'post-historical' time in the closure of history as a 'single, coherent, evolutionary process', and the universal triumph of capitalist liberal democracy (pp. xii–xiii). See further Nicholas Lash, 'The end of history?' *Concilium* (1994), 6/47–56.

5 In fact, Jencks announced it at least two years earlier in 'The rise of post-modern architecture', *Architectural Association Quarterly*, 7/4 (1975), 3–14. Nicolaus Pevsner had already written of 'post-modern' architecture in 1961, though in a somewhat different sense to Jencks. See Margaret A. Rose, *Parody*, pp. 199 and 233.

6 Architects like Bernard Tschumi, Peter Eisenman and Frank Gehry may be considered deconstructivists. See Andrew Benjamin and Christopher Norris, *What is Deconstruction?* (London: Academy Editions, 1988).

characters but life-styles). It is also a sensibility (kitsch), a philosophy (nihilism) and a theology.

How postmodernism is theology is the question of this chapter. Below I shall consider two possible answers. One embraces postmodernism as described above. The other redeems postmodernism by finding in it, not the end of time, but the re-appearing of what may be called the 'future now'. Before proceeding to these answers, however, we may better understand postmodernism by considering what comes before.

MODERNISM

As its name suggests, postmodernism comes after the modern and its cult: modern*ism*. But what is/was that? Accounts of modernism are as various as those of postmodernism. For some the modern world arrives in the eighteenth century with the industrial revolution, while for others it begins in the seventeenth century with the scientific revolution occasioned by Copernicus, Kepler, Galileo and Newton. Some trace it further back, to the sixteenth century and the Protestant Reformation, to the religious revolution that, according to Max Weber, inaugurated the capitalist ethic. If we think of the modern as not so much a period as a mode of cultural sensibility, we may trace its emergence back to St Augustine and his *Confessions*.[7] Here I have space to offer only one brief description, from a postmodern vantage point.

The modern is the idea that humanity is the maker of its own destiny, of progress toward technological and social utopia. Newton produced the idea of constructing clear and powerful models of the world's working. He provided a paradigm for scientific precision and success. Everyone who came after him wanted to be the Newton of their chosen field, he modelled the stars; Darwin modelled the species. Marx

[7] This is suggested by Jean-François Lyotard in *The Postmodern Explained to Children: Correspondence 1982–1985* (London: Turnaround, 1992), pp. 35–6. He is following Erich Auerbach in *Mimesis: The Representation of Reality in Western Literature*, translated by Willard R. Trask (Princeton, New Jersey: Princeton University Press, 1953), pp. 67–76 and 300.

modelled society; Freud modelled the mind. Others followed. Ferdinand Saussure modelled language and Claude Lévi-Strauss modelled myth. Above all, there is Hegel and his story of the world as the self-realisation of Spirit. In the modern moment, in the mind of the European philosopher, Spirit achieves consummation in a moment of perfect modelling or story-telling – telling it as it truly is. The modern is thus imbued with a great sense of its own importance, of its ability to comprehend the world and make it new. In this it is spurred on by its ability to transform the material environment through technology, and through commerce the matrix of society.

Here are some twentieth-century examples of the modern spirit. In the late 1920s a group of like-minded mathematicians and philosophers formed themselves into the Vienna Circle and published a manifesto, *The Scientific Conception of the World* (1929). The Circle was zealous for new ways of thought and living, for a scientific future and a socialist utopia. Wherever people turned to science and empiricism, there the spirit of the scientific world-conception was at home. 'We witness the spirit of the scientific world-conception penetrating in growing measure the forms of personal and public life, in education, upbringing, architecture, and the shaping of economic and social life according to rational principle. *The scientific world-conception serves life, and life receives it.*'[8] They preached emancipation through science.

The architect Le Corbusier also wrote a manifesto, *Towards a New Architecture* (1927). It declared that the question of modern architecture was a question of morality. The question was one of architecture or revolution, and Le Corbusier believed that revolution could be avoided. Europe needed a new scientific architecture suited to the factory animal, endowed with the engineer's aesthetic. 'The Engineer, inspired by the law of Economy and governed by mathematical calculation, puts us in accord with universal law. He achieves

[8] In Otto Neurath, *Empiricism and Sociology*, edited by M. Neurath and R. S. Cohen (Dordrecht: D. Reidel Publishing Company, 1973), pp. 317–18.

harmony.'[9] The design of ocean liners, aeroplanes and automobiles showed the way; the modern architect would design machines for living in, houses that would be as 'healthy' and 'moral' as the 'big-business' that had transformed society.[10]

Science, engineering, architecture, medicine and morality; these were the weapons of the social revolutionary. With these, as the young poet W. H. Auden declared, they would harrow the houses of the dead and renew civilisation – 'New styles of architecture, a change of heart.'

MODERN AND POSTMODERN STORIES

One way of understanding the modern is as the telling of a master story with scientific rigour. A master story or grand narrative is a tale which comprehends everything, telling us not only how things are, but how they were and how they will be, and our place among them. Such stories tell us who we are. Religious stories are often said to be like this. The Christian story of Creation, Fall and Redemption places the individual soul within a divine drama of human possibility, of salvation or damnation. The modern is not the end of such stories, only their transformation. Marxism places us within the unfolding dialectic of history; Darwinism writes us into the epic of evolution; Freud locates us in the theatre of the psyche. Cosmology wants to tell us how the world began and how it will end.

When modern master stories are avowedly political they are decidedly utopian; they tell us that society will be better under their narration. Such stories are always true because they make the world fit the narrative. We can be characters within them because we can be mastered by them. And it would seem that most of us want to be within such a story; we want to be mastered or written into a narrative that is larger, longer, and stronger than our own. This is because stories are secure

9 Le Corbusier, *Towards a New Architecture*, translated by Frederick Etchells (London: The Architectural Press, 1927), p. 7.

10 Le Corbusier, *Towards a New Architecture*, p. 264.

places. We know how they begin and how they end. 'Once upon a time . . . happily ever after.' But what happens when these stories begin to break down; when their narrators lose confidence and forget what comes next?

The French philosopher Jean-François Lyotard tells us that postmodernism is what happens when master stories lose their appeal and become incredible.[11] When the grand narratives of religion began to lose their credibility, the modern world invented itself by re-telling the old stories in a new way. It didn't tell stories about God, but about history, evolution, the psyche, about stars and scientific progress, about genetic manipulation and a master race: about human emancipation through enlightenment and 'technoscience'. These stories, however, are now also incredible, undesirable, horrible. And it seems that now there are no master stories left. We have to make up our own individual, little stories. We have to be our own story-tellers, our own little masters. And this is something good, something to be happy about; or so the story goes.

Here we are as postmoderns! We are our own little story-tellers, living among the ruins of our former grand narratives. We tell stories purely for pleasure. Today we tell one story and tomorrow we will tell another. Stories are fashionable; we change them with the seasons, as we change our clothes. Perhaps because this is a new game, we make our stories out of the rubble of the old narratives we find lying around.[12] We mix and match, liking the fun of spotting where the bits have come from. Our novels and films are full of quotes and allusions; our buildings are a little classical, a little rococo, a little gothic, and even, sometimes, a little modernist. Our values and morals are equally various, equally changeable, commodities like everything else.[13]

11 Jean-François Lyotard, *The Postmodern Condition: A Report on Knowledge*, translated by Geoff Bennington and Brian Massumi (Manchester: Manchester University Press, 1984), p. xxiv.

12 Fredric Jameson, *Postmodernism, or the Cultural Logic of Late Capitalism* (London: Verso, 1991), p. 96.

13 Alasdair MacIntyre, *After Virtue: A Study in Moral Theory*, second edition (London: Duckworth, 1985).

So there it is: the story of modernism as the attempt to build a better tomorrow without aid of the divine, and of how the master stories of yesterday lost their appeal, turned sour. Now there are only little stories. But this history is also a story, and a rather grand one. Postmodernism cannot escape the master narrative. If it is to understand itself it has to understand everything; it has to establish its place in the world.[14]

POSTMODERN THEOLOGY

Christian theology has responded to postmodernism in several ways. Some theologians are hostile, others curious, and others extremely enthusiastic, declaring themselves to be post-modern theologians. A few have done so because it is fashionable, but most because they believe that theology must become postmodern if the Church is not to be permanently eclipsed by modernity. Here I am concerned with enthusiastic theologians only, and of the three groups I discern among them – the fashionable but still liberal, the textualist but finally nihilist, and the narrativist but really orthodox – I am concerned with the second and third. Mark C. Taylor and Don Cupitt are representative of textualist theologians (though I shall discuss mostly Cupitt), while narrativist theology is well represented in the work of George A. Lindbeck and John Milbank.[15]

NIHILIST POSTMODERN THEOLOGY

Mark C. Taylor is perhaps America's best known post-modernist theologian. Noted for his work on Søren

[14] Lyotard, *Postmodern Explained*, pp. 40–1.

[15] Hans Küng and David Ray Griffin are representative of fashionable but still liberal 'postmodernist' theologians. Their work is modernist liberal theology, despite its appearance in *The Post-Modern Reader*, edited by Charles Jencks (London and New York: Academy Editions and St Martin's Press, 1992), pp. 373–82; 409–16. Jencks also seems to think Matthew Fox a postmodernist theologian (pp. 35–6).

Kierkegaard,[16] he came to prominence with his book *Erring: A Postmodern A/Theology* (1984). He had already published *Deconstructing Theology* (1982) and has since published *Altarity* (1987), *Disfiguring* (1992) and *Nots* (1993).[17] *Erring* is an accomplished celebration of deferral, of the way in which meaning is always one step ahead of the signs in which we try to entrap it. For Taylor, language is like a vast and endless maze, in which we are forever running, turning this way and that, but never finding a centre or an exit.[18] We never find God, self or meaning, for they are dispersed throughout the labyrinth, noticeable by their absence.

Don Cupitt, who announced that he was *Taking Leave of God* in 1980, has gone on to provide a brilliant if at times hasty manifesto for nihilist postmodern theology. Like Taylor he believes that the old certainties have been dispersed across the surface of language. There are no longer any heights or depths, only a cultural skin of endlessly proliferating signs on which we must lightly tread, like *The Long-Legged Fly* (1987). In such a situation, religious values, like all values, have to be created out of nothing through the telling of stories, through make-believe. These themes are rumbustiously celebrated in

16 Mark C. Taylor, *Journeys to Selfhood: Hegel and Kierkegaard* (Berkeley: University of California Press, 1980).

17 The last two works suggest a move from 'a/theology' to cultural studies, confirmed in Taylor's recent work with Esa Saarinen, *Imagologies: Media Philosophy* (London: Routledge, 1994).

18 Though, as Gillian Rose notes, 'Taylor has put a unicursal maze on his cover – which offers no choice of route – as opposed to a multicursal maze – with choice of route.' For Rose, this picture is telling of the tyranny that is the obverse of postmodern freedom: 'on the cover of *Erring* we look down on a maze, and are placed not in joyous disempowerment but in panoptic dominion, notwithstanding that in the text, the maze is celebrated as "the horizontality of a pure surface", and we are said to be situated "in the midst of a labyrinth from which there is no exit" . . . [But] it is the beginning and the end which give authority to the way, and meaning to being lost – especially to any conceivable relishing of being lost. If the beginning and end are abolished, so that all is divine middle – *Mitte ist überall* – joyful erring would not be achieved nor would pure virtue "without resistance"; one would be left helpless in the total domination of the maze, every point equally beginning and end. This is to encounter not pure freedom but pure power and to become its perfect victim.' (Gillian Rose, *The Broken Middle: Out of Our Ancient Society* (Oxford: Blackwell, 1992), pp. 286–7.)

Cupitt's most recent trilogy: *Creation Out of Nothing* (1990), *What is a Story?* (1991) and *The Time Being* (1992).[19]

For both Taylor and Cupitt postmodernity is welcome and irreversible, and for both it has to do with the radical textuality of reality. Both of them are deeply influenced by twentieth-century philosophies of language: by structuralism, post-structuralism and deconstructionism, and by the people who invented, developed or promoted these 'isms': Ferdinand de Saussure, Claude Lévi-Strauss, Roland Barthes, Jacques Derrida. Both Taylor and Cupitt believe that Christian faith and practice must adopt the new postmodern understanding of the human condition. Cupitt, especially, champions a new sort of Christianity. 'We want a new religion that makes liberation and bliss out of the way the world is . . . for a beliefless world that is *rightly* beliefless, we'll need a beliefless religion.'[20] What is this new blissful and beliefless religion of liberation?

Textualism is the idea that finally there is only language, understood as a vast and proliferating system of signs. Cupitt calls it 'culturalism' – the flowing together of language and world as a sea of signs in which we float and swim and have our being.[21] Meaning is produced as the difference between signs. It is not something other than signs, to which signs are somehow stuck, so that I know what the sign 'cat' means because it has been stuck onto cats, or what 'idea' means because it has been stuck onto ideas. I know what 'cat' means because it is different from 'hat' and 'mat' and from other words of the lexicon, and because it is different from other words in the sentence in which I find it, located in a certain order of signs. These strings of signs have meaning because I know how to use them to do things within my language community. I can tell someone to get the cat off the mat.

The basic idea of textualism can be grasped by looking up

19 Cupitt has since published *After All: Religion Without Alienation* (London: SCM Press, 1994).

20 Don Cupitt, *The Time Being* (London: SCM Press, 1992), p. 117.

21 Cupitt, *Time Being*, p. 64.

the meaning of a word in a dictionary. You want to know what the word means, but all you find are other words, other signs. The meanings of words can only ever be other words: the difference between words. Meaning is not outside, but wholly inside language. This does not have to mean that there is nothing except language in the world. When I hit my foot against a stone it is not a word that causes my pain. But 'foot', 'stone' and 'pain' are all signs. If the world is to have meaning for me, it must come into language, into meaningful being. It must be placed under a description, categorised and indexed. Without language I would hit my foot against a stone and feel pain, but I would not know that I was feeling 'pain', that my 'foot' had struck a 'stone'. The event would be painful but without meaning, for I would be without language. 'When I seem to see red', Cupitt writes, 'I am already interpreting what I see, for I am classifying it. I am seeing it through a word. And unless I see through words I don't see at all.'[22]

The meaning of a word is always another word or words – the differential relation between words – and the meaning of those words yet other words. Meaning is always one word away; it is always different and deferred. In language we can never have the thing itself; we can never stop the endless drift of meaning from one sign to the next, from one sign-string to another. This, of course, is why language is so wonderful. As we move the signs around, putting them in new orders, producing new sign-strings – as in the shifts of metaphor, the sign-strings of poetry – we provide new routes for the ceaseless drift of meaning, and thus create new meanings and understandings: new patterns of difference. But it is also why language is so frustrating, why it is so difficult to say what we want to say or stop what we have said from meaning something else. Meaning is always one word away: we are never fully in control.

Control, however, is one of our dearest desires, for when we are in control we are safe. Thus is born one of our dearest myths: escape from language to a place where meaning is

[22] Cupitt, *Time Being*, p. 56.

self-present, where the truth is not different and deferred from the sign, where the sign is the truth. Here, then, is a route for escape: back from the written sign to the spoken word, from the spoken to the silent word of inner speech, from the silent word to the pure thought. If we can retrace the route by which thought came to language, we can arrive at the truth itself. Jacques Derrida has named this desire logocentrism, and finds it throughout the Western tradition. It is finally a desire for God conceived ontotheologically, as a being or as Being itself. It is nowhere better expressed than in the twelfth-century *Didascalicon* of Hugh of St Victor.

> The unsubstantial word is the sign of man's perceptions; the thing is a resemblance of the divine Idea. What, therefore, the sound of the mouth, which all in the same moment begins to subsist and fades away, is to the idea in the mind, that the whole extent of time is to eternity. The idea in the mind is the internal word, which is shown forth by the sound of the voice, that is, by the external word. And the divine Wisdom, which the Father has uttered out of his heart, invisible in Itself, is recognised through creatures and in them. From this is surely gathered how profound is the understanding to be sought in the Sacred Writings, in which we come through the word to a concept, through the concept to a thing, through the thing to its idea, and through its idea arrive at Truth.[23]

This – so textualism teaches – is the great myth of language. It holds, as Jesse M. Gellrich writes of Hugh of St Victor, that 'language is a transparency through which meaning may be reached by ascending the hierarchy to the origin of truth; signification is identified with a parent word or an original language before the taint of differentiation and mediation'.[24] It is a myth because there is no escape from language. Pure thought, truth present to itself, these are nothing more than ideas generated by the differences between signs. Meaning

[23] *The Didascalicon of Hugh of St Victor: A Medieval Guide to the Arts*, translated by Jerome Taylor, Records of Western Civilization (New York: Columbia University Press, [1961] 1991), pp. 121–2.

[24] Jesse M. Gellrich, *The Idea of the Book in the Middle Ages: Language Theory, Mythology, and Fiction* (Ithaca and London: Cornell University Press, 1985), p. 101.

does not stop when it comes to these signs, but moves on through them, one step ahead, because they also have meaning only because they too are different from other signs, different from other sign-strings. They would not mean anything at all if they were not so related, if they were not part of a sign system which allows them to have meaning.

Story and narrative are fashionable topoi for theology, and Cupitt takes to them with relish.[25] Everything is a story, for stories produce every significant thing. Stories produce desire. They manipulate and channel our emotions, directing them toward objects we might otherwise find unexciting. Stories produce reality, establishing certain orders and relations between things and people and other people. They establish the significance of age and gender, of skin colour, class and accent: of all the things that matter and that could be otherwise, if told in a different story. Narratives produce time, the positioning of things before and after, the placing of the present at the complex intersection of individual and communal time-narratives. And stories produce us, our sense of self-hood, of being an 'I' with a past and a future, a narrative trajectory.

Religion, needless to say, is also a product of narrative; it is only a story. But it is an important one, for religious stories provide our lives with significance; they inspire moral endeavour and conquer the Void.[26] In the past we thought that God wrote the story, but now we know that we ourselves have written God. Now the religious task is to keep up the fiction, and not with a heavy but with a light touch. We must be 'cheerfully fictionalist'.[27] For the heavy hand produces a master story that weighs upon the soul. Instead we must be 'continually improvising, retelling, embroidering, making it up as we go along'.[28]

For the textualist theologian, such as Taylor or Cupitt, God is also a sign; one which, like any other, depends for its

[25] Don Cupitt, *What is a Story?* (London: SCM Press, 1991).

[26] Cupitt, *What is a Story?*, p. 80.

[27] Cupitt, *What is a Story?*, p. 96

[28] Cupitt, *What is a Story?*, p. 154.

meaning on all the rest. God is not outside language, in a place where meaning and truth are self-present, for language has no outside. God is wholly inside language, make-believe like everything else; God is language. God is the play of signs upon the Void.

> The Void is just movement, change. Semiosis, signification, is a temporal moving process . . . Just reading a sentence, we should be able to feel on our pulses the way life and meaning continually come out of the Void and return into it. That's the new religious object. That's what we have to learn to say yes to . . . life's urgent transience . . . The sign is our only metaphysics, our little bit of transcendence.[29]

The textualist's vision is a dark one. As Taylor's image of language as a maze suggests, we are forever enclosed, wandering in the labyrinth. No matter how long our piece of thread, there is no way out and nowhere to go. Cupitt, in a telling moment, imagines a reversed Platonic myth in which there is no way out of the cave. All we can do is to make it bigger. But no matter how much we dynamite and tunnel, we are still surrounded by rock, as dark as night. Cupitt complements this story with that of a house with no exterior doors or windows. We never go outside, and nothing ever enters. We never see a dawn or feel a breeze.[30] Cupitt insists that he is not imagining a prison. But he is imagining a space without light; and without light human beings cannot long survive.

Cupitt's anti-Platonic stories answer to the postmodern condition of consumerist society. His windowless house and interminable cave could be descriptions of the modern shopping mall, which is already of indefinite extension, without windows and almost entirely hermetic. Fredric Jameson describes such places as 'postmodern hyperspace', a space which has 'finally succeeded in transcending the capacities of the individual human body to locate itself, to organise its immediate surroundings perceptually, and cognitively to map

[29] Cupitt, *Time Being*, p. 61 and p. 95. [30] Cupitt, *Time Being*, p. 33.

its position in a mappable external world.'[31] He gives the example of the Western Bonaventure Hotel in Los Angeles and its lobby space, which 'takes on those who still seek to walk through it.'[32] Jameson suggests that such spaces are analogues of 'that even sharper dilemma which is the incapacity of our minds, at least at present, to map the great global multinational and decentred communicational network in which we find ourselves caught as individual subjects.'[33] But postmodern nihilism delights in precisely this network of disorientation.

PROBLEMS

The chief problem with textualist theology is that it is not textualist enough. It tells us that there are only stories, but it tends to obscure the fact that in that case, textualism also is only a story; and it tends to obscure the fact that it is a nihilist and not a Christian story. Here it is: 'The world remains fictional, as it must . . . Outside our stories there is still nothing but formlessness.'[34] For textualism it is the story of 'formlessness' that goes all the way down. For textualist theology we tell stories *against the Void*. There is nothing beyond our stories except white noise.[35] This is the master narrative: that there is, finally, only nothing. This radically differs from the Christian story, which teaches that really there is nothing whatsoever beyond God's story. It is the love of God that goes all the way down, really.

For someone like Cupitt, religious stories are tales told to keep the darkness at bay, until the night comes. We must ask: Are there no better stories we can tell, stories less complacent about contemporary society, less pessimistic about the human condition, more hopeful of change? There is some reason to think that the old ecclesial story of God's self-gift in Christ and Church is such a tale, since in the telling it looks for the coming of the dawn.

[31] Jameson, *Postmodernism*, p. 44.

[32] Jameson, *Postmodernism*, p. 43.

[33] Jameson, *Postmodernism*, p. 44.

[34] Cupitt, *What is a Story?*, p. 80.

[35] Cupitt, *What is a Story?*, p. 93.

ORTHODOX POSTMODERN THEOLOGY

The Church's old story is maintained by those theologians I am calling narrativists, of whom George A. Lindbeck and John Milbank are representative. They are narrativists because, like the textualists, they accept the ubiquity of language. They believe that our sense of the world is formed by the socially constructed discourses in which we find ourselves, and to which we contribute. We are embedded in language, as is language in us. There is a reciprocal relation between story and story-teller. As I recount my life-story, my story produces the 'I' which recounts it. I tell the story by which I am told. And since I am part of a larger community – one in which others tell stories about me, just as I tell stories about them – I am the product of many inter-related narratives, as is everyone else.

Narrativists also believe that stories go all the way down. Finally our deepest convictions about the world and ourselves are constituted in stories only. As such, stories are human constructions, socially enacted. When the stories that society tells about itself change, so does society. The world changes when we tell different stories about it.

> What is taken to be reality is in large part socially constructed and consequently alters in the course of time. The universe of the ancient Near East was very different from that of Greek philosophy, and both are dissimilar from the modern cosmos . . . In one world, for example, the origin of things is pictured in terms of a Babylonian myth; in another, in terms of Plato's Timaeus tale; and in a third, in terms of a scientific account of cosmic evolution.[36]

However, narrativists, unlike textualists, believe that what matters most in story-telling is not the telling itself – narrativity or textuality – but the stories told, the particular narratives unfolded. They are concerned not so much with the fictionality of the world, as with the particular world fictioned.

36 George A. Lindbeck, *The Nature of Doctrine: Religion and Theology in a Postliberal Age* (London: SPCK, 1984), p. 82.

Thus Lindbeck and Milbank are both orthodox theologians because they believe that the Christian story of Christ and his Church is preferable to all others. It is a story to live by.

In 1984 George Lindbeck published a short, powerful and provocative study on *The Nature of Doctrine*. In the book he sought to outline an ecumenical theory of doctrine as the neutral 'grammar' of varied Christian discourses. Doctrines are understood not as propositions, but as regulations for our talk of divine matters, of God and Christ and Church. They are second-order rules for first-order talk. The creeds of the Church are regulative in that they tell us how to speak about Father, Son and Spirit, and about Jesus the Christ; or rather, they tell us how not to speak about them. Whatever we say of the Father, Son or Spirit we must say of the other two, but we must not suggest that one is the same as the other two. Whatever we say of Jesus, we must not suggest that he was only a man or only God, nor that he was some sort of hybrid God-Man.[37]

Doctrines are rules for the imagining of God and world, in our story-telling, pray-acting and in our common-living. 'Doctrines regulate truth claims by excluding some and permitting others, but the logic of their communally authoritative use hinders or prevents them from specifying positively what is to be affirmed.'[38] Therefore, in addition to the rules of Christian imagining, we need a vocabulary of imagined stories for them to rule; stories which are also human lives, individual and communal.

The vocabulary of 'symbols, concepts, rites, injunctions and stories' for a doctrinally ruled Christian imagining, comes largely from the Bible.[39] The canonical Scriptures provide the basic narratives for how the Church imagines the world and itself in the world. The Church imagines itself within the narrative-world of the Bible, a written-world into which people can be 'inscribed'. Rather than understanding the Bible in worldly terms, the Christian understands the world in biblical

[37] Lindbeck, *Nature of Doctrine*, p. 94.

[38] Lindbeck, *Nature of Doctrine*, p. 19.

[39] Lindbeck, *Nature of Doctrine*, p. 81.

ones; the Christian takes the biblical narratives, above all the narratives of Christ, as the fundamental story by which all others are to be understood, including his or her own story. 'The cross is not to be viewed as a figurative representation of suffering nor the messianic Kingdom viewed as a symbol for hope in the future; rather, suffering should be cruciform, and hopes for the future messianic.'[40] The biblically formed narratives of Christ and his Church become the story which literally makes the world; it goes all the way down.[41]

One can develop Lindbeck's idea by saying that when a person enters the scriptural story he or she does so by entering the Church's performance of that story: he or she is baptised into a biblical and ecclesial drama. It is not so much being written into a book as taking part in a play, a play that has to be improvised on the spot. As Rowan Williams puts it, people are 'invited to "create" themselves in finding a place within this drama – an improvisation in the theatre workshop, but one that purports to be about a comprehensive truth affecting one's identity and future.'[42]

On Lindbeck's postliberal view, language and story come first, world and experience second. We only recognise the world as *world* because we can say 'world'. Experience occurs within language. All that we have has been given in *words*. This is much the same as textualism. But where narrativist theology differs is in its master story. Whereas for textualist nihilism it is the movement of signs upon the surface of the Void, for Lindbeck it is the story of Christ and his Church. One could say that the difference between these stories is the difference between Nothing and Everything, between ultimate darkness and hoped-for dawn, between violence and harmony. This last way of stating the difference is after John

40 Lindbeck, *Nature of Doctrine*, p. 118.

41 Here, one may be reminded of Karl Barth, whose theology is properly postmodern (Lindbeck, *Nature of Doctrine*, p. 135). See further, Graham Ward, 'Barth and postmodernism', *New Blackfriars*, 74 (1993), 550–6.

42 Rowan D. Williams, 'Postmodern theology and the judgement of the world', in *Postmodern Theology: Christian Faith in a Pluralist World*, edited by Frederic B. Burnham (New York: Harper Collins, 1989), p. 97.

Milbank, who has made the difference between malign and benign postmodernism a theme of his magisterial study, *Theology and Social Theory* (1990).

Milbank argues that all stories stage themselves; that is, they imagine a context for their telling, they imagine how the world must be for the story to make sense. As we have seen, Cupitt's story of shifting signs makes sense upon the stage of the Void. Milbank, however, argues that nihilism imagines not just an impassive Void but an incessant contest between powers. For where there are only differences, and no common ground, each difference is set against all the rest.

Nihilism condemns us to endless violence, as alone appropriate to its story. The Christian narrative, on the other hand, imagines the possibility of harmonious difference and peace as the inner dynamic of the triune God. The Church imagines people remaining in their 'many different cities, languages and cultures, yet still belonging to one eternal city ruled by Christ', in whom all humanity is fulfilled.[43] It is the idea of difference in music. 'For Christianity, true community means the freedom of people and groups to be different, not just to be functions of a fixed consensus . . . but a consensus that is only in and through the inter-relations of community itself, and a consensus that moves and "changes": a *consentus musicus*.'[44]

Christianity is postmodern because it is not founded on anything other than the performance of its story. It cannot be established against nihilism by reason, but only presented as a radical alternative, as something else altogether.[45] It is also postmodern because its story – God's story – imagines a world 'out of nothing', a world of becoming, in which people are not fixed essences but life-narratives with a future. The story of Jesus Christ gives us the pattern of peaceful existence. It is an 'atoning' peace of mutual forgiveness and the bearing of one another's burdens. This peace is sought in the nomadic city of

[43] John Milbank, *Theology and Social Theory* (Oxford: Basil Blackwell, 1990), p. 227.

[44] Milbank, *Theology and Social Theory*, p. 228.

[45] John Milbank, '"Postmodern critical Augustinianism": a short summa in forty-two responses to unasked questions', *Modern Theology*, 7 (1991), 225–37 (p. 389).

the Church, an open-ended tradition of charity, of 'differences in a continuous harmony'.[46]

DIFFICULTIES

From the point of view of Christian theology, narrativist orthodoxy is preferable to textualist nihilism, but postmodern narrativist theology has its difficulties. Firstly, is it possible to affirm the reality of God while allowing that such an affirmation can take place only within a story, albeit a master story which is said to go all the way down, without remainder?

Cupitt believes that any talk of transcendent realities, of things beyond or outside language, is rendered 'silly' by the fact that it is *talk*, and thus wholly within language.[47] If God appears in a story – as he does in the Bible – he must appear as a human-like, gendered and speaking character, with ideas and assumptions appropriate to his time, with feelings and intentions, 'behaving in general like an extra-powerful and demanding king'.[48] He will be all too human. And won't it be odd that people can write about him, as if from God's point of view?[49] Who was around when God made the heaven and the earth, to tell us about it? The whole thing is artifice.[50]

Jacques Derrida famously said that there is nothing outside the text, no outside-text: *il n'y a pas de hors-texte*.[51] But he did not mean that there is only text. He meant, among other things, that whatever we know, we know in and through language.[52]

[46] Milbank, *Theology and Social Theory*, p. 417.
[47] Cupitt, *Time Being*, p. 90.
[48] Cupitt, *What is a Story?*, p. 114.
[49] Cupitt, *What is a Story?*, pp. 118–19.
[50] 'Whatever our ideas may be about the natural way to tell a story, artifice is unmistakably present whenever the author tells us what no one in so-called real life could possibly know.' Wayne C. Booth, *The Rhetoric of Fiction* (Chicago and London: the University of Chicago Press, 1961), p. 3.
[51] Jacques Derrida, *Of Grammatology*, translated by Gayatri Chakravorty Spivak (Baltimore and London: Johns Hopkins University Press, [1967] 1976), p. 158.
[52] 'The doctrine that there is nothing outside the text is neither esoteric nor difficult: it is merely that there is no knowledge, of which we can speak, which is unmediated.' Kevin Hart, *The Trespass of the Sign: Deconstruction, Theology and Philosophy* (Cambridge: Cambridge University Press, 1989), p. 26.

But one of the things that we know *in* language is that there are things *outside* language. Though words are used to talk about things, we can use them to talk about things other than words. Cupitt, it seems, forgets this, confusing words with the things we use words to talk about. No one should pretend that talk of God is easy, but nor should they think it impossible. Of course God is a human-like character in the biblical narrative. But this does not mean that God is a human being. Of course the first story of Genesis is narrated from an impossible standpoint, it is a work of imagination after all. But this does not mean that it is not an 'inspired', profound and true depiction of the world as creation. (See further below chapter 4.)

Truth is said to be another problem for narativism. How can there be true stories when it is said that there are only stories? For it is supposed that a true story is one that matches up to reality, to the way things are. But if the way things are can never be known, because all we can ever know are stories of one sort or another, we can never match stories against reality, but only against one another. Thus it is said that science is not so much the matching of scientific theories against reality, as the matching of theories against experimental data, observation statements and so forth, which are always already theory-laden. Science matches theory-stories against observation-narratives.

Whatever the case with science, Christian truth has never been a matter of matching stories against reality. It has always been a matter of matching reality-stories against the truth: Jesus Christ. For the Christian Church it has always been a life-story that comes first, against which all other things are to be matched. This life-story is what 'truth' means in Christianity. Nor is this a matter of making up the truth, because it is the truth that makes up the story. The story is imagined for us before it is re-imagined by us: the story is *given* to us. That, at any rate, is the Church's story.

It is said that narrativist theology renders the Church sectarian. For it denies that reason provides an autonomous language in which everything can be discussed; rather it supposes a multiplicity of self-sustaining language communities.

There is no common language the Church can use to express itself to an unbelieving world. Postmodern theology rejects the idea that Christian discourse can be translated into alien tongues without ceasing to be Christian. But then it seems that Christian discourse is the in-language of an in-group, cut off from a larger commonwealth. But this is to forget that people can learn to speak more than one language without recourse to some 'common' tongue. Moreover, it is to forget 'that the history called Christ is the encompassing history within which all things live and move and have their being.'[53]

Finally, it is said that despite all the talk about 'harmony' and 'peace', narrativist theology is itself violent in thinking the Christian story a master narrative that positions all other stories. It is the violence of having the last word. It must be remembered, however, that the Christian story is always provisional because not yet ended. It is performed in the hope that the one of whom it speaks will return again to say it. The last word is yet to be said; and when it is, the Church also will find itself positioned. Thus the Christian story resists mastery by being the prayerful tale of one who came in the form of a servant and who will return as a friend. (See further chapter 7.)

FUTURE NOW

In nihilist postmodernism we find the curious conjunction of paganism and modernity. It is pagan because it sets the world against the Void: a play of signs upon the surface of nothingness. But it is modern because instead of finding this a reason for despair or resignation, it finds it an occasion for delight and joy. The realisation of the Void is the moment of human emancipation.

> The world is only an endlessly shifting purely contingent order of signs in motion, a Sea of Meanings . . . And just the ability to see this and say it is precisely what gives us our new and joyful freedom . . .

[53] Robert W. Jenson, 'The Hauerwas project', *Modern Theology* 8 (1992), 285–95 (p. 293).

Your God is only your faith in him, your values are only your commitment to them. That is liberation. You're free.[54]

Whether in the expanse of the open market, epitomised in the spaces of the shopping mall, or in the mazes and caverns of textualism, pagan modernity announces that the end of the story has arrived, human freedom and emancipation achieved. Ironically it is the triumph of Hegelianism, the myth of perfect self-realisation, the conjunction of sign and meaning. Meaning no longer slips away, one word ahead, because now the meaning is the sign: the medium is the message. This is why nihilist postmodernism is a realised eschatology. We are at the end of the story; the end of the world.

However, such postmodernism is really only paganized modernity. Its exponents, including its theologians, have not superseded modernism. They still believe in the story of human emancipation humanly achieved, and because they understand the narrative as one of emancipation rather than of formation, they conceive its conclusion only negatively, as freedom from rather than freedom for. But the narrativist theologians hold out the possibility of a true postmodernism, a story that is neither pagan nor modernist, but Christian. It is a story about the possibility of human formation for harmonious and charitable union with God. And this ancient story is truly postmodern because it is a story about the future, of what is to come after the present. At the same time it partakes of the paradox which Lyotard locates in the word 'postmodern': 'the future (*post*) anterior (*modus*)'.[55] The future now.

The postmodern work, according to Lyotard, is not governed by the past, and cannot be judged by present rules, precisely because it calls past rules into question. The rules that govern the work are made in its production. The writer or artist works 'without rules, and in order to establish the rules for what *will have been made*.'[56] Thus the work is an event, ahead

[54] Cupitt, *Time Being*, p. 66.

[55] Lyotard, *Postmodern Explained*, p. 24.

[56] Lyotard, *Postmodern Explained*, p. 24.

of its time. This is true of God's work, which cannot be governed by the past. It is always ahead of its time: *postmodern*. The Church is a postmodern event because it exists to establish the 'rule' of love for what will have been made: the peace and harmony of Christ's coming Kingdom.

It is only a story because it is only one way of telling the world – as Creation rather than Void, as Light rather than Darkness. The Church tells its story as best it can. Some like it and believe, and others don't. The Church moves on and tells it somewhere else. At the end of the world it's a matter of telling different stories. When the postmodernist culture of late capitalism tells us that the end of human striving arrives when society is indistinguishable from a market, when everything can be bought and sold and the good life is a matter of efficient management; then it's the difference between having the Kingdom of God now, shopping on a Sunday, or still waiting, hoping and praying, for the return of one who loves us for what will have been made.

PART I

Consuming text

Then the voice that I had heard from heaven spoke to me again, saying, 'Go, take the scroll that is open in the hand of the angel who is standing on the sea and on the land.' So I went to the angel and told him to give me the little scroll; and he said to me, 'Take it, and eat; it will be bitter to your stomach, but sweet as honey in your mouth.' So I took the little scroll from the hand of the angel and ate it; it was sweet as honey in my mouth, but when I had eaten it, my stomach was made bitter.'

Revelation 10.8–10

CHAPTER 2

Around Christ

The medievals conceived the world as a book written by God, the plot of which is given in God's other book, the Bible.[1] Today, however, the world is plotted by different narratives, either humanly authored (modernism) or authorless (post-modernism). Now the world writes itself; or better, it is writing itself.

The world is all that we know. It is the ground beneath our feet, the sky above our heads, the people with whom it is shared. The world is our parents, siblings and children; our lovers, friends and neighbours. It is the stories we tell and are told; tales of distant times and far places; of terrible deeds and delightful things. It is stories of war and famine, of slavery and despair; but also of resistance and liberation, of peace and joy. It is stories of where we have come from and are going to; and of who 'we' are. It is our politics and economics, our science, philosophy and religion. Through the telling of stories the world is what we make it. It is also what makes us.

Who can fight the world? Who can resist its reality, inevitable and recalcitrant? The world is as it is: unchanging and unchangeable. There is no other way. Harsh reality is unavoidable. The world is dominated by master narratives,

[1] See Marjorie Reeves, 'The Bible and literary authorship in the middle ages', in *Reading the Text: Biblical Criticism and Literary Theory*, edited by Stephen Prickett (Oxford: Basil Blackwell, 1991), pp. 12–63. This essay provides an introduction to the medieval conception of the Bible as the book of the world, showing in particular how Joachim of Fiore (c. 1135–1202) and Dante (1265–1321) in the *Divina Commedia* read 'history in biblical terms' (p. 37).

above all economic and political ones, which dictate what is important, what matters and counts, what is real. Or so it was. But now that the once feared and powerful narrative – the emancipation of the people through state socialism – has ceased to be told with any conviction, and the space for the telling of many little stories – the market of the free world – has been extended yet again, the age of the master narrative, of the emancipatory project, seems finally finished.[2] The announced passing of modernity – and socialism was nothing if not modern – heralds the end of the world as a dominant coding, a system rendering all life identical. Jean-François Lyotard, as we have seen, announces the end of grand narrative and the coming of little singular tales, a delirium of difference. Surely this will make for a more hospitable, changeable, plural world? An unsystematic world that no one can be against?[3]

But perhaps the telling of many little stories is itself dependent on a rather larger tale; one that cannot be controverted because dissembled as the space in which all the little stories are told, as *telling* itself? As Terry Eagleton (and others) proclaim, postmodern society – or late capitalist society – is a tyrannous space of freedom, at once 'libertarian and authoritarian, hedonist and repressive, multiple and monolithic'.

The logic of the market-place is one of pleasure and plurality, of the ephemeral and discontinuous, of a great decentred network of desires of which individual consumers are the passing functions. Yet to hold all this anarchy in place requires a political, ethical and ideological order which is a good deal less laid-back and dishevelled, wedded as it is to absolute values, autonomous human subjects and metaphysical foundations. . . . Capitalism is the most pluralist order history has ever known, restlessly transgressing boundaries and pitching diverse life-forms together. If it has need of the 'unified

[2] See John Paul II, *Centesimus Annus* (London: Catholic Truth Society, 1991).

[3] See Don Cupitt, 'Unsystematic ethics and politics', in *Shadow of Spirit: Postmodernism and Religion*, edited by Philippa Berry and Andrew Wernick (London: Routledge, 1992), pp. 147–55 (p. 154).

subject' in the classroom or law-court, it has little enough time for it in the media or market-place.[4]

Eagleton insists that it is no good setting diversity against uniformity, plurality against univocity, seeking to undermine the latter by the former, for the former are already in the service of the latter: 'difference, transgressiveness and multiplicity . . . are as native to capitalism as cherry pie is to the Land of the Free.'[5] The delirium of free-market consumerism is made possible by the iron fist of capitalist technoscience that brooks no dissenters.

Lyotard argues that capitalist technoscience, while claiming to complete the project of Enlightenment emancipation, is in fact its destruction. For it has no end in view other than its own replication, accumulating facts and commodities for no other purpose than their accumulation. 'Success is the only criterion of judgement technoscience will accept. Even so, it is incapable of saying what success is, or why it is good, just or true, since success is self-proclaiming, like a ratification of something heedless of any law.'[6]

Since modernity makes the people, rather than God, the author of the world, the world no longer has a legitimating authority, for the people are only one people among many.

What is the source of legitimacy in modern history going to be after 1792? Supposedly the people. But the people is an Idea – arguments and battles strive to establish what the right Idea of the people is, and to make it prevail. That is why there is a spread of civil war in the 19th and 20th centuries, and why even modern war between nations is always civil war: I, government of the people, contest the legitimacy of your government. At 'Auschwitz', a modern sovereign, a whole people was physically destroyed. The attempt was made to destroy it. It is the crime opening postmodernity, a crime of violated

[4] Terry Eagleton, 'Discourse and discos: theory in the space between culture and capitalism', *Times Literary Supplement*, 15 July 1994: 3–4 (p. 4).

[5] Eagleton, 'Discourse and discos', p. 4.

[6] Jean-François Lyotard, *The Postmodern Explained to Children: Correspondence 1982–1985*, translated by Julian Pefanis and Morgan Thomas (London: Turnaround, 1992), p. 30.

sovereignty – not regicide this time, but populicide (as distinct from ethnocide).[7]

Lyotard sees the problematic of the world as a 'crisis of delegitimation'. God, king and people are all dethroned. 'The people's prose – the real prose I mean – says one thing and its opposite: "Like father, like son" and "To the miserly father, a prodigal son". Only Romanticism imagined this prose to be consistent, to be guided by the task of expressivity, emancipation, or the revelation of wisdom. Postmodernity is also the end of the people as sovereign of their stories.'[8] There remains only the strife of contesting powers, which is alone legitimate. (All the great modernist narratives – Darwinism, Marxism, Freudianism – are modalities of one economic narrative: the contest of market exchange.)

It is said that each individual is now his or her own storyteller, his or her own source of legitimacy: I author myself. But this is a delusion, for no one stands alone. For Lyotard, the modern world is one vast interconnected field, where humanity studies and manipulates both nature and itself, the 'imbrication of subject and object'. The human being is 'only a very sophisticated node in the general interactions of emanations constituting the universe.'[9] But this also, is only a story. It is one moreover that serves to legitimate certain interests. Lyotard may wish to contest totality,[10] but it is not evident that secular postmodernism is other than its legitimation under the name of difference. That which delegitimates all divine and human authority, legitimates itself as the necessary condition of 'freedom'. The world is not writerless when it is no longer written by God; it is written by powers and dominions.

It is against this background – of the world writing itself –

[7] Lyotard, *Postmodern Explained*, pp. 30–1.

[8] Lyotard, *Postmodern Explained*, pp. 31–2.

[9] Lyotard, *Postmodern Explained*, p. 32.

[10] Jean-François Lyotard, *The Postmodern Condition: A Report on Knowledge*, translated by Geoff Bennington and Brian Massumi, Theory and History of Literature 10 (Manchester: Manchester University Press, 1984), p. 82.

that the Church continues to tell the story of God's Christ. It does so because it believes that only the story of a world written out of love of what is written, and written into that love, serves to delegitimate all authorities – including the economy of strife – while at the same time granting legitimacy to what is written in all its difference. The Christian story is a grand narrative of delegitimating legitimation. In Christ the world is affirmed, freed from the need to write itself, loved simply as that which is written.

NARRATIVE THEOLOGY

Long before it was fashionable to be non-foundational,[11] Hans Frei (1922–1988) had learnt from Karl Barth (1886–1968) that Christian faith rests not upon universal reason or human self-consciousness, but is sustained through and as commitment to a story. The story is not supported by anything else, by another story, theory or argument. The story is simply told, and faith is a certain way of telling it, a way of living and embodying it; a habit of the heart. But it is not the way of modern theology, whether liberal or evangelical.

Hans Frei argues that for nearly three hundred years, from the end of the seventeenth century until today, modern theology has sought to establish the *possibility* of a divine manifestation or revelation in the world. It has argued that if it is possible for God to be known, then it is possible that God is known and the claims of Christianity are at least reasonable and at most credible. This is theology as apologetics. 'A bold apologetics proves to a particular generation the intellectual necessity of the theological principles taken from the Bible or from Church dogma or from both; a more cautious apologetics proves at least their intellectual possibility.'[12] Modern theology has sought to fit the story of God into whatever has

[11] See D. Z. Phillips, *Faith After Foundationalism* (London and New York: Routledge, 1988).

[12] Karl Barth, *Protestant Thought: From Rousseau to Ritschl*, translated by Brian Cozens (New York: Harper Brothers, 1959), p. 320.

been the prevailing story of the world. It has tried to show that the former can be a part of the latter. If the world is rendered by natural science, then natural theology shows how knowledge of the world, its design and evolution, leads to knowledge of God.[13] If the world is rendered by Marxist dialectics, then liberation theology shows that God is on the side of the proletariat.[14] And if the world is rendered by free-market economics, then theology shows that God is whatever the consumer places in his or her personal shrine.[15] 'In the self assured world of modernity, people seek to make sense of the Scriptures, instead of hoping, with the aid of the Scriptures, to make some sense of themselves.'[16]

Against the prevailing current of modern theology, Hans Frei follows Karl Barth in advocating a diametrically opposed theology, one that seeks to fit the world into the story of God rather than God into the story of the world. Both Barth and Frei believe that such a theology is wholly congruent with the greater part of the Christian tradition, with the theology of the Reformers, the Fathers and the Apostolic writers. 'Narrative theology' is an appropriate term for their approach, and it is after Barth and Frei that it is used in this book. Frei himself describes Barth as a narrative theologian, insofar as Barth came to see that who Jesus was and what he did and under-

[13] See Peter Byrne, *Natural Religion and the Nature of Religion: The Legacy of Deism* (London and New York: Routledge, 1989).

[14] See Gustavo Gutierrez, *A Theology of Liberation* (London: SCM Press, 1983). See further John Milbank, *Theology and Social Theory: Beyond Secular Reason* (Oxford: Basil Blackwell, 1990), pp. 232–55; and compare Nicholas Lash, 'Not exactly politics or power?' *Modern Theology*, 8 (1992), 353–64.

[15] See Michael Novak, *The Spirit of Democratic Capitalism* (London: Institute of Economic Affairs Health and Welfare Unit [1982] 1991) and John Hick, *An Interpretation of Religion: Human Responses to the Transcendent* (London: Macmillan, 1989). For an indication of how Novak's 'empty shrine' and Hick's 'Real' conspire together see Gerard Loughlin, 'Noumenon and phenomena', *Religious Studies*, 23 (1987), 493–508 (pp. 504–8); and for a liberal attempt to save the 'empty shrine' or 'square' for a tolerant but robust theology see Ian S. Markham, *Plurality and Christian Ethics*, New Studies in Christian Ethics (Cambridge: Cambridge University Press, 1994). For the present author it remains unapparent that tolerance is a Christian virtue; patience and peaceableness are.

[16] Nicholas Lash, 'When did the theologians lose interest in theology?' in *Theology and Dialogue: Essays in Conversation with George Lindbeck*, edited by Bruce D. Marshall (Notre Dame, Indiana: University of Notre Dame Press, 1990), 131–47 (p. 143).

went are united in his person as a 'self-enacted agency or performative project'.[17] In the same sense Frei would have accepted the description of himself.[18]

Unlike most modern theology, narrative theology does not look to the world and its possibilities, but to the actuality of God's story as it is told in the Church's Scripture. It does not seek to show the possibility of revelation, but its actuality; not that God can and may speak, but that God has spoken. Indeed both Barth and Frei teach that unless God has spoken we could not know that there is God, let alone that God could speak. It is the possibility that follows from the actuality, and not the other way around.[19]

Narrative theology begins with the literal reading of the Bible as inspired testimony to God's revelation: as Scripture.[20] How it reads the Bible literally is the subject of chapter 5, and how it understands biblical inspiration and its relation to revelation is the subject of chapter 4. Ingredient in the idea that narrative theology is a way of reading the Bible is the idea of the readers who read it in that way. Thus narrative

[17] Hans Frei, *Theology and Narrative: Selected Essays*, edited by George Hunsinger and William C. Placher (New York and Oxford: Oxford University Press, 1993), p. 184. See David Ford, *Barth and God's Story: Biblical Narrative and the Theological Method of Karl Barth in the 'Church Dogmatics'*, Studies in the Intercultural History of Christianity 27 (Frankfurt am Main, Berne: Verlag Peter Lang, 1981). On the narrative identity of Jesus Christ see further chapter 3.

[18] Kevin J. Vanhoozer argues that 'strictly speaking' Frei is not a narrative theologian. 'Frei is not a narrativist if by this we mean someone who builds an epistemology or an ontology of human being on a narrative substructure. Rather, Frei is an Anselmian theologian who is seeking to understand the Christian faith, particularly its central narrative expression, on its own terms.' (*Biblical Narrative in the Philosophy of Paul Ricoeur: A Study in Hermeneutics and Theology* (Cambridge: Cambridge University Press, 1990), p. 178.) It is however Frei's concern with the 'central narrative expression', and his conviction that the expression is constitutive of what it expresses, that makes narrative and narrativist appropriate terms for his theology. On the distinction between liberal and 'Anselmian' narrativism see the beginning of chapter 3.

[19] Frei, *Theology and Narrative*, p. 30. 'Barth said very simply and consistently that the possibility and even the necessity for God's assuming man unto himself by incarnating himself may be affirmed and explored because he did so and only for that reason' (*Theology and Narrative*, p. 170).

[20] I propose using 'Bible' and 'Scripture' to designate the difference between reading the Church's canonical writings as one would any other book and as an inspired testimony to God's condescension in Christ.

theology cannot begin with the Bible without at the same time beginning with its readers: the Church. Those who read and that which is read are mutually related in the event of reading. The Scripture makes the Church and the Church makes the Scripture; they are mutually constitutive.[21] The next chapter is concerned with the Church as reading community, but in the rest of this chapter I want to explore what it is for the Church to read its Scripture as narrative, as the story of God's revelation in history.

OVERCOMING REALITY

Erich Auerbach tells us that the Bible, and in particular the Mosaic authorship, is like no other ancient book. Homer, in contrast, creates a world we can enter and enjoy; but it serves no other purpose. The 'Homeric poems conceal nothing, they contain no teaching and no secret second meaning.'[22] They cannot be interpreted. The biblical narratives are different. They demand interpretation, and since so much in them is 'dark and incomplete', and since the reader knows that 'God is a hidden God', efforts to interpret them constantly find 'something new to feed upon'. But more importantly, the narratives disclose a world that makes an absolute, tyrannical claim upon us: 'it insists that it is the only real world, is destined for autocracy.' We are to be either its subjects or rebels. 'Far from seeking, like Homer, merely to make us forget our own reality for a few hours, it seeks to overcome our reality: we are to fit our own life into its world, feel ourselves to be elements in its structure of universal history.'[23] The Old Testament begins with the creation of the world and ends with Malachi's prophecy of final judgement. 'Everything else that happens in the world can only be conceived as an element in

[21] I will suggest that this aspect of Scripture is underestimated by Hans Frei and even George Lindbeck, who led Frei to pay it more attention.

[22] Erich Auerbach, *Mimesis: The Representation of Reality in Western Literature*, translated by Willard R. Trask (Princeton, New Jersey: Princeton University Press, 1953), p. 13.

[23] Auerbach, *Mimesis*, p. 15.

this sequence; into it everything that is known about the world, or at least everything that touches upon the history of the Jews, must be fitted as an ingredient of the divine plan'.[24]

The demand of the Old Testament that extra-biblical history should be incorporated within its story does not stop with either the Old Testament or with Jewish history, but is a demand made by the whole Bible, extending to all history.[25] The book is omnivorous. The 'need for interpretation reaches out beyond the original Jewish-Israelitish realm of reality – for example to Assyrian, Babylonian, Persian, and Roman history'.[26] And as it does so, the Bible itself changes, forges new links and enlarges. The linking of the Hebrew Scriptures to the Church's own early writings is the most striking interpretation of this sort. Now the book engulfs the entire Roman world and relates everything to Jesus Christ. Nothing short of the world's destiny is written into its pages.

Auerbach's understanding of the Bible as seeking to 'overcome our reality' has been influential in the development of narrative theology. Hans Frei, in particular, has used the idea of the Bible as a consuming text to articulate the primacy of the biblical story for theology. The Bible sets forth a story of the world, from its beginning to its ending. It is the only true story of the world, all other stories being at best partial renditions of the world story disclosed in the Bible. Consequently, all other stories must be inscribed into the biblical story, rather than the biblical story into any one of them. Insofar as we allow the biblical story to become our story, it overcomes our reality. We no longer view the world as once we did; we view it from the point of view of a character in the Bible's story.

Reading the Bible in this way, Frei argues, is consistent with the greater part of the Christian tradition, from Augustine to

24 Auerbach, *Mimesis*, p. 16. Presumably it is the Church that will fit the 'history of the Jews' into the Old Testament, since the Hebrew Bible ends not with Malachi but with II Chronicles, looking not to the end of the world but to the rebuilding of Solomon's Temple.

25 Auerbach uses 'Old Testament' and 'Bible' either synonymously or carelessly.

26 Auerbach, *Mimesis*, p. 16.

Barth.[27] On Frei's reading of Barth's *Church Dogmatics*, the Bible depicts the 'temporal world of eternal grace' as a 'world with its own linguistic integrity, much as a literary art work is a consistent world in its own right, one that we can have only under a depiction, under its own particular depiction and not any other'. But unlike other depicted worlds – in Homer or elsewhere – 'it is the one common world in which we all live and move and have our being'. The Bible's 'narrated, narratable world is at the same time the ordinary world in which we are responsible for our actions'.[28] For Frei, Barth uses exegesis, ethics and *ad hoc* apologetics,[29] in order to show how the biblical world is our world. Barth is a 'poet'; his work the product of 'dogmatic imagination', using 'second-order talk merged with imaginative restatements . . . of parts of the original narrative', the two 'carefully crafted together' and 'governed by the controlling subject matter'.[30] While this way of reading the Bible goes against the spirit of the modern age, which is narrated by other stories, and against liberal theology, which is engulfed by them, it is the reading to which the Church has long been committed and to which it is recalled by both Barth and Frei.

George Lindbeck, in the preface to his important study on *The Nature of Doctrine* (1984), expresses his indebtedness to the work and encouragement of Hans Frei.[31] That indebtedness shows in Lindbeck's discussion of 'extra-' and 'intratextuality'.

[27] Frei, *The Eclipse of Biblical Narrative: A Study in Eighteenth and Nineteenth Century Hermeneutics* (New Haven: Yale University Press, 1974), p. 1.

[28] Hans Frei, 'Eberhard Busch's biography of Karl Barth', in *Types of Christian Theology*, edited by George Hunsinger and William C. Placher (New Haven and London: Yale University Press, 1992), pp. 147–63 (p. 161).

[29] George Hunsinger (Afterword in Frei, *Theology and Narrative*, p. 247) describes *ad hoc* apologetics as 'essentially a matter of clarifying the meaning rather than demonstrating the truth of a particular claim or set of claims.' The latter is *bad* apologetics.

[30] Frei, *Types*, p. 162. Maurice Wiles suggests that Barth should be read as a poet in *The Remaking of Christian Doctrine* (London: SCM Press, 1974), p. 24.

[31] George A. Lindbeck, *The Nature of Doctrine: Religion and Theology in a Postliberal Age* (London: SPCK, 1984), pp. 12–13. As William Placher notes, Lindbeck is more influenced by Frei's work than the 'relatively sparse references' to him in Lindbeck's book suggest (William C. Placher, Introduction to Frei, *Theology and Narrative*, p. 20 n. 1).

Once again, as with Barth and Frei, the distinction turns on where theology stands to view the world: outside or inside the religious text or semiotic system. Is the signification of 'God' determined by the reality to which it refers or the experience it symbolises, or does its meaning depend upon how it is used, and thus how it helps to shape the experience of people within the Church? Does its meaning depend upon something outside the Christian system (extratextual), or upon the system itself (intratextual)?

Unlike Barth and Frei, Lindbeck advances a general theory of religion.[32] In brief, Lindbeck's theory states that religion is a 'medium' or 'framework' that shapes the entirety of a believer's life. The discourses and practices of religion, its 'language-games' and 'forms of life', provide a 'scaffolding' for religious feeling and experience.[33] Religion is an 'external word, a *verbum externum*, that moulds and shapes the self and its world, rather than an expression or thematization of a pre-existing self or preconceptual experience.'[34] On this view, religious experience arises out of religious practice, rather than the other way around. 'First comes the objectivities of the religion, its language, doctrines, liturgies, and modes of action, and it is through these that passions are shaped into various kinds of what is called religious experience.'[35]

[32] Lindbeck's account of religion is intended to be broadly philosophical and 'social-scientific' in character, while remaining advantageous to, and fruitful for, 'theological purposes'. *Nature of Doctrine*, pp. 7–8. D. Z. Phillips ('Lindbeck's audience', *Modern Theology* 4 (1988), 133–54; reprinted in *Faith After Foundationalism*, pp. 195–224) points out that Lindbeck's theory only makes sense within a certain 'ecumenical tradition', and not across religions as suggested (p. 136). Phillips also notes that Lindbeck, having shown the confusions in other 'theories' (cognitivist and expressivist) continues to talk of them as valid options (p. 144).

[33] See Ludwig Wittgenstein, *On Certainty*, edited by G. E. M. Anscombe and G. E. von Wright, translated by G. E. M. Anscombe (Oxford: Basil Blackwell, [1967] 1981), p. 211.

[34] Lindbeck, *Nature of Doctrine*, p. 34.

[35] Lindbeck, *Nature of Doctrine*, p. 39. Lindbeck describes his preferred theory of religion as 'cultural-linguistic', and sets it against the cognitivist-propositional (religion as propositions concerning religious objects) and the experiential-expressivist (religion as expression of religious experience). See further Gerard Loughlin, 'See-saying/say-seeing', *Theology* 91 (1988), 201–9. For a general overview of Lindbeck's theology and of responses to it, see Gordon E. Michalson Jr., 'The response to Lindbeck', *Modern Theology* 4 (1988), 107–20.

Allied to this account of religion is Lindbeck's general theory of meaning, which draws a distinction between meaning that is internal to a system and meaning that is dependent on something external to the system.

> One does not succeed in identifying the 8.02 to New York by describing the history or manufacture of trains or even by a complete inventory of the cars, passengers, and conductors that constituted and travelled on it on a given day. None of the cars, passengers, and crew might be the same the next day, and yet the train would be self-identically the 8.02 to New York. Its meaning, its very reality, is its function within a particular transportation system.[36]

In a sense all meaning is intratextual or intrasemiotic, insofar as any meaningful thing is a sign and all signs signify through their location in a semiotic system. Yet within the category of 'meaning systems' Lindbeck seems to want to distinguish between semiotic and non-semiotic systems (e.g. transportation systems),[37] and within semiotic systems, greater and lesser degrees of intratextuality. Languages, cultures and religions are the most intratextual of all because in a system like French or English one can transcribe all other systems, including the system itself, reflexively. 'One can speak of all life and reality in French, or from an American or Jewish perspective; and one can also describe French in French, American culture in American terms, and Judaism in Jewish ones.'[38] In other words – though Lindbeck does not make this explicit – there is really no such thing as extratextuality: there is nothing outside the text.[39] But what Lindbeck wants to

[36] Lindbeck, *Nature of Doctrine*, p. 114.

[37] Though surely a transportation system is also a semiotic system, as Lindbeck's example of the 8.02 to New York suggests?

[38] Lindbeck, *Nature of Doctrine*, p. 114.

[39] Again, this does not mean that there are no non-textual realities, but that insofar as they are meaningful they are encoded within a language, a semiotic system. This, perhaps, destabilises Lindbeck's distinction between intra- and extratextual meaning. If a theology determines the meaning of 'God' by reference to a reality external to the religious system, it can do so only in the sense that it is extra or supplemental to the particular system, not that it is textually uncoded. But as a supplement it will be both extra to, and necessary for, the completion of

show, is that his general theory of meaning permits the consumption of the world by a religious text, understood in this instance as a religious culture.[40] It is possible for 'theology to be intratextual, not simply by explicating religion from within but in the stronger sense of describing everything as inside, as interpreted by the religion'.[41]

Religious cultures are literally intratextual insofar as they live within a textual world, a 'semiotic universe paradigmatically encoded in holy writ.'[42] Thus we arrive at Lindbeck's rendition of Auerbach's tyrannical text. But here the contrast is drawn not with Homer, but with Sophocles and Tolstoy, and it is not so much a contrast as a similitude. Like *Oedipus Rex* and *War and Peace*, the Bible evokes its own 'domain of meaning', with its own events and characters. In order to be understood it does not have to be related to other stories, histories and theories. It shapes the 'imagination and perceptions of the attentive reader so that he or she forever views the world to some extent' through its lenses. To describe the meaning of the book is an 'intratextual task'. If these considerations apply to plays and novels, they apply 'even more forcefully to the preeminently authoritative texts that are the canonical writings of religious communities. For those who are steeped in them, no world is more real than the ones they create. A scriptural world is thus able to absorb the universe.'[43]

the system. Lindbeck's argument must be that the system does not need supplementing. This would seem to be the position of Hans Frei when he writes that the narrative description of God in Scripture is adequate for knowing, obeying and trusting God: 'we do not need more.' (Frei, *Theology and Narrative*, p. 210.) Yet the history of the Church shows Scripture's ceaseless supplementation.

40 Lindbeck follows Clifford Geertz in describing religions as complex, comprehensive and reflexive cultures that require 'thick description' (Lindbeck, *Nature of Doctrine*, p. 115). See Clifford Geertz, *The Interpretation of Cultures: Selected Essays* (New York: Basic Books, 1973).

41 Lindbeck, *Nature of Doctrine*, p. 114–15.

42 Lindbeck, *Nature of Doctrine*, p. 116.

43 Lindbeck, *Nature of Doctrine*, p. 117. See further Bruce D. Marshall, 'Absorbing the world: Christianity and the universe of truths', in *Theology and Dialogue: Essays in Conversation with George Lindbeck*, edited by Bruce D. Marshall (Notre Dame, Indiana: University of Notre Dame Press, 1990), pp. 69–102. Mark I. Wallace identifies Lindbeck's absorbant Bible as 'the cornerstone' of Yale theology (*The*

Like Frei, Lindbeck also seeks to relate his account of an absorbent Scripture to the greater part of the Christian tradition. Augustine struggled to 'insert everything from Platonism and the Pelagian problem to the Fall of Rome into the Bible.' Aquinas also assumed that 'Scripture creates its own domain of meaning and that the task of interpretation is to extend this over the whole of reality.' And even Schleiermacher struggled to get 'German romantic idealism' into the Bible.[44]

FIGURING IN

While Auerbach presents the Old Testament as an imperious narrative, claiming absolute truth for its reality and denying all others – eating up the world – it is not so much the Bible that does this as its readers. The continued consumption of nations and powers – Assyria, Babylon, Persia, Rome – and the growth of the Bible, could not be accomplished without people to feed it. Hans Frei's interest in the history of the Bible's reading leads to a less fanciful account than Auerbach's, which constantly treats the Bible as an agent, seeking, insisting, and subjecting. Above all, Frei pays attention to the Church's reading of Scripture, noting that figuration was the chief means for reading the histories of others into the biblical story. It was used first to link narratives within the Bible, especially Old to New Testament stories, and then biblical stories to histories outside the Bible.[45]

Second Naiveté: Barth, Ricoeur and the New Yale Theology, Studies in American Biblical Hermeneutics 6 (Macon, GA: Mercer University Press, 1990), p. 104). For Wallace's critique of Frei and Lindbeck see chapter 5 below.

44 Lindbeck, *Nature of Doctrine*, p. 117. See Marshall, 'Absorbing the world', pp. 76–7.

45 Hans Frei, *Eclipse*, p. 3. As Marjorie Reeves notes, the 'reality of sacred history is brought under pressure to yield every possible "sign" along the road which humanity is treading into the future'. She describes a remarkable example of 'figuring in' provided by the medieval Spiritual Franciscan, Angelo Clareno: 'His sense that St Francis had inaugurated the new age led him to adapt New Testament words applied to Christ to contemporary experience in an astonishing manner: "God has in times past spoken to us in Fathers, Apostles, Prophets, Martyres, Doctors and Saints, but in these newest days He has spoken to us in his

The Jewish texts are taken as 'types' of the story of Jesus as their common 'antitype', an appropriating procedure that begins in the New Testament, notably in the letters of Paul, the letter to the Hebrews, and the synoptic Gospels, and then becomes the common characteristic of the Christian tradition of scriptural interpretation until modern times.[46]

The effect of figural or typological reading, which permits not only the relation of otherwise independent biblical narratives, but of biblical and extrabiblical stories, including one's own, is to render the Bible not only all-consuming, but coherent: a single unified story rather than a collection of disparate narratives and other writings. 'Figuration was at once a literary and a historical procedure, an interpretation of stories and their meanings by weaving them together into a common narrative referring to a single history and its patterns of meaning.'[47] Figuration thus serves to overcome one of the criticisms made of narrativist theology, that it supposes the Bible a single narrative when manifestly it is not.

Maurice Wiles insists that there is no 'necessary unity' to the Bible apart from the fact that the Church has chosen to ascribe it 'an authoritative status as scripture.'[48] He notes that narrativists such as George Lindbeck, Charles Wood and

Seraphic Son Francis whom he has constituted heir of all things following . . . who, being in this world in the form of Christ crucified, humbled himself . . . wherefore God has exalted him and given him a name . . . ".' Reeves, 'The Bible and literary authorship', pp. 33–4. See also Averil Cameron, *Christianity and the Rhetoric of Empire: The Development of Christian Discourse* (Berkeley: University of California Press, 1991), pp. 47–119.

46 Frei, *Theology and Narrative*, p. 120. Frei relies on Auerbach's analysis of typological figuration: 'Figural interpretation establishes a connection between two events or persons in such a way that the first signifies not only itself but also the second, while the second involves or fulfils the first. The two poles of a figure are separated in time, but both, being real events or persons, are within temporality. They are both contained in the flowing stream which is historical life, and only the comprehension, the intellectus spiritualis, of their interdependence is a spiritual act.' *Mimesis*, p. 73. See further Erich Auerbach, 'Figura' (1944) in *Scenes from the Drama of European Literature*, Theory and History of Literature vol.9 (Manchester: Manchester University Press, 1984), pp. 11–76.

47 Frei, *Eclipse*, p. 2; see also p. 28.

48 Maurice Wiles, 'Scriptural authority and theological construction: the limitations of narrative interpretation', in *Scriptural Authority and Narrative Interpretation*, edited by Garret Green (Philadelphia: Fortress Press, 1987), 42–58 (p. 46).

Ronald Thiemann choose to read it as a unified text,[49] but thinks this an arbitrary decision. 'For it amounts simply to saying that it is a decision to go on regarding Scripture as it has been regarded in the past, whatever new insights about its nature may have arisen in the meantime.'[50] Nor is it a 'straightforward' matter to unify the Bible under the term of narrative. While narrative 'can be wide ranging and allow for various subplots within an ordered whole', the 'term when applied to the whole of Scripture has been stretched beyond the point at which such precise description is appropriate.'[51] Wiles is critical of reading the Bible as 'one vast, loosely structured non-fictional novel'; a way of reading the Bible that David Kelsey ascribes to Barth, and which Lindbeck endorses.[52]

Wiles is doubtful that one can read the Bible as a unified story. Even in those parts that are more clearly narrative than others, the gospels, the story of Jesus is always in danger of losing its coherence and of collapsing into multiple conflicting narratives. The Church has strained to maintain the single story. Wiles suggests that the problem is simply aggravated if we try to read the entire Bible as telling the story of God, and concludes 'that even if the concept of reading the Bible as one story is allowed, it is not at all clear what that one story is.'[53]

But the Church has read its Scriptures as narrating one story, and has had little difficulty in determining what that story is. The Church has found the focus or centre of the biblical narratives in the story of Jesus Christ, the story of his life, death and resurrection. It reads the Bible 'around

[49] See Lindbeck, *Nature of Doctrine*, pp. 120–1; Charles M. Wood, *The Formation of Christian Understanding: An Essay in Theological Hermeneutics* (Philadelphia: Westminster Press, 1981), p. 70; and Ronald F. Thiemann, *Revelation and Theology: The Gospel as Narrated Promise* (Notre Dame, Indiana: University of Notre Dame Press, 1984), pp. 65–6.

[50] Wiles, 'Scriptural authority', p. 47. It is unclear why choosing to read the Bible as it has been read in the past is arbitrary; it seems highly determined.

[51] Wiles, 'Scriptural authority', p. 47.

[52] David H. Kelsey, *The Uses of Scripture in Recent Theology* (Philadelphia: Fortress Press, 1975), p. 48. See Lindbeck, *Nature of Doctrine*, pp. 120–1.

[53] Wiles, 'Scriptural authority', p. 48.

Christ'.[54] For St Augustine, the Scripture serves to teach us *caritas*; love of God and love of neighbour for the sake of God. It does so by leading us to Christ crucified, who came to show us the way of charity; the way to God in whom alone we can take true enjoyment.[55] Christ shows us the way by being 'a pattern of holy life in the form of our own humanity'. He is the way by which we shall 'reach our home'.[56]

Scripture is a text with a centre; it is to be interpreted in the light of Christ crucified and only so . . . with the coming of Christ and his passion and resurrection the full scope of divine and human *caritas* appears, so that the previous history in the light of which Christ is intelligible, and which he in turn makes newly intelligible, is seen to serve, to be 'useful', in relation to this decisively liberating event.[57]

It is this same centre and focus of Scripture – the life and death of Christ as the way of love to God – that narrativists such as Barth, Frei and Lindbeck, also discern. Lindbeck could be summarising Augustine when he writes that the 'primary focus is not on God's being in itself, for that is not what the text is about, but on how life is to be lived and reality construed in the light of God's character as an agent as this is depicted in the stories of Israel and of Jesus.'[58] If the Church, from Augustine to Lindbeck, and of course from before Augustine, has been able to identify the story of Scripture as the story of Christ crucified, how is it that Wiles finds it so difficult?

[54] Rowan Williams, *Open to Judgement: Sermons and Addresses* (London: Darton, Longman and Todd, 1994), p. 160.

[55] Augustine, *On Christian Doctrine*, in *A Select Library of the Nicene and Post-Nicene Fathers*, edited by Philip Schaff, vol.2 (Grand Rapids, Michigan: William B. Eerdmans Publishing Company, [1886] 1977), Book 1, chapter 22 (p. 527).

[56] Augustine, *On Christian Doctrine*, Book 1, chapter 11 (p. 525).

[57] Rowan Williams, 'Language, reality and desire in Augustine's *De Doctrina*', *Literature and Theology* 3 (1989), 138–50 (p. 146). See also Williams, 'The literal sense of Scripture', *Modern Theology*, 7 (1991), 121–34 (pp. 130–1).

[58] Lindbeck, *Nature of Doctrine*, p. 121. Augustine also stresses that the Bible is not about 'God's being in itself', which is ineffable. *On Christian Doctrine*, Book 1, chapter 6 (p. 524).

The answer is simple enough. Barth, Frei and Lindbeck are bound by the past, as was Augustine. More precisely, they are bound, or bind themselves, by rules of engagement with the text, by reading regulations. Augustine's *De Doctrina Christiana* is about 'rules for the interpretation of Scripture.'[59] It is to such a ruled reading of Scripture that Wiles objects, asserting that 'the grammatical rules for reading the Christian story (as Lindbeck regards them) have served the cause of institutional control at least as much as the cause of religious truth.'[60] The story of Scripture becomes difficult to discern once one abandons the traditional reading rules; the Church's scriptural grammar.

SCRIPTURE RULES

The Church reads its Scripture according to certain rules or doctrines. For Lindbeck, doctrines are the 'communally authoritative teachings regarding beliefs and practices that are considered essential to the identity and welfare' of the Church.[61] They thus cover the reading of Scripture. Lindbeck's rule theory of doctrine, which seeks to show 'how doctrines can be both firm and flexible, both abiding and adaptable',[62] suggests that the function of doctrine is purely regulative. Doctrines *qua* doctrines are second-order propositions which make 'intrasystematic rather than ontological truth claims'.[63] They may function otherwise in the Church, as symbols or as first-order propositions making ontological claims, but then they are not functioning as doctrines, as norms of 'communal

[59] Augustine, *On Christian Doctrine*, Preface (p. 519).

[60] Wiles, 'Scriptural authority', p. 51. Lindbeck notes that the 'modern mood is antipathetic to the very notion of communal norms . . . The suggestion that communities have the right to insist on standards of belief and practice as conditions of membership is experienced as an intolerable infringement of the liberty of the self. This reaction is intensified by the growing contradiction between traditional standards and the prevailing values of the wider society as communicated by education, the mass media, and personal contacts.' (*Nature of Doctrine*, p. 77.)

[61] Lindbeck, *Nature of Doctrine*, p. 74.

[62] Lindbeck, *Nature of Doctrine*, p. 79.

[63] Lindbeck, *Nature of Doctrine*, p. 80.

belief or practice'.[64] Doctrines are propositions functioning as rules.

Doctrines are not the most fundamental rules governing religious discourse and practice. They merely 'reflect' the more basic grammar that regulates the vocabulary of 'symbols, concepts, rites, injunctions and stories' which go to make up the discourses and practices of religion. They 'illustrate correct usage rather than define it. They are exemplary instantiations or paradigms of the application of rules.' Thus faithfulness to doctrine is not a matter of adhering to it as such, but to the grammar it illustrates or exemplifies.[65]

Doctrines are imperfect rules, attempts after the event to model in a formal system the vagaries of the Church's language, the 'deep grammar' of which may 'escape detection'. They are no more than useful guides which must, on occasion, give way to the 'wisdom of the competent speaker'. 'Yet, despite these inadequacies, the guidance offered by the grammar or the doctrine of the textbooks may be indispensable, especially to those who are learning a language, to those who have not mastered it well, or to those who, for whatever reason, are in danger of corrupting it into meaninglessness.'[66]

Following Bernard Lonergan, Lindbeck asserts that the rule theory of doctrine is ancient in the Church. 'The Christians learned from the Greeks the technique of operating on propositions, of formulating propositions about propositions.'[67] Thus for Athanasius, the 'consubstantiality' of Father and Son is a proposition about propositions concerning the Father and the Son; it is a rule for their deployment. As Lonergan has it: 'what is said of the Father is also to be said of the Son, except that the Son is Son and not Father'.[68] 'Thus the theologian most responsible for the final triumph of Nicea thought of it,

64 Lindbeck, *Nature of Doctrine*, p. 80.

65 Lindbeck, *Nature of Doctrine*, p. 81.

66 Lindbeck, *Nature of Doctrine*, p. 82.

67 Lindbeck, *Nature of Doctrine*, p. 94.

68 Bernard Lonergan, *The Way to Nicea: The Dialectical Development of Trinitarian Theology*, translated by Conn O'Donovan (London: Darton, Longman and Todd, 1976), p. 103. See also *Method in Theology* (London: Darton, Longman and Todd, 1972), p. 277.

not as a first-order proposition with ontological reference, but as a second-order rule of speech.'[69]

Doctrines as rules or grammar operate on the 'surface' and at 'depth' (when they are described as 'principles').[70] Surface grammar is but an indication of what lies below. Thus Lindbeck suggests that beneath the ancient credal rules lie three other, deeper rules, which 'have been abidingly important from the beginning in forming mainstream Christian identity.'[71] These rules or principles propose that (1) there is only one God; that (2) Jesus was an actual human person and that (3) every possible importance should be ascribed to him which is not inconsistent with the first two rules.[72] It is these three deep principles – monotheism, historical specificity and Christological maximalism – that finally have doctrinal authority. The authority of the creeds derives from the underlying principles which are permanently embodied, if anywhere, in the Scripture that shapes the practice of the Church.[73]

The relationship between Lindbeck's deep grammatical principles and specific doctrinal rules is unclear. The supposition of such principles seems to serve the purpose of relativising any particular doctrine, which at best can only be the effect of a prior rule which is finally unstatable. This follows from Lindbeck's distinction between doctrine and formulation, content and form.[74] He argues that Christianity has always distinguished between the content of faith and its expression. 'No particular words or specific interpretive notions are uniquely sacrosanct.'[75] But there is a problem with stating the content as distinct from its forms. Lindbeck notes

[69] Lindbeck, *Nature of Doctrine*, p. 94.

[70] Lindbeck, *Nature of Doctrine*, p. 94. Lindbeck's terminology is nothing if not fluid.

[71] Lindbeck, *Nature of Doctrine*, p. 95. Terrence F. Tilley ('Incommensurability, intratextuality, and fideism', *Modern Theology* 5 (1989), 87–117) suggests that Lindbeck's three principles could as easily give rise to Arianism as to orthodoxy, and therefore need the additional principle of the 'sufficiency of salvation' in Jesus Christ (pp. 103 and 111 n. 31).

[72] Lindbeck, *Nature of Doctrine*, p. 94.

[73] Lindbeck, *Nature of Doctrine*, p. 96.

[74] Lindbeck, *Nature of Doctrine*, p. 92.

[75] Lindbeck, *Nature of Doctrine*, p. 92.

that though it is possible to have different statements of the same proposition – the 'fact that so-and-so has jaundice can be affirmed in the idiom of Galen's medical theories (an imbalance of humours) or that of modern science (a viral infection)' – it is not possible to state the proposition apart from its formulations.[76] This problem leads Lindbeck to say that one 'can grasp the self-identical content as distinct from the form only by seeing that the diverse formulations are equivalent and, usually in a second step, by stating the equivalency rules.'[77] This is no doubt correct. But it is not obviously equivalent to distinguishing between content and form. The latter notion involves the supposition of an unstatable proposition which underwrites the equivalency of formulations; whereas the former idea requires only the *judgement* of equivalency. Thus different doctrinal formulations are judged to be equivalent, not in virtue of stating one and the same proposition, itself not otherwise statable, but in virtue of the *judgement* that they are equivalent. To this one may respond that there must be something in virtue of which the judgement is made. Lindbeck suggests that one may judge the equivalency of doctrines in virtue of their 'equivalent consequences'.[78] But once again, how can one judge the *equivalency* of the consequences, without so *judging*? Judgement is a basic practice which *makes* distinctions and equivalences or observes the equivalences and distinctions made by other judgements.[79]

Lindbeck's understanding of doctrine as the rule of faithful practice, recalls medieval understanding of grammar as the

76 Lindbeck, *Nature of Doctrine*, p. 93. Is it so obvious that having jaundice, an imbalance of humours or a viral infection are one and the same thing?

77 Lindbeck, *Nature of Doctrine*, p. 93.

78 Lindbeck, *Nature of Doctrine*, p. 93.

79 This does not mean that one cannot give reasons for judging equivalency. It means only that equivalency is not a determinant, but a result of the judgement. As Stanley Fish puts it, judgements are made *within* and not *with* a practice of judgement. Stating *why*, as distinct from *how*, a judgement was made, is a matter of the 'complex of rhetorical gestures to which one has recourse when a decision, already made, must be put into presentable form.' *Doing What Comes Naturally: Change, Rhetoric, and the Practice of Theory in Literary and Legal Studies* (Oxford: Clarendon Press, 1989), p. 389.

'motherly' care of reading and writing, the 'nurse' that guards against mistake and impropriety, correcting bad form and nurturing good.[80] Also popular in medieval thought was the idea that grammar limited the confusion of languages after Babel, the misunderstanding that arises from the 'babbling chaos of tongues'.[81] Jesse M. Gellrich suggests that medieval appeals to the necessity of the *Ars grammatica* and the *Institutiones grammaticae* – and to Hebrew as 'mother tongue' – were attempts to stabilise semantics and arbitrate discourse, to shore up 'meaning against the ruin of misreading.'[82] It is in this sense that doctrines are rules for the reading of Scripture.

The Church learns the ruled reading of Scripture through catechesis and liturgy, and above all through the creeds which are taught in the first and prayed in the second. The worship of the Church is where the creed is primarily and most properly used, above all in baptism and Eucharist, which are themselves enacted construals of the Scripture story (see further chapter 3). The Nicene creed summarises the story of Scripture, focused around the death and resurrection of Christ. 'What the Scriptures say at length, the creed says briefly.'[83] It relates Christ to those who came before him, to the prophets who foretold his advent, and to those who come after him, who look for his return and the resurrection of the dead. It relates Christ to the mystery of God, to the Father and the Spirit with whom he is 'consubstantial'. If you know the creed you know how to read the Scripture.

The creed is the rule of Scripture, but a rule means nothing without that which it rules. Thus, as Nicholas Lash insists, it is only if you know the Scripture that you know how to read the creed; you 'only discover the meaning of the creed in the

80 Jesse M. Gellrich, *The Idea of the Book in the Middle Ages: Language Theory, Mythology, and Fiction* (Ithaca and London: Cornell University Press, 1985), pp. 96–8.

81 *The Metalogicon of John of Salisbury*, translated by Daniel D. McGarry (Berkeley: University of California Press, 1955), p. 28.

82 Gellrich, *The Idea of the Book*, p. 99.

83 Nicholas Lash, *Believing Three Ways in One God: A Reading of the Apostles' Creed* (London: SCM Press, 1992), p. 8.

measure that the Bible stays an open book.'[84] It is to Scripture that the Church turns in order to know what it means to confess Father, Son and Spirit as consubstantial; to confess Christ's death and resurrection, and to have hope of the body's resurrection. Thus creed and Scripture, rule and text, are mutually implicated, folded within one another.[85]

Again, the ruled reading of Scripture is ancient in the Church. St Irenaeus, seeking in the second century to differentiate catholic from gnostic Christianity, deployed the 'rule of faith' or 'canon of truth' as a measure for the reading of Scripture. The Irenaean 'rule' was closely related to the Church's later creeds, but it was not itself a creed. As Frances Young argues, it was rather an 'overall framework' which gave expression to the Church's understanding of the 'unitive story' narrated in the Scriptures, and to the Church's 'tradition of appropriate performance of the text'.[86] It is through the traditioned performance of the Scriptures in the liturgy of the Church that the ruled reading of Scripture is given and learned, the creeds serving to sustain the 'identity and oneness of the Christian Church in obedience to the One confessed as God and in service of the oneness of the world and of the human race.'[87]

This discussion of Scripture's reading rules began as an answer to the question of how one determines the story of the Bible from among its many different writings, its myths and chronicles, laws, proverbs and poems. Having shown that the Church does so by practising a reading discipline, I now turn to consider *how* it is possible for the Bible to tell many narratives, but only one story.

[84] Lash, *Believing*, p. 9.

[85] For further discussion of the enfolding of rule and text see Gerard Loughlin, 'Christianity at the end of the story or the return of the master-narrative', *Modern Theology* 8 (1992), 365–84 (pp. 377–8).

[86] Frances Young, *The Art of Performance: Towards a Theology of Holy Scripture* (London: Darton, Longman and Todd, 1990), p. 48. See Irenaeus, *Against the Heresies*, 1.10.1.

[87] Lash, *Believing*, pp. 7–8. The creeds are 'communally authoritative . . . identity-sustaining rules of discourse and behaviour governing Christian uses of the word "God"' (p. 8).

STORY/NARRATIVE/NARRATOLOGY

The working of narrative is of increasing interest to biblical scholars. Against earlier forms of scholarship which read the biblical narratives as merely deposits or traces of past events, the new scholarship seeks to understand the storied nature of the narratives.[88] Thus there has developed a biblical narratology.[89] The following is a sketch, after Gérard Genette, of what is involved in such an enterprise. It is by no means exhaustive, and is chiefly intended to explore the distinction between 'story' and 'narrative' that is framed at its conclusion.[90]

In *Narrative Discourse* (1980), Gérard Genette proffers a narrative mechanics, a detailed exposition of how narrative works to configure its elements. He analyses five mechanisms of configuration – order, duration, frequency, mood and voice, but fundamental to his argument is a distinction between two sorts of time, story time and narrative time. There is the time of the story *told* and the time of its *telling*. In the case of written narrative, telling becomes reading, the time of 'consumption'.

[88] 'Today, narrative criticism has all but replaced redaction criticism in many circles as the dominant methodology for study of Mark's Gospel' (Mark Allan Powell, 'Toward a narrative-critical understanding of Mark', *Interpretation* 47 (1993), 341–6 (p. 342)). See further Stephen D. Moore, *Literary Criticism and the Gospels: The Theoretical Challenge* (New Haven and London: Yale University Press, 1989).

[89] On narratology see Robert Scholes and Robert Kellog, *The Nature of Narrative* (New York: Oxford University Press, 1966) and Mieke Bal, *Narratology: Introduction to the Theory of Narrative*, translated by C. von Boheemen (Toronto: University of Toronto Press, 1985). On biblical narratology see Robert Alter, *The Art of Biblical Narrative* (London and Sydney: George Allen and Unwin, 1981) and Meir Sternberg, *The Poetics of Biblical Narrative: Ideological Literature and the Drama of Reading* (Bloomington, Indiana: Indiana University Press, 1985); and for brief and accessible introductions see Elizabeth Struthers Malbon, 'Narrative criticism: how does the story mean?' in *Mark and Method: New Approaches in Biblical Studies*, edited by Janice Capel Anderson and Stephen D. Moore (Minneapolis: Fortress Press, 1992), pp. 23–49 and Mark Allan Powell, *What is Narrative Criticism? A New Approach to the Bible* (London: SPCK, 1993).

[90] Readers reading for the argument may like to pass over this section, but they should note its conclusions.

Produced in time, like everything else, written narrative exists in space and as space, and the time needed for 'consuming' it is the time needed for crossing or traversing it, like a road or a field. The narrative text, like every other text, has no other temporality than what it borrows, metonymically, from its own reading.[91]

For Genette, the time of consumption is a pseudo time, standing in for the true time of the story. The difference between pseudo and true time constitutes the first three mechanisms of his narrative analytics. Firstly, there is the difference between the 'order' or 'succession' of events in story (true time) and in narrative (pseudo time); secondly, the variable 'duration' or 'speed' of the events in both story and narrative; and thirdly, the 'frequency' or 'repetition' of the story and narrative events.[92]

While the time of the narrative is a pseudo-time, the time of the story is fictive insofar as it has to be inferred from the narrative. Such inference or reconstitution is not always possible, as in the novels of Robbe-Grillet or in many of the biblical narratives. (When is the Temple cleansed, at the beginning or end of Christ's ministry?)[93] But for the most part reconstitution is possible and necessary.

When a narrative segment begins with an indication like 'Three months earlier, . . .' we must take into account both that this scene comes *after* in the narrative, and that it is supposed to have come *before* in the story: each of these, or rather the relationship between them (of contrast or of dissonance) is basic to the narrative text.[94]

The daughter of Herodias dancing before Herod comes *after* the arrest of John the Baptist in Matthew's narrative, but *before* the arrest in the story.[95]

[91] Gérard Genette, *Narrative Discourse*, translated by Jane E. Lewin (Oxford: Basil Blackwell, 1980), p. 34. Genette applies his narratology to Marcel Proust's *A la recherche du temps perdu* (1913–1927); I minimally apply it to biblical narrative, in particular the gospels.

[92] Genette, *Narrative Discourse*, p. 35.

[93] Compare John 2.13–25; Matthew 21.12–17; Mark 11.15–19; and Luke 19.45–8.

[94] Genette, *Narrative Discourse*, p. 35.

[95] Matthew 14.3–12. See also Mark 6.14–29 and Luke 9.7–9.

Genette calls the difference between the order of events in the story and in the narrative, *anachrony*, and suggests a trajectory of anachronistic possibility: from a point of absolute zero where story and narrative order perfectly agree, to a point of maximum disagreement between the two orderings. Both points are ideals, but Genette suggests that traditional or folklore narrative most nearly approaches zero degree, while the Western literary tradition typically effects discordance. Indeed the tradition is 'inaugurated by a characteristic effect of anachrony. In the eighth line of the *Iliad*, the narrator, having evoked the quarrel between Achilles and Agamemnon that he proclaims as the starting point of his narrative, goes back about ten days to reveal the cause of the quarrel in some 140 retrospective lines'.[96] Genette calls such retrospection *analepsis*, and as a way of beginning a narrative in the middle rather than at the beginning of the story, it becomes a recurring *topos* of Western literature.

Analepsis is a narrative 'manoeuvre' or mechanism, by which the narrative renders or evokes an event that occurred earlier to the point of narration. For example, it is only when Mark narrates the crucifixion of Jesus, and tells us of the women who stayed with him, that we learn that they 'used to follow him and provided for him when he was in Galilee'.[97] *Prolepsis*, on the other hand, is a 'narrative manoeuvre that consists of narrating or evoking in advance an event that will take place later'.[98] These are the two principle forms of discordant anachrony, and both of them can be further analysed in terms of their 'reach' and 'extent'. The 'reach' of anachrony consists in the 'distance' of the story event from its point of narration. It may be a few days or several years. The 'extent' of anachrony consists in the 'duration' of the narrated event, which again may be anything from a few moments to many years.

[96] Genette, *Narrative Discourse*, p. 36.

[97] See Mark 15.40–1. 'So the implied reader learns at the last hour that Jesus had other followers, women followers, from the first. Moreover, these surprising followers stay to the last – although at a distance. Three of them are at the empty tomb as well.' Malbon, 'Narrative criticism', p. 33.

[98] Genette, *Narrative Discourse*, p. 40.

Anachrony can be understood as the grafting or embedding of a second narrative into a first narrative, and the levels of such embedding may be as complex as the author can contrive. Secondary narratives may be 'external' or 'internal' to the first narrative. They can narrate events that occurred either before or after the beginning of the first narrative. Internal anachronies can narrate events that are either extraneous or integral to the main story. Thus when a new character enters a story, and the first narrative breaks off to tell us something of his or her past, we have a case of an internal analepsis that Genette describes as *heterodiegetic*.[99] In Acts the story of Philip in Samaria is interrupted by that of Simon 'who had practised magic in the city and amazed the people of Samaria.'[100] When the main narrative stops to tell us something about the past of its central characters, then we have a case of *homodiegetic* internal analepsis.

Genette distinguishes two forms of homodiegetic analepsis. The first is a 'completing' analepsis which fills in a gap in the narrative. It either fills in a narrative *ellipsis*, a missing part of the story, or a *paralipsis*, a missing element in part of the story.[101] Matthew, having told us about the death of Herod, then fills in a missing part of the story by telling us that Herod had previously 'killed all the children in and around Bethlehem who were two years old or under'.[102] The second sort of homodiegetic analepsis that Genette notes is a 'repeating' analepsis, where the narrative 'retraces its own path.'[103] The retelling of Matthew's story in Mark, Luke and John, may be considered an example of repeating analepsis.

Under the heading of 'duration' Genette discusses narrative 'speed'. This is the measure of how long a narrative takes to tell its story. The speed of a narrative is 'defined by the relationship between a duration (that of the story, measured in seconds, minutes, hours, days, months and years) and a

99 Genette, *Narrative Discourse*, p. 50.

100 Acts 8.9–11. See also the interpolated story of Simeon in Luke 2.25–6.

101 Genette, *Narrative Discourse*, p. 52.

102 Matthew 2.15–18.

103 Genette, *Narrative Discourse*, p. 54.

length (that of the text, measured in lines and in pages).'[104] As with 'order' one can construct a table of possible speeds. Zero degree is *isochronous* narrative, with unvarying speed, neither accelerating nor slowing down. This is an ideal point, and no such narrative exists. All narratives require variations of speed, *anisochrony* or *rhythm*. Variations occur between, on the one hand, the infinite speed of the *ellipsis* and the 'absolute slowness of descriptive *pause*, where some section of narrative discourse corresponds to a nonexistent diegetic duration.'[105] These speeds constitute two of the four speeds or movements that Genette identifies as basic. Between *ellipsis* and *pause* comes *scene* and *summary*. In the scene there is equality between story and narrative time. A scene is typically a piece of dialogue, as between Jesus and his various interlocutors, friendly and hostile. The speed of summary is extremely variable, but the narrative is always faster than the story.[106] The genealogical list in the first chapter of Matthew is a good example of fast summary.

Stories and narratives repeat. An event recurs, perhaps a few times, perhaps every day. The sun rises, the sun sets; winds blow and rains fall. Births and deaths are common; but the birth and death of a particular person occurs only once. However, narrative can tell such events many times. Genette discusses this type of slippage between story and narrative under 'relation of frequency'. 'Schematically, we can say that a narrative, whatever it is, may tell once what happened once, *n* times what happened *n* times, *n* times what happened once, once what happened *n* times.'[107] *Singulative* narrative tells once what happened once (1N/1S); *anaphoric* narrative tells *n* times what happened *n* times (*n*N/*n*S), and is a form of the

[104] Genette, *Narrative Discourse*, pp. 87–8.

[105] Genette, *Narrative Discourse*, pp. 93–4.

[106] Pause: $NT = n$, $ST = 0$. Thus $NT \infty > ST$
Scene: $NT = ST$
Summary: $NT < ST$
Ellipsis: $NT = 0$, $ST = n$. Thus $NT < \infty ST$
(NT = narrative time; ST = story time; $\infty >$ = infinitely greater; $< \infty$ = infinitely less)

[107] Genette, *Narrative Discourse*, p. 114.

singulative. Telling *n* times what happened once is *repeating* narrative (*n*N/1S), beloved of children and modern fiction, as Genette notes, but also of the Bible. And telling once what happened *n* times (1N/*n*S) is *iterative* narrative.[108]

A story can be narrated from a number of different perspectives, each giving a different view of the events, each giving more or less information (and sometimes disinformation) about the story. These differences are like seats in a theatre; stalls, circle and balcony are at differing distances from the stage and provide different angles of vision. Some seats allow clear views, others partial or restricted vision. From some seats you can see all the action on the stage and from others only part of what happens. The view of the stage is regulated by the position of the seat. In the same way, narrative regulates the view of the story. It is this regulation that Genette calls narrative 'mood'.

> Narrative 'representation', or, more exactly, narrative information, has its degrees: the narrative can furnish the reader with more or fewer details, and in a more or less direct way, and can thus seem (to adopt a common and convenient spatial metaphor . . .) to keep at a greater or lesser distance from what it tells. The narrative can also choose to regulate the information it delivers, . . . according to the capacities of knowledge of one or another participant in the story (a character or group of characters), . . . the narrative seems . . . to take on, with regard to the story, one or another perspective. 'Distance' and 'perspective' . . . are the two chief modalities of that regulation of narrative information that is mood.[109]

Genette traces the question of 'distance' back to Plato, who distinguished between pure narrative (*diegesis*) – when the poet is the speaker, and imitation (*mimesis*) – when the poet speaks as if he or she were someone else.[110] Pure narrative or

[108] Genette, *Narrative Discourse*, pp. 114–16.

[109] Genette, *Narrative Discourse*, p. 162.

[110] Plato, *The Republic*, translated by Desmond Lee, revised second edition (Harmondsworth: Penguin Books, 1987), pp. 149–54 (lines 392b–395e). Aristotle makes diegesis a variety of mimesis. See Aristotle, *On The Art of Poetry* in *Classical Literary Criticism*, translated by T. S. Dorsch (Harmondsworth: Penguin Books, 1965).

diegesis, is more 'distant' than mimesis, which is above all the art of the theatre.[111] Genette suggests that all narrative mimesis is an illusion of mimesis, since 'narration, oral or written, is a fact of language, and language signifies without imitating'. Language can imitate only language. 'The truth is that mimesis in words can only be mimesis of words. Other than that, all we have and can have is degrees of diegesis.'[112]

Genette notes that the translation of mimesis into diegesis usually results in *condensation*, chiefly through the elimination of incidental detail, of what Roland Barthes termed *reality effects*. This leads to a consideration of how narratives produce the illusion of imitation. Incidental detail produces the effect of reality because it seems as if its only reason for being in the narrative is that it was there in the story: it just happened to be the case. 'A useless and contingent detail, it is the medium par excellence of the referential illusion, and therefore of the mimetic effect: it is a *connotator of mimesis*.'[113] When the soldiers came to arrest Jesus it just so happened that a 'young man was following him, wearing nothing but a linen cloth'. Never mentioned before or after the incident, the boy is caught by the soldiers, 'but he left the linen cloth and ran off naked.'[114]

Profusion of detail and suppression of the informer are typical of the mimetic illusion; 'mimesis being defined by a maximum of information and a minimum of the informer, diegesis by the opposite relationship.' The informer is effaced so that the story appears to tell itself, showing through the narration. 'Pretending to show is pretending to be silent.'[115] Who informs us about the creation of the world in Genesis, or of Christ tempted in the wilderness?

[111] Genette, *Narrative Discourse*, p. 163. [112] Genette, *Narrative Discourse*, p. 164.

[113] Genette, *Narrative Discourse*, p. 165.

[114] Mark 14.51–2. See Frank Kermode, *The Genesis of Secrecy: On the Interpretation of Narrative* (Cambridge, Massachusetts and London: Harvard University Press, 1979), p. 56. Having noted that the naked boy might be a 'reality effect' or Mark himself – a 'reticent signature, like Alfred Hitchcock's appearances in his own films' – or suggested by Genesis 39:12 and Amos 2:16, Kermode muses on the need to explain the incident (p. 64). For Kermode, the labour of explanation, of reducing fortuity, seems only to render the text more impenetrable.

[115] Genette, *Narrative Discourse*, p. 166.

In the mimesis of language, of speech and dialogue, Genette notes three degrees of distance. *Narrated* speech is the most distant, and generally the most reduced. *Reported* speech is the least distant, the most mimetic – 'Jesus said to them: . . . ' – and, despite Plato's teaching, the most successful and authoritative.[116] At median distance is *transposed* speech – 'Then he began to teach them that . . . '.[117]

Genette discusses 'perspectives' under the category of 'focalization', otherwise known as 'point of view'. Where does the narrator stand to see the story, outside or within? Where does the narrator stand in relation to the story's characters? A narrative has zero focalization when the narrator knows more than the characters (N > C); it has internal focalization when the narrator knows or says what a given character knows (N = C), and this internal focalization may be fixed, variable or multiple. External focalization is where the narrator knows less than the characters (N < C).[118] Biblical narratives are focalized from different distances. The gospel narrators, for example, sometimes know more than the characters, sometimes what one or another knows, and always less than is known by the central character.

The category of 'voice' concerns the 'narrating instant': the point from which a narrative is narrated. The instant of narration is tensed, because the time of the story must be present, past or future to its narration.[119] Genette suggests that we are more likely to know *when*, rather than *where* a story is told.[120] While most narratives are *subsequent* to the story, some are *prior* (predictive) and others *simultaneous*. Genette categorises the distance between the story and the narrating instant in terms of levels. 'Any event a narrative recounts is at a diegetic level immediately higher than the level at which the narrating act producing this narrative is

[116] 'Up to the end of the nineteenth century, the novelistic scene is conceived, fairly piteously, as a pale copy of the dramatic scene: mimesis at two degrees, imitation of imitation.' Genette, *Narrative Discourse*, p. 173.

[117] Mark 8.31.

[118] Genette, *Narrative Discourse*, pp. 189–90.

[119] Genette, *Narrative Discourse*, p. 215.

[120] Genette, *Narrative Discourse*, p. 216.

placed.'[121] Mark's gospel, for example, is narrated at a first, *extradiegetic* level. The events in his narrative, such as the telling of a parable by Jesus, occur at another, *intradiegetic* level. And the events in the parable told by Jesus, occur at yet another, *metadiegetic* level.[122] And so on. Luke telling his readers what Jesus told his auditors Abraham said to Lazarus, is an example of meta-metadiegesis.[123]

Under 'voice', Genette also discusses the 'person' of the narrator.[124] He insists that whether a narrative is told in the first or third person, the 'person' of the narrator is 'invariant'. 'Insofar as the narrator can at any instant intervene as such in the narrative, every narrating is, by definition, to all intents and purposes presented in the first person'.[125] Genette, as is his wont, goes on to outline four ways in which a narrator may appear in his or her narrative.[126] These are plotted along two axes: that of narrative level – where the narrator is either outside or inside the narrative (*extra-* or *intradiegetic*), and that of narrative relationship to the story – where the narrator may or may not be a character in the story (*hetero-* or *homodiegetic*). Thus a narrator may tell a story at the first (*diegetic*) level from which he or she is absent (*extradiegetic-heterodiegetic*) – the Gospel of Matthew; a story at the first level in which he or she

[121] Genette, *Narrative Discourse*, p. 228.

[122] Genette, *Narrative Discourse*, p. 228. For Genette, the *metadiegetic* or *metanarrative* is a narrative within a narrative, rather than a narrative outside and about another narrative. Genette notes that the latter usage is common to 'logic and linguistics' (p. 228 n. 41). It is also usual in theology.

[123] Luke 16.19–31.

[124] Narrator and author are not the same. 'John' is the narrator of Revelation (1.1), but we can only surmise the identity of its author. Narratology also distinguishes between the real author and the implied author. The latter is the author whom the text seems (to the real reader) to imply. Usually implied author and narrator are the same. To all these authoring characters are corresponding recipients or readers. There is the narratee – the 'seven Churches that are in Asia' in Revelation (1.4); the implied reader to whom the text seems (to the real reader) to be addressed (again, implied reader and narratee are often the same); and finally the real reader. Thus:

Real Author	>	Implied Author	>	Narrator	>	Narratee	>	Implied Reader	>	Real Reader

[125] Genette, *Narrative Discourse*, p. 244.

[126] Genette, *Narrative Discourse*, p. 248.

is the principal character – autobiography (*extradiegetic-homodiegetic*) – parts of Paul's letters;[127] a story at the second (*intradiegetic*) level from which he or she she is largely absent (*intradiegetic-heterodiegetic*) – Stephen telling the story of Israel to the Jewish council;[128] and finally a story at the second level in which he or she is the principal character – (*intradiegetic-homodiegetic*) – Paul telling his story to Agrippa.[129]

What is the function of the narrator? Clearly to tell the story (*narrative function*). But the narrator can also direct the reader to certain aspects of the narrative, pointing out connections and offering clarifications (*directing function*).[130] Then there is the relationship of the narrator to the narratee (*narrating situation*), and the relationship of the narrator to the story (*testimonial* and *ideological functions*).[131]

The narratee, who is not necessarily the same as the reader (or implied reader) – for example, the Jewish council listening to Stephen; Agrippa listening to Paul – is constituted at the same level as the narrator. This is usually the diegetic level – Luke addressing Theophilus (who is also the implied reader) – but where there are intradiegetic narrators there are also corresponding narratees – the auditors of Jesus' parables. Thus the intradiegetic narrator can aim only at the intradiegetic narratee, and the extradiegetic narrator 'can aim only at the extradiegetic narratee, who merges with the implied reader and with whom each real reader can identify.'[132]

There is much more to biblical narratology than the above. A fuller discussion would, for example, have to say something

[127] If Mark is the naked boy of his gospel, and John the beloved disciple of his, then these also are *extradiegetic-homodiegetic* narrations.

[128] Acts 7.2–53.

[129] Acts 26.2–23.

[130] This occurs many times in John's gospel.

[131] Genette, *Narrative Discourse*, p. 256. See Luke 1.1–4; John 21.24–5.

[132] Genette, *Narrative Discourse*, p. 260. But is this correct in regard of the Church's reading of the Bible? Does Jesus, as intradiegetic narrator, address only his intradiegetic narratees? Insofar as the Church has found itself addressed by Christ in Scripture, might it be that Christ is not confined to one narrative level? Traditionally, of course, the transition from one level to another has been effected by allegorical reading.

of plot and character.[133] But my deployment of Genette's narratology should be sufficient to show not only the rudiments of narrative mechanics, but how the Bible's many narratives, and in particular the gospels, can tell one story. Genette's complex categorisation of order, duration and frequency, mood and voice, all depend on the distinction, the gap and slippage, between story and narrative.

The story is not given apart from its telling in narrative, but the narrative is not the same as the story.[134] The order of the narrative can be different from that of the story; the narrative's duration is nearly always different from the story's duration; the narrative can tell many times what happened only once, and tell once what happened many times; and the distance between narrative and story can differ greatly, as also the instant of telling. Given these differences between story and narrative, we can see how the Bible can tell one story in variously different ways. It does not narrate every part of the story – there are ellipses, as well as pauses;[135] while other parts are told repeatedly, and from different instants of narration.

That the Bible does tell one story, and what that story is, are not, of course, given by narratology (which is only a mechanics). The story that the Bible tells is given, as we have

[133] For fuller discussion see Adele Berlin, *Poetics and Interpretation of Biblical Narrative* (Sheffield: Almond Press, 1983); R. Alan Culpepper, *Anatomy of the Fourth Gospel: A Study in Literary Design* (Philadelphia: Fortress Press, 1983); Robert W. Funk, *The Poetics of Biblical Narrative* (Sonoma, California: Polebridge Press, 1988); Werner H. Kelber, *Mark's Story of Jesus* (Philadelphia: Fortress Press, 1979); Jack Dean Kingsbury, *Matthew as Story*, second edition (Philadelphia: Fortress Press, 1988); David Rhoads and Donald Michie, *Mark as Story: An Introduction to the Narrative of a Gospel* (Philadelphia: Fortress Press, 1982); and Robert C. Tannehill, *The Narrative Unity of Luke-Acts: A Literary Interpretation* (Philadelphia: Fortress Press, 1986).

[134] It is perhaps a problem of certain literary attempts to read the Bible as a unified whole that they work at the level of the narratives (and other writings) and not at the level of the story. Furthermore – as David Norton suggests – any unity they do espy must seem either arbitrary or an act of covert faith (*A History of the Bible as Literature*, 2 vols. (Cambridge: Cambridge University Press, 1993), Vol. II, p. 393). The Church's account of the Bible's unity depends upon its explicit faith given in the ruled *reading* of the text.

[135] Perhaps laws, proverbs, psalms and songs are narrative 'pauses'.

already seen, through the Church's ruled reading of the Bible as Scripture. It is the story and the communal aspect of the story – as constituting and constituted by the Church – that is the subject of the next chapter.

CHAPTER 3

Character/circumstance/community

Why narrative? Why attend to the narrative function, to the telling of stories? Why insist that Christian convictions are best conveyed in story, rather than in proposition and maxim? One answer would be to say that narrative is basic in human life, beyond culture and rooted in nature. Stephen Crites has offered such an account, a narrativist phenomenology in which human consciousness arises out of the narrative depths, the deep 'unutterable cadences' of 'sacred stories'. People 'awaken to a sacred story, and their most significant mundane stories are told in the effort, never fully successful, to articulate it.'

> For the sacred story does not transpire within a conscious world. It forms the very consciousness that projects a total world horizon, and therefore informs the intentions by which actions are projected into that world. The style of these actions dances to its music. . . . every sacred story is creation story . . . the story itself creates a world of consciousness and the self that is oriented to it.[1]

Crites's sacred stories are like the consuming text of the Bible – 'people live in them'[2] – but they precede all actual texts and narratives – 'even the myths and epics, even the Scriptures, are mundane stories'[3] – they precede consciousness

[1] Stephen Crites, 'The narrative quality of experience', in *Why Narrative? Readings in Narrative Theology*, edited by Stanley Hauerwas and L. Gregory Jones (Grand Rapids, Michigan: William B. Eerdmans Publishing Company, 1989), pp. 65–88 (p. 71).

[2] Crites, 'Narrative', p. 70.

[3] Crites, 'Narrative', p. 71.

itself. Human consciousness mediates between sacred and mundane stories and 'is itself an incipient story'. The 'form' of consciousness, which allows for 'coherent experience', is in a 'rudimentary sense narrative'.[4] Crites argues that memory is ingredient in the form of human consciousness, allowing us to escape the ignorance of the present moment and know ourselves in time. 'Without memory, in fact, experience would have no coherence at all. Consciousness would be locked in a bare, momentary present, i.e., in a disconnected succession of perceptions which it would have no power to relate to one another.'[5] Prior to storytelling, memory chronicles past events.[6] And before we outline future plans, consciousness produces scenarios of anticipation – the 'framing of little stories about how things may fall out'.[7] The narrativising of past and future is always-already underway.

The sense of 'self' arises from memory and anticipation, from combining chronicle and scenario into a single story. It is the narrative form of consciousness which allows for the holding together of a determined past and an indeterminate future in the present moment.[8]

> The conscious present is that of a body impacted in world and moving, in process, in that world. In this present, action and experience meet. Memory is its depth, the depth of its experience in particular; anticipation is its trajectory, the trajectory of its action in particular. The *praesens de praesentibus* [the present of things present] is its full bodily reality.[9]

For many there will seem to be something profoundly right in Crites's claim that 'experience is moulded, root and branch, by narrative forms, that its narrative quality is altogether

[4] Crites, 'Narrative', p. 72. 'The narrative quality of experience has three dimensions, the sacred story, the mundane stories, and the temporal form of experience itself: three narrative tracks, each constantly reflecting and affecting the course of the others' (p. 81).

[5] Crites, 'Narrative', p. 73.

[6] Crites, 'Narrative', pp. 75–6.

[7] Crites, 'Narrative', p. 77.

[8] Crites, 'Narrative', p. 78.

[9] Crites, 'Narrative', p. 79.

primitive'.[10] But the idea that there are deep, unutterable stories underlying human consciousness cannot be demonstrated without begging the question.[11] However, Crites's subterranean stories are not necessary for the idea that human experience is narratively structured,[12] but the latter idea must also beg the question, since one cannot go outside of textuality. No matter how vague Crites's use of terms, they are all highly determined. If narrative is always-already underway – as part of Crites's argument seems to suggest – can one finally distinguish between depth and surface, sacred and mundane? The latter terms are always-already at play in the former. This does not count against the claim that experience is narratively construed, only that such construal is not determinable other than within a culture. The narrative quality of experience may be specific to certain traditions which make story central to their negotiation of the world, as in Christianity.[13] It is not, however, considerations such as these that lead Hans Frei to reject an experiential foundation for narrative theology.

'There is a liberal sense of using the term, narrative theology, which generally says that to be human is above all to have a story.'[14] Liberal narrative theology seeks to found itself

[10] Crites, 'Narrative', p. 84. Paul Ricoeur can be read as offering a more sophisticated version of Crites' argument. See *Time and Narrative*, 3 vols., translated by Kathleen McLaughlin and David Pellauer (Chicago and London: University of Chicago Press, 1984–88). For discussion of Ricoeur see chapter 5 below.

[11] Crites acknowledges that his argument is circular: experience is incipiently narrative because it arises from a basal story: there is a basal story because experience is incipiently narrative. 'Narrative', p. 72 n. 6.

[12] Crites's idea of 'sacred story' becomes more problematic the more he expounds it: 'Certainly the sacred story to which we give this name cannot be directly told. But its resonances can be felt in many of the stories that are being told, in songs being sung, in a renewed resolution to act.' 'Narrative', p. 87.

[13] Herbert N. Schneidau seeks to show that the 'feeling that everyone's life is a "story", if only it can be told' is a 'paradigm' that pervades Western history. See *Sacred Discontent: The Bible and Western Tradition* (Baton Rouge: Louisiana State University Press, 1976), pp. 182–3.

[14] Hans Frei, *Theology and Narrative: Selected Essays*, edited by George Hunsinger and William C. Placher (New York and Oxford: Oxford University Press, 1993), p. 208. See Paul Brockelman, *The Inside Story: A Narrative Approach to Religious Understanding and Truth* (Albany, NY: State University of New York Press, 1992), which seeks to 'think through the specific nature of religious understanding and truth in light of [the] basic, narratively structured self' (p. 17). All specific religious stories are then but thematisations of the self's story.

upon a general theory of human experience. It thus begins with the world. Frei insists that theology must begin with the scriptural word; with the *particular* story that the Bible has to tell. It is because there is this particular story that there is theology at all. (In this sense, all theology is narrative theology.) Rather than starting with a theory of the narrative self, of which Christ's story is but an example, it is the scriptural story that comes first, upon which individual and communal stories are then shaped. For Frei, the scriptural story comes first and last; we have no need of anything more. 'The truth to which we refer we cannot state apart from the biblical language which we employ to do so. And belief in the divine authority of scripture is for me simply that we do not need more. The narrative description there is adequate.'[15]

Furthermore, narrative is not an accidental form for the expression of Christian faith in Jesus Christ. For insofar as it is faith in the person of Jesus, his identity as God's Christ is given in his life, death and resurrection, and that can be given to us only in story. Who is Jesus Christ? is answered by the scriptural story, which is fitted to the telling of his identity. This is because some of the biblical narratives, especially the four gospels, and in particular the passion narratives, have the form of what Frei calls 'realistic narrative'. It is that form of narrative in which 'character, circumstance and theme are nothing without each other and become themselves only in their mutual reaction.'[16] Jesus Christ is the 'interactive unity' of what he did, the way that he did it, and what was done to him; and all that cannot be explained, only described.

One can, up to a point – and only up to a point – render a description, but not a metaphysics, of such interactive unity. It is done by the rendering of certain formal categories; but finally, the categories themselves are outstripped, and then all one can and must do is *narrate* the unity . . . [F]inally one can only have recourse

[15] Frei, *Theology and Narrative*, p. 210.
[16] Frei, *Theology and Narrative*, p. 34.

to the story of the interaction itself for supplying the understanding of it.[17]

Before proceeding to further consider realistic narrative and the narrative identity of Jesus Christ, we should note an instability in Frei's procedure. As we have seen, Frei after Barth – and behind him such figures as Augustine and Aquinas – wishes to start only with the Word of God in the word of Scripture. He thus resists any attempt to found theology on prior theory, whether of experience or narrative. 'Frei is best understood, therefore, as a theologian who seeks to approach the gospel narratives in an Anselmian way, letting them make sense in their own way.'[18] It is this that Frei attempts in *The Identity of Jesus Christ* (1975), making 'every effort to let the text speak for itself rather than casting it into an alien conceptual framework such as existentialism'.[19] Yet his account of realistic narrative seems dependent on a general theory of literature. Kevin Vanhoozer rehearses this problem:

> Is not an approach to the Gospels which subsumes them under the category of 'realistic narrative' itself an instance of a reading that forces an extratextual category onto the biblical narratives? To make the Gospels a type of the category 'realistic narrative' is to operate with what one might call an 'analogy of being' on the level of narrative. One first determines how realistic narrative in general works, and then proceeds to an interpretation of the Gospels.[20]

[17] Frei, *Theology and Narrative*, p. 35. 'Who is Jesus in the gospel story, and under what identification or description do we know him? He is who he is by what he does and undergoes, and chiefly we must say that he is Jesus crucified and raised' (p. 37).

[18] Kevin J. Vanhoozer, *Biblical Narrative in the Philosophy of Paul Ricoeur: A Study in Hermeneutics and Theology* (Cambridge: Cambridge University Press, 1990), p. 154. 'Anselm, as Barth has shown, represents a form of theology that seeks to describe Christian faith on its own terms. Barth argues that Anselm's theological method seeks to explain the logic of biblical language rather than transposing it into a philosophical conceptuality, such as Aristotelianism or Platonism.' Vanhoozer provides a most clear and illuminating discussion of the differences between Ricoeur's and Frei's biblical hermeneutics, between 'mediating' (liberal) and Anselmian theology.

[19] Vanhoozer, *Biblical Narrative*, p. 161.

[20] Vanhoozer, *Biblical Narrative*, p. 164.

Vanhoozer rehearses the problem after Frei himself, who, in his essay 'The "Literal Reading" of Biblical Narrative in the Christian Tradition' (1986), comments on his earlier work, and notes the resemblance between his account of realistic narrative and the literary theory of 'Anglo-American "New Criticism"'. 'Both claim that the text is a normative and pure "meaning" world of its own which, quite apart from any factual reference it may have, and apart from its author's intention and reader's reception, stands on its own with the authority of self-evident intelligibility.' They both seek a low-key interpretation that 'leaves the text sacrosanct', offering a formal analysis of its stylistic devices.[21] However, Frei does not think this similarity fatal for his understanding of narrative theology as an intratextual response to the scriptural story.

There may or may not be a class called 'realistic narrative', but to take it as a general category of which the synoptic Gospel narratives and their partial second-order redescription in the doctrine of the Incarnation are a dependent instance is first to put the cart before the horse and then cut the lines and claim that the vehicle is self-propelled.[22]

The 'New Criticism' is a generalisation of a specifically Christian way of reading the gospels, and while it may offer a reading of them, 'it is in fact a disguised Christian understanding of them and not a reading under a general theory'.[23] Frei admits that the Church's reading of Scripture will have to share categories with other kinds of reading, but insists that it will bend them to its own ends; and it will be the Church rather than a literary school that does so.[24] Finally all categories must give way to the 'specific set of texts and the most specific context [the Church], rather than to a general class of texts ("realistic narrative") and the most general

[21] Frei, *Theology and Narrative*, p. 140.

[22] Frei, *Theology and Narrative*, pp. 142–3.

[23] Frei, *Theology and Narrative*, p. 143. For further discussion of this claim see chapter 5 below.

[24] Frei, *Theology and Narrative*, pp. 143–4.

context ("human experience").'[25] This is to repeat a point Frei had already made in a lecture of 1967 and which is quoted above: 'finally, the categories themselves are outstripped, and then all one can do is to *narrate* the unity [of character, circumstance and theme].'[26] Even a minimal narrative theory must give way to the telling of the story.

FRAUGHT WITH BACKGROUND

Realistic narrative permits a form of representation not otherwise possible: the representation of character as engagement with contingent circumstance. This is not just the idea of character engaging with contingency, but of character constituted in and by such an engagement. It is a case where character and circumstance are so related that the character is the story of his or her engagement with the vicissitudes of life, and cannot be known or portrayed otherwise.[27] Such a character is 'fraught with background'.[28]

In *Mimesis: The Representation of Reality in Western Literature* (1953), Erich Auerbach contrasts two styles of ancient storytelling, the Greek and the Hebrew, Homer and Moses. The former illumines its characters with an even light, presenting them clearly in the foreground, while the latter provides intermittent illumination, its characters sometime in full light, sometime in shadow, moving between foreground and background.

> On the one hand fully externalized description, uniform illumination, uninterrupted connection, free expression, all events in the foreground, displaying unmistakable meanings, few elements of historical development and of psychological perspective; on the other hand, certain parts brought into high relief, others left obscure, abruptness, suggestive influence of the unexpressed, 'background quality', multiplicity of meanings and the need for

[25] Frei, *Theology and Narrative*, p. 144.
[26] Frei, *Theology and Narrative*, p. 35.
[27] Frei, *Theology and Narrative*, p. 37.
[28] Erich Auerbach, *Mimesis: The Representation of Reality in Western Literature*, translated by Willard R. Trask (Princeton, NJ: Princeton University Press, 1953), p. 12.

interpretation, universal-historical claims, development of the concept of the historically becoming, and preoccupation with the problematic.[29]

While the Homeric heroes have many adventures, they remain essentially the same people, distinguishable by certain marks of body and temperament. They do not become but are heroes. As Georg Lukács writes, they are 'life become essential'.[30] The characters of the Mosaic authorship, on the other hand, carry the trace of their past and the expectation of their future. Tragedy is a possibility for them.[31]

Abraham's actions are explained not only by what is happening to him at the moment, nor yet only by his character (as Achilles' actions by his courage and his pride, and Odysseus' by his versatility and foresightedness), but by his previous history; he remembers, he is constantly conscious of, what God has promised him and what God has already accomplished for him – his soul is torn between desperate rebellion and hopeful expectation; his silent obedience is multilayered, has background. Such a problematic psychological situation as this is impossible for any of the Homeric heroes, whose destiny is clearly defined and who wake every morning as if it were the first day of their lives: their emotions, though strong, are simple and find expression instantly.[32]

Much befalls the Greek and Hebrew heroes, but only the latter are changed by their histories. 'Odysseus in his return is exactly the same as he was when he left Ithaca two decades earlier. But what a road, what a fate, lie between the Jacob who cheated his father out of his blessing and the old man whose favourite son has been torn to pieces by a wild beast!'[33] It is the road followed that makes Abraham or Jacob the person he is. 'The old man, of whom we know how he has become what he is, is more of an individual than the young

[29] Auerbach, *Mimesis*, p. 23.

[30] Georg Lukács, *The Theory of the Novel: A Historico-Philosophical Essay on the Forms of Great Epic Literature*, translated by Anna Bostock (London: Merlin Press, 1971), p. 35.

[31] See Lukács, *Theory of the Novel*, pp. 35–6.

[32] Auerbach, *Mimesis*, p. 12.

[33] Auerbach, *Mimesis*, p. 17.

man; for it is only during the course of an eventful life that men are differentiated into full individuality'.[34]

It is because the Hebrew narratives render characters who are the cumulation of circumstance and are strung between memory and expectation – 'fraught with their development, sometimes even aged to the verge of dissolution'[35] – that they have a realistic or historical quality.

Abraham, Jacob, or even Moses produces a more concrete, direct, and historical impression than the figures of the Homeric world – not because they are better described in terms of sense (the contrary is the case) but because the confused, contradictory multiplicity of events, the psychological and factual cross-purposes, which true history reveals, have not disappeared in the representation but still remain clearly perceptible.[36]

This ability of the Hebrew narratives to render the historical, to show characters who are constituted through engagement with confused and contradictory events, is further developed in the 'Jewish-Christian literature' of the gospels.[37] In them Auerbach finds a counter-example to the 'antique realism', not only of the Greek Homer, but of a Latin Petronius or Tacitus. They portray characters for whom nothing is certain and everything is possible, triumph and defeat.[38] Moreover they are characters who emerge from the 'common people, from within the everyday occurrences of contemporary life', yet partake in a 'spiritual movement' of world-historical significance.[39] The grand theme does not detract from the mundaneties of life in which it is constitutively enacted; it 'clings to the concrete'.[40] For Auerbach, they are unique in ancient literature.

The New Testament writings are extremely effective; the tradition of the prophets and the Psalms is alive in them, and in some of them – those written by authors of more or less pronounced Hellenistic

[34] Auerbach, *Mimesis*, p. 18.
[35] Auerbach, *Mimesis*, p. 18.
[36] Auerbach, *Mimesis*, p. 20.
[37] Auerbach, *Mimesis*, p. 40.
[38] Auerbach, *Mimesis*, p. 42.
[39] Auerbach, *Mimesis*, p. 43.
[40] Auerbach, *Mimesis*, p. 44.

culture – we can trace the use of Greek figures of speech. But the spirit of rhetoric – a spirit which classified subjects in *genera*, and invested every subject with a specific form of style as the one garment becoming it in virtue of its nature – could not extend its dominion to them for the simple reason that their subject would not fit into any of the known genres. A scene like Peter's denial fits no antique genre. It is too serious for comedy, too contemporary and everyday for tragedy, politically too insignificant for history – and the form which was given it is one of such immediacy that its like does not exist in the literature of antiquity.[41]

It is this understanding of a unique narrative form, suited to a unique subject, that Hans Frei develops under the category of 'realistic narrative', and applies above all to the gospel narratives concerning Jesus of Nazareth.

THE NARRATIVE IDENTITY OF JESUS CHRIST

As we have already seen, characters in 'realistic narrative' are constituted through their engagement with contingency. They are neither abstract subjects nor a series of events, but persons.[42] They are actors who engage in the world, who act and are acted upon, and in whose actions and reactions is found their identity. They are what they do and is done to them, and their identity is given by a narrative description of their doing. Thus Frei can say that Jesus of Nazareth 'was what he did and underwent'.[43] 'Jesus *is* his story.'[44]

Narrative identity is unsubstitutable; it cannot be given to someone else. There are no two people of whom the same narrative can be told; no two people who do and undergo the same acts and circumstances. Names, titles and offices are identities which apply to more than one person, but there is no narrative of sufficient depth, 'fraught with background', that picks out more than one person. This is why the gospel

[41] Auerbach, *Mimesis*, p. 45. Auerbach suggests that much of the gospels' immediacy is due to the use of 'direct discourse', 'numerous face-to-face dialogues' (p. 46).

[42] Frei, *Theology and Narrative*, p. 50.

[43] Frei, *Theology and Narrative*, p. 57.

[44] Frei, *Theology and Narrative*, p. 42.

narratives are not simply stories of a saviour figure, similar to other stories of the period in which they were written. The gospels' saviour figure is a particular unsubstitutable person, a man living at a particular time and place. It is not so much the idea of a saviour that identifies Jesus, as Jesus who gives circumstantial and concrete identity to the saviour figure.[45]

> If one identifies the saviour figure with a fully human being, the story cannot be retold by substituting somebody else as its hero who is then made to be fully identical with that original person. No matter who the saviour may be, if he is *a* person, once the identification is made he is *that* person and no one else.[46]

Narrative characters are agents, at least some of whose actions are intentional actions. Their identity is the unique 'intention-action pattern' they perform in the vicissitudes of life.[47] 'A person's identity is constituted (not simply illustrated) by that intention which he carries into action.'[48] Thus the identity of Jesus is given by his intention to 'enact the good of men on their behalf in obedience to God.'[49] Intention and action have to be understood together. 'We must . . . not abstract one from the other: as if, in the New Testament, the event of the crucifixion were anything without Jesus' resolve, or the resolve anything without the event in which it took concrete shape!'[50] For Frei, Jesus is most himself in his resolve to go to Jerusalem, to drink the cup his Father gives him.

> In his general intention to enact, in obedience to God, the good of men on their behalf, and at the crucial juncture in his specific resolve to do so if necessary in this terrifying way – and in the event in which this intention and resolve were enacted – Jesus was most of all himself in the description of the Gospels. This was his identity. He was what he did and underwent: the crucified saviour.[51]

[45] Frei, *Theology and Narrative*, p. 48.
[46] Frei, *Theology and Narrative*, p. 55.
[47] Frei, *Theology and Narrative*, p. 57.
[48] Frei, *Theology and Narrative*, p. 63.
[49] Frei, *Theology and Narrative*, p. 51.
[50] Frei, *Theology and Narrative*, p. 57.
[51] Frei, *Theology and Narrative*, p. 57.

Frei is aware that intention is a troublesome thing. I know my own intentions, but how do I know the intentions of others? Is it by inference or analogy or is it more like knowing a character in a story? Despite these problems, Frei insists that the ideas of intention and action are ingredient in one another. 'To describe an occurrence as an action I must describe it as explicit intention; to describe an intention as just that and not as a putative mental "thing", I must describe it as an implicit action.'[52] Intending to act is not a second, separable act, to the act itself (an action in the mind); but nor is it a function of the act. Intention is one pole of an event of which action is the other, and it is the occurrence of such events that constitutes a person's distinctive identity. 'The identity of Jesus is focused *in* the circumstances of the action and not in back of them. He is what he does and undergoes. It is an intention-action sequence. Indeed, in and by these transpirings he becomes what he is.'[53]

The description of character that 'realistic narrative' permits – identity as an 'intention-action sequence' – is equally possible in both historical and fictional narratives. The 'realistic' style, 'fraught with background', is as much a feature of fiction as of history.

> What they have in common is their insistence that the direct interaction of character and circumstance not be abstracted from each other. And whatever theme there is – and there is bound to be a unifying theme in a historical as in a fictional narrative – emerges from this interaction rather than as an independent, *a priori* moral.[54]

Auerbach suggests that the gospel narratives are more like realistic novels of the nineteenth century than they are like other antique writings.[55] Frei follows him in this,[56] and

52 Frei, *Theology and Narrative*, p. 63.

53 Frei, *Theology and Narrative*, pp. 73–4.

54 Frei, *Theology and Narrative*, p. 34.

55 See Auerbach, *Mimesis*, pp. 31 and 40.

56 Frei, *Theology and Narrative*, p. 59.

notes that the novel and short story owe much to the gospels 'in the first place'.[57]

While character, circumstance and theme are handled alike in historical and fictional narrative, the latter is better able to present the relation of intention to action. 'The novelist knows his subject from the inside in a more intimate way than the historian, because he knows . . . the unity of private and public life, of character and circumstance, in the whole web of the novel's transactions and in the case of each character.' But since a person's identity is first and last what he does and is done to him, as opposed to only what he thinks and says, the relation of the latter to the former is known only insofar as it is known how 'a character is firmly ingredient in his public life'. This is why the identity of Jesus is better understood from what he did and underwent than from what he said.[58]

Mention of the difference and similarity between fiction and history reminds us that the Jesus of the gospels is not just a fictional character but an historical person. The difficulties raised by this simple observation are discussed in chapter 5. The identity of Jesus Christ is given in his complete story, which includes his death, resurrection and ascension, and the continuing story of the Church. The resurrection of Christ is further discussed in chapter 7 and the Church in 'Continuing the story' below. But I want to conclude discussion of the

[57] Frei, *Theology and Narrative*, p. 56. The novel as successor to the Bible has been the theme of a number of studies. See Georg Lukács, *The Theory of the Novel*, pp. 83–8; and C. A. Patrides, *The Grand Design of God: The Literary Form of the Christian View of History* (London: Routledge and Kegan Paul, 1972).

[58] Frei, *Theology and Narrative*, p. 36. Frei's final privileging of action over intention in the 'intention-action-sequence' goes some way to meet John Milbank's robust refusal of the gospels as realistic narratives and Jesus as a character within them. For Milbank the gospels have no interest in the intentions of Jesus, who is barely more than a 'cipher' for the 'universal significance' vertically invested in him by the deployment of certain metaphors – Jesus as way, word, truth, life, water, bread. It is only the name of 'Jesus' that gestures toward an historical reference. The gospels are more the story of a new community, of whom Jesus is the founder, than they are of an individual person. See John Milbank, 'The name of Jesus: incarnation, atonement, ecclesiology', *Modern Theology*, 7 (1991), 311–33 (pp. 315–17). The present book seeks to resist Milbank's alternative, reading the 'vertical' metaphors as more closely folded within the 'horizontal' narratives than does he.

narrative character of Christ's identity by considering how his identity is *discerned* in the scriptural story.

NORMATIVITY AND FOLLOWABILITY

In his early work in the 1960s, Hans Frei sought to show how his reading of the scriptural story – as disclosing the identity of Jesus Christ – was what he called a normative or aesthetic reading of the biblical texts: a reading that the texts themselves force upon us.

> Normative interpretation is a matter of the structure of the narrative itself and seeing if the text *as given* has a genuine structure . . . The formal structure of the narrative itself is the meaning, not the author's intention nor an ontology of language nor yet the text's impact.[59]

If we attend to what the text gives, rather than to what we or someone else – perhaps the author – give to the text, we will find that 'the meaning of the narrative is, indeed, Christological in a very strong sense, and Christological in a sense that is focused on Jesus, and either not at all or only from him on the story focused on our relation to him.'[60] This is the logic of the story. It becomes clear when we adopt a minimal hermeneutic that allows the text to speak for itself. In this way we find the normative and authoritative meaning of the scriptural story. Otherwise we would have to rely on authority (Catholicism?) or submit to relativism and perspectivism (liberalism).

> In the absence of that authority – and there is no way in which tradition can establish its authority except by authoritarian means – the story seems to mean whatever you want, depending on what 'perspective' or 'modern view of man' you happen to come from as you read the story and want to find substantiated there.[61]

[59] Frei, *Theology and Narrative*, pp. 33–4.
[60] Frei, *Theology and Narrative*, p. 40. [61] Frei, *Theology and Narrative*, p. 40.

There is something structuralist about Frei's 'aesthetic model', with its appeals to the logic and structure of the text, seeking a meaning that 'remains the same no matter what the perspectives of succeeding generations of interpreters may be.'[62] It was of course a naive conception – that a reader travelling light, without hermeneutic baggage, could discern the simple meaning of the tale. Frei, as he indicates, was led to affirm it in seeking to avoid authoritarianism on the one hand and relativism on the other. In subsequent years, however, Frei came to see that only some form of 'authority' could save his 'normative' reading from finally collapsing into the perspectivism he wished to avoid. By the 1980s, and under the influence of George Lindbeck, Frei came to regard the Church's tradition of the *sensus literalis* as alone affording a normative and authoritative reading of the scriptural texts. It is not so much the text, as the Church's rule for the reading of the text, that gives it a high Christological meaning.

The creed, 'rule of faith' or 'rule of truth' which governed the Gospels' use in the Church asserted the primacy of their literal sense. Moreover, it did this right from the beginning in the *ascriptive* even more than the *descriptive* mode. That 'Jesus' – not someone else or nobody in particular – is the subject, the agent, and patient of these stories is said to be their crucial point, and the descriptions of events, sayings, personal qualities, and so forth, become literal by being firmly predicated of him. Not until the Protestant Reformation is the literal sense understood as authoritative – because perspicuous – in its own right, without authorisation from the interpretive tradition.[63]

[62] Frei, *Theology and Narrative*, p. 32. Frei himself offers a complex genealogy: Wittgenstein and J. L. Austin; William Empson, William Wimsatt and Cleanth Brooks; William Dray, W. B. Gallie and Arthur Danto; Gilbert Ryle, Stuart Hampshire, Peter Strawson and Elizabeth Anscombe; Austin Farrer and Karl Barth (*Theology and Narrative*, pp. 33–5).

[63] Frei, *Theology and Narrative*, pp. 122–3. See George Hunsinger, 'Afterword: Hans Frei as Theologian', in *Theology and Narrative*, pp. 235–70 (p. 259). Frei's belated attention to the 'interpretative tradition' answers Lynn M. Poland's concern (in *Literary Criticism and Biblical Hermeneutics: A Critique of Formalist Approaches*, AAR Academy Series 48 (Chico, California: Scholars Press, 1985), pp. 120–37) that Frei 'seems to exclude interpretative activity altogether' (p. 136). Poland rightly notes that if 'Frei maintains the complete autonomy of the biblical narratives, we are

The development in Frei's thought, from an aesthetic to a communal reading of the scriptural text, demonstrates what we already found in the last chapter, where we argued that it is possible to discern a unified story in the biblical narratives and other writings only by dint of a community that so reads them. It is to a consideration of that community – constituting and constituted by the Scripture – that I now turn; but before doing so there is one further objection to the reading of the Bible as the telling of God's story to which we must attend.

I began this chapter by arguing for the grounding of narrativist theology in the specific scriptural story of God's Christ, rather than in a general theory of narrative experience, which not only begs the question but makes anthropology the foundation of theology. Beginning with the scriptural story means that theology does not have to counter those theories which insist that experience is inherently chaotic and unfollowable, rather than orderly and readable. But it does mean that narrativist theology insists on the orderability of the world and experience through the following of God's story. In other words, it holds that the claimed unfollowability of the world is itself only a story, and it is possible to tell a different, followable story. (The world is followable because the story is, and not the other way around.)

It may be noted that this is to suppose that the world is as God's story says it is; but it is not to suppose a third, ontological narrative which underwrites or legitimates the Church's story and contradicts nihilism. For that would not only ground theology in ontology (an absurdity), it would be unnecessary. The story that legitimates God's story – that says how the world must be for God's story to be true – is, for faith, simply God's story. As Frei would say, we need no more.

left with a puzzle as to how their meaning is actually discerned' (p. 137). Situating the narratives within the Church's tradition resolves this 'puzzle', as well as avoiding the individualism inherent in Poland's stress on the reader rather than the reading community. See also the discussion of Frei in Kenneth Surin, *The Turnings of Darkness and Light: Essays in Philosophical and Systematic Theology* (Cambridge: Cambridge University Press, 1989), pp. 206–12. Against textual autonomy Surin argues for the necessity of a 'Church poetics' (pp. 213–21).

What narrativist theology does have to show, however, is that the scriptural story is indeed followable, and not, as some have argued, unfollowable. The challenge is not that the Bible tells many disparate stories rather than a single tale; but that the single tale it tells is unfollowable, despite our best efforts. The more we look the less we see; the more we read the less we understand. We want to be insiders, privy to the meaning of the text; but we are forever outsiders, imperceptive and heedless.

And he said to them, 'To you has been given the secret of the Kingdom of God, but for those outside, everything comes in parables; in order that they may indeed look, but not perceive, and may indeed listen, but not understand; so that they may not turn again and be forgiven.'[64]

We are those outsiders. This, of course, is the 'secret' revealed in Frank Kermode's *The Genesis of Secrecy* (1979). We look but do not perceive, listen but do not understand. Everywhere we find the necessity of interpretation, and everywhere an indeterminacy of meaning. In the Gospel of Mark, Kermode finds 'something irreducible, therefore perpetually to be interpreted; not secrets to be found out one by one, but Secrecy.'[65] And for Kermode this is true not only of Mark or the Bible, but of all texts, including the text of the world.

The world is our beloved codex. We may not see it, as Dante did, in perfect order, gathered by love into one volume; but we do, living as reading, like to think of it as a place where we can travel back and forth at will, divining congruences, conjunctions, opposites; extracting secrets from its secrecy, making understood relations, an appropriate algebra . . . World and book, it may be, are hopelessly plural, endlessly disappointing; we stand alone before them, aware that they may be narratives only because of our impudent intervention, and susceptible of interpretation only by our hermetic tricks.[66]

64 Mark 4.11–12. What is the meaning of this hard saying?

65 Frank Kermode, *The Genesis of Secrecy: On the Interpretation of Narrative* (Cambridge, Massachusetts and London: Harvard University Press, 1979), p. 143.

66 Kermode, *Genesis of Secrecy*, p. 145.

Written in a more confident and strident tone, without hesitation, this would be the master narrative of nihilism: that world and book are plotless, without significance, our reading but 'impudent intervention'. But Kermode's more tentative manner is perhaps more unsettling: not certainty but suspicion, which finds comfort in kindly but ironic observation of our plight: 'Hot for secrets, our only conversation may be with guardians who know less and see less than we can; and our sole hope and pleasure is in the perception of a momentary radiance, before the door of disappointment is finally shut on us.'[67]

Hans Frei rightly insists that theology must resist such an understanding of our hermeneutic lot, at least in regard to the word of Scripture read as the Word of God. Theology is committed to saying that a certain reading of the biblical text will not disappoint. Frei observes that indeterminacy of meaning gathers strength from weakening the relationship between meaning and truth, and that most 'recent secular interpreters of the Bible' do not want 'its interpretation to be governed by a criterion of meaning that is strongly connected to one of truth.'[68] Frei believes there is some virtue in this, in that 'a good interpretation of a text is one that has "breathing space", that is to say, one in which no hermeneutic finally allows you to resolve the text – there is something that is left to bother, something that is wrong, something that is not yet interpreted.'[69] But at the same time, the Church reads for the Word that is more than words, the truth that is at the same time transcendent and incarnate.[70] 'The textual world as witness to the Word of God is not identical with the latter, and yet, by the Spirit's grace, it is "sufficient" for the witnessing.'[71] The Christian reader cannot finally sever meaning from truth,

[67] Kermode, *Genesis of Secrecy*, p. 145. Kermode is alluding to Kafka's parable 'Before the Law', told to K by a priest in *The Trial*. See Kermode, *Genesis of Secrecy*, pp. 27–8.

[68] Frei, *Theology and Narrative*, p. 162. For Frei, Derrida's *Il n'y a pas de hors-texte* is a 'drastic summary expression' of this view.

[69] Frei, *Theology and Narrative*, p. 162.

[70] Frei, *Theology and Narrative*, p. 163.

[71] Frei, *Theology and Narrative*, p. 164.

the text from what the text is about; nor collapse the two, so that the text is about the text itself.

The text is not to be interpreted 'without residue', but it is to be interpreted. Textuality and truth are different but related, and for Christian reading, the one is sufficient for the other. 'There is a fit due to the mystery of grace between truth and text.'

> The Reformers saw the place where that fit was realised in the constant reconstitution of the Church where the word is rightly preached and where the sacraments are rightly administered. *There* is where that fit takes place and there alone – and there without any guarantees.[72]

I now turn to a consideration of that 'place' which promises – but does not guarantee – something more than a momentary radiance before final disappointment.

CONTINUING THE STORY

The story of Jesus is also the story of the Church; or rather, the story of Jesus opens onto the Church's story, so that the two stories are one story. This is because Jesus' story does not come to an end with his death, but continues, and does so variously. The story of Jesus continues because no one human life-story is isolate, entire onto itself. All human life-stories are woven out of and into other life-stories; the stories of parents and children, of friends and enemies, of all whom we have touched and who have touched us, however fleetingly. Thus Jesus' story is also the stories of those who cared for him and who taught him, who befriended him and who hated him; as it is also the stories of those for whom he cared, whom he taught and loved. And each one of their stories is woven into the stories of the people with whom they had to do. Thus we can think of the story of Jesus as linked to, or woven with,

[72] Frei, *Theology and Narrative*, p. 166.

many others; all of them interwoven so that together they make one story: ultimately the story of humanity.

But in what sense can we call the story of humanity, imagined as the interweaving of all stories, the story of Jesus? Surely as much can be said of any individual life-story, naming the whole by a part? In what sense is Jesus's story continued rather than dissipated through its interweaving with others? For there is no need of a single thread to run through the entire cloth in order to make it one piece. Perhaps the idea of a pattern in the cloth will permit us to do so. The pattern is woven in the Scriptures; threads of narrative and other writings interwoven with the gospels and the early history of the Church, and then, through later writings, with the larger Christian story that continues to the present day. And Christ is the pattern in the Scripture. But this Christ-pattern is the pattern of the world only insofar as it is woven into the world-cloth; woven in such a way as to transform the whole.

But even if we can determine a particular patterned story, and name it the story of Christ, we still have to ask with Hans Frei how this storied pattern is to be understood. 'Shall we, as it were, radiate out from the Gospels with their firm meaning (in the interaction of character and circumstance) to the earlier and later story (that of the Old Testament and that of human history since Jesus Christ)?'[73] Or shall we close in on the gospels from the wider context of history and experience? Shall we seek to understand the whole from the part, or the part from the whole? Again, this is the central problematic that narrativist theology poses to the Church in the twentieth century: do we start from the Word or the world? The question, which perhaps presupposes that we will end where we began, opens two possible routes through what it recognises as the one wor(l)d. However, it would be a mistake to suppose that these two routes are the same path traversed in different directions. Frei doubts that 'history and experience . . . themselves constitute even incipiently a unified story or narrative

[73] Frei, *Theology and Narrative*, pp. 42–3.

pattern'.[74] That would mean that one could never move from the whole to the part without covertly deploying a particular story (which is the *agon* of the Enlightenment). The whole has no discernible pattern. Thus Frei suggests that the Church should continue to do what it has always done, moving from the particular to the whole, from the story of the Word to that of the world.

Why not proceed the way the Church has traditionally done, even if the Gospels are bound to be an *incomplete* clue to the rest of Scripture, and a necessarily *ambiguous* clue to the experience of history, both as narrated in the Old Testament and as we, simply as members of the human race, experience it. Incomplete, even ambiguous – yes, but not without meaning, as long as we understand that in the Gospels Jesus *is* nothing other than his story, and that this both is the story of God with him and all mankind, and is *included* in that story.[75]

Here we must press further the idea that the story of Jesus Christ continues in the story of the Church, and is thus not ended; or, as Frei has it, that the stories of all are included in the story of Christ, so that the end of his story is the end of all stories. The story of Christ continues in the story of the Church because the Church is precisely constituted as the continuation of Christ's story. Christ leaves so that the Spirit may come to lead the Church in 'a little while' to Christ.[76] Everything given to Christ is given to the Church;[77] and the Church sent out 'into the world'.[78] The Church is the community that tells Christ's story by being itself the continuing story of Christ; embodying the story of Christ in the circumstances of its day.

As Christ is his story, so the Church is its story. 'Images such as "body of Christ", or the traditional marks of "unity, holiness, catholicity, and apostolicity", cannot be first defined and then used to specify what is and what is not the Church. The story is logically prior. It determines the meaning of

[74] Frei, *Theology and Narrative*, p. 43.
[75] Frei, *Theology and Narrative*, p. 43. [76] John 16.7–24.
[77] John 17.7–8. [78] John 17.18.

images, concepts, doctrines, and theories of the Church rather than being determined by them.'[79] The identity of the Church – like that of an agent in a realistic narrative – is constituted through the engagement of character and circumstance, and given in the narratives of that engagement. In the case of the Church, the character is that of a community or communities; the circumstance anything and everything that life has to offer. The Church does not escape the circumstantial, for it is first and foremost groups of people struggling with the contingencies and vicissitudes of earthly existence, in all its messiness.

The Church *is* its story, but that story is shaped by the story of Christ. On Lindbeck's exegesis of the New Testament, Church and Israel are both types of the one antitype: 'the kingdom already present in Christ'.[80] In different ways, Church and Israel embody the one body that is 'God with us'. They share the one story that is the story of Christ, in whom both are fulfilled. 'Christ is depicted as the embodiment of Israel (e.g., "Out of Egypt have I called my son"; Matthew 2.15), and the Church is the body of Christ. Thus, in being shaped by the story of Christ, the Church shares (rather than fulfils) the story of Israel.'[81] However, Israel and Church are differently shaped by the story of Christ. Israel precedes, whereas the Church proceeds from Christ as their common antitype. The shape of Israel is retrospectively known, while that of the Church is known prospectively. Or so it would be if this were not a story, and a matter of 'shapes' in time rather

[79] George Lindbeck, 'The story-shaped Church: critical exegesis and theological interpretation', in *Scriptural Authority and Narrative Interpretation*, edited by Garrett Green (Philadelphia: Fortress Press, 1987), pp. 161–78 (p. 165).

[80] Lindbeck, 'Story-shaped Church', p. 166.

[81] Lindbeck, 'Story-shaped Church', p. 166. In construing both Church and Israel as types of Christ, Lindbeck wants to suggest a way forward for the Church in relation to Judaism today, that would be a return to an earlier story. 'Christendom is passing and Christians are becoming a diaspora. The antagonism of the Church to the synagogue has been unmasked (we hope definitively) for the horror it always was. Christian pretensions to fulfilment have become obnoxious to vast numbers of Catholics and Protestants alike. Some of the reasons for distorting the story are disappearing, and perhaps its original version is again applicable.' (p. 174).

than space. If Christ shows Israel's shape, he shows the Church not what it is but what it is called to be. The Church is called to be the shape of Israel-fulfilled-in-Christ, finding its own fulfilment in continuing Christ's story.

The story of Christ is not finished. It includes the stories of all those people who were touched by him, and of the people touched by them, and so on through the Church's touching history: through the laying on of hands. But there is another more important sense in which Christ's story is not over but continuing. It is the sense in which Jesus Christ is not dead but alive, having left the past in order to return from the future. The Church is not to look for the living among the dead, modelling itself upon a memory,[82] for Jesus has gone on ahead, awaiting those who follow after.[83] The Church is shaped by a story that is even now being told. It is shaped *within* a story that it has also shaped and is shaping: the story of the body of Christ.[84]

BODY SHAPING

The Church is a Christ-shaped people; its shaping a matter of virtuous discipline, a pedagogy of the body. It is a community in which people learn how to embody the story of Jesus Christ.[85] The Church can only tell the story of Christ if it has first read Christ's story, consumed it in such a way that it nourishes and shapes the Church as consumer, reader and teller of the story. One might say that before the scriptural story can consume the world, the Church must consume the story in order to become its embodiment or 'bearer'.[86] Entering the story, becoming a character within its storied

82 Luke 24.5.

83 Mark 16.6–7. On the resurrection see further chapter 7 below.

84 I return to the theme of the Church in chapters 6 and 7.

85 See Stephen E. Fowl and L. Gregory Jones, *Reading in Communion: Scripture and Ethics in Christian Life* , Biblical Foundations in Theology (London: SPCK, 1991), p. 29.

86 For the Church as 'bearer' of the scriptural world see Stanley Hauerwas, *A Community of Character* (Notre Dame, Indiana: University of Notre Dame Press, 1981), p. 57.

world, is then a matter of becoming part of the body that embodies the story.

Learning how to consume the scriptural story so that it nourishes and strengthens the body – how to read it in order to tell it aright – is a matter of disciplined practice, of ecclesial (narrative) ethics. On such an account, ecclesial ethics is concerned with nourishing and shaping the Christian body through care of its consumption and exercise of its members. The aim is to shape characters fitted for life in the story of Christ; characters who, shaped in and after the body of Christ, are able to follow him into his Kingdom. Such shaping consists in the formation of virtuous habits through communal practices.

> Because our lives are to be patterned in relation to the One confessed in Scripture to be the Word incarnate, we need to be more than simply disciplined in our use of words; we need also to be disciplined by the Word made flesh. Being disciplined by the Word entails allowing our lives to be patterned in Christ. . . . [I]t involves a willingness to have our lives formed and transformed in and through particular Christian communities so that the words we use become means of pointing to the Word who we follow . . . We are called into such communities by the Triune God to whom the scriptural texts bear witness. Hence Christian communities provide the contexts whereby we learn – as the body of Christ through the power of the Holy Spirit – to interpret, and to have our lives interrogated by, the scriptural texts such that we are formed and transformed in the moral judgement necessary for us to live faithfully before God.[87]

One of the most important lessons in learning the scriptural story of Christ is learning its story of the world; learning to see the world as it is envisioned in Scripture: as the gift of God. This first requires that we learn our sinfulness. 'The Christian story trains us to see that in most of our life we act as if this is not God's world and therein lies our fundamental sin.'[88] Our

[87] Fowl and Jones, *Reading in Communion*, p. 34.

[88] Stanley Hauerwas, *The Peaceable Kingdom: A Primer in Christian Ethics* (London: SCM Press, [1983] 1984), p. 30.

sinfulness has to be learned, and we learn it in the same story in which we learn that the world is God's gift and that we are convicted and forgiven sinners. It is the story in which we learn, as Stanley Hauerwas puts it, that we are both the friends of the crucified, and his crucifiers.[89]

> The story Christians tell of God exposes the unwelcome fact that I am a sinner. For without such a narrative the fact and nature of my sin cannot help but remain hidden in self-deception. Only a narrative that helps me place myself as a creature of a gracious God can provide the skills to help me locate my sin as fundamentally infidelity and rebellion.[90]

It is the scriptural story of Christ which teaches us that for the most part we live in other stories than his, stories of our own making. 'Sin consists in our allowing our characters to be formed by the story that we must do everything (pride) or nothing (sloth).'[91]

This account of ecclesial ethics, which seeks to understand the Christian life according to certain tropes – as the reading, consuming and embodying of the Word in the word of Scripture in order to be read, consumed and embodied in the life of Christ – has much in common with the revived interest in virtue ethics following the work of people like Alasdair MacIntyre. It is, however, ancient in the Church, and MacIntyre traces its development from Augustine to Aquinas, after Aristotle.

It is an important part of the Church's body ethics that it is not an ethics for the world: 'Christians cannot pretend to do ethics for anyone.'[92] Christians do ethics for the Church; or better, Christian ethics are the Church.[93] 'By virtue of the distinctive narrative that forms their community, Christians are distinct from the world. They are required to be nothing less than a sanctified people of peace who can live the life of the forgiven.'[94] For some this is to render the Church a

89 Hauerwas, *Peaceable Kingdom*, p. 30.
90 Hauerwas, *Peaceable Kingdom*, p. 31.
91 Hauerwas, *Peaceable Kingdom*, p. 48.
92 Hauerwas, *Peaceable Kingdom*, p. 34.
93 Hauerwas, *Peaceable Kingdom*, p. 99.
94 Hauerwas, *Peaceable Kingdom*, p. 60.

sectarian group concerned with its own shaping, rather than with the reshaping of the world. This criticism, however, not only overlooks the incipient violence contained in the claim to be the harbinger of a universal ethic,[95] it misunderstands the shape of the Church patterned upon Christ. As a 'sanctified people of peace' the Church is called to a life of 'service and sacrifice'.[96] It is called to be the sacrament or foretaste of the Kingdom of God; 'a holy people – that is, a people who are capable of maintaining the life of charity, hospitality, and justice.'[97] This means that far from turning its back on the world, it turns to the world as the sign of the world's contradiction, serving the world by being other than the world. It is those forms of Christianity which seek compromise with the world – erastian and liberal – which abandon the world.[98]

Narrativist theology – as exemplified in the work of George Lindbeck and Stanley Hauerwas – is charged not only with sectarianism, but with irrationalism. It is to this further and related complaint that we must now turn.

AUDACIOUS DOGMATISM

In the October 1870 issue of *The Edinburgh Review*, John Tulloch concluded his anonymous review of John Henry Newman's *Essay in Aid of a Grammar of Assent*, by noting that while it was the product of Romanism's perhaps 'finest mind', it was a work of 'intellectual havoc and the audacious yet hopeless dogmatism which it teaches.'[99] Newman, his mind 'intensely dogmatic and authoritative', abandons not only reason but argument in 'reference to his faith', and refuses to 'look

[95] 'When Christians assume that their particular moral convictions are independent of narrative, that they are justified by some universal standpoint free from history, they are tempted to imagine that those who do not share such an ethic must be perverse and should be coerced to do what we know on universal grounds they really should want to do.' Hauerwas, *Peaceable Kingdom*, p. 61.

[96] Hauerwas, *Peaceable Kingdom*, p. 60.

[97] Hauerwas, *Peaceable Kingdom*, p. 109.

[98] See Fowl and Jones, *Reading in Communion*, pp. 67–80.

[99] [John Tulloch], 'Dr Newman's *Grammar of Assent*', *The Edinburgh Review*, 132 (October 1870), 382–414 (p. 414).

around'.[100] He attempts to render faith secure from criticism simply by refusing its claims. Tulloch, of course, was not the first to say this of Newman's thought, nor the last;[101] nor Newman the only person of whom the charge has been made. The same criticism is made of narrativist theology in general, and of George Lindbeck's postliberal intratextualism in particular. It is a criticism that Lindbeck himself confronts at the end of his book, *The Nature of Doctrine*: 'Intratextuality seems wholly relativistic: it turns religion, so one can argue, into self-enclosed and incommensurable intellectual ghettos.'[102]

Mark Corner, in his review of Lindbeck's book, brings charges similar to those brought by Tulloch against Newman. Corner accuses Lindbeck of ruling 'out of court the sort of critique of the Christian religion which seeks to expose the inadequacy of its truth claims.'[103] Corner appears to believe that religion must be *reasonable* or, as Lindbeck puts it, *intelligible* and *credible* to the modern world. It must lay itself open to rational assessment. In Corner's view, Lindbeck's cultural-linguistic approach to religion, which insists that the text interprets the world rather than the world the text, is profoundly conservative and 'totalitarian'.[104] He ominously notes that Lindbeck's book 'effectively shuts the door on the criticism of religion'. According to Corner, the 'cultural-linguistic view of religion denies the possibility of falsifying

100 Tulloch, 'Dr Newman's *Grammar of Assent*', pp. 391–2.

101 See M. Jamie Ferreira, *Doubt and Religious Commitment: The Role of the Will in Newman's Thought* (Oxford: Clarendon Press, 1980), p. 11; and Nicholas Lash, *Newman on Development* (London: Sheed and Ward, 1975), pp. 148–9. Newman, of course, was not a fideist, but a non-foundationalist for whom the intellect does not provide the 'first principles' on which it works. In science these are given by the senses; but in religion we must 'interrogate our hearts.' *Letters and Diaries of John Henry Newman*, edited by C. S. Dessain and Thomas Gornall SJ, vol. 25 (Oxford: Clarendon Press, 1973), pp. 275–6; cited in Nicholas Lash's 'Introduction' to *An Essay in Aid of a Grammar of Assent* (Notre Dame, Indiana: University of Notre Dame Press, [1870] 1979), pp. 1–21 (p. 9).

102 Lindbeck, *Nature of Doctrine*, p. 128.

103 Mark Corner, Review of George Lindbeck's *The Nature of Doctrine*, *Modern Theology* 3 (1986), 110–13 (p. 112).

104 Corner, Review of Lindbeck, p. 112.

religion by the perception of a mismatch between reality and its interpretation within the religious community', since the community's self-understanding is independent of what lies outside.[105] Corner is afraid that Lindbeck forecloses on the prophetic spirit, promotes indoctrination and locks the Church into an 'Orthodox time warp, forever immersed in a totalitarianism of tradition.'[106]

How valid are these criticisms? It is clear that Lindbeck is far from sanguine about rendering religion credible for modernity. How does one assess the reasonableness of religion? Lindbeck does not question the idea of universal rationality, but he does question the possibility of formulating its criteria or 'norms of reasonableness'. For he doubts that we live in a world with such universally agreed criteria. It is likely that we live amidst a plurality of incommensurable norms and standards.[107] Yet he allows that we do make judgements and decisions according to set norms, but that these are specific to particular contexts and frameworks such as provided by a religious tradition. Further, we can make decisions and judgements as between such frameworks and contexts, but what we cannot do is to provide a clear and analytic account of how we do it. 'Reason places constraints on religion as well as on scientific options even though these constraints are too flexible and informal to be spelled out in either foundational theology or a general theory of science.' Thus Lindbeck is led to suggest that 'the reasonableness of a religion is largely a function of its assimilative powers, of intelligible interpretation in its own terms of the varied situations and realities adherents encounter.'[108] The reasonableness of a religion is

105 Corner, Review of Lindbeck, p. 113.

106 Corner, Review of Lindbeck, p. 113. Compare Tulloch, who cites Newman as a 'single example' that 'Romanism . . . has lost the key to the door of the world's progress, and can only grope amidst the strewn wreck – the dogmatic débris – of the path by which man has advanced.' ('Dr Newman's Grammar of Assent', p. 414.)

107 Lindbeck, *Nature of Doctrine*, p. 130.

108 Lindbeck, *Nature of Doctrine*, p. 131. Bruce D. Marshall ('Absorbing the world: Christianity and the universe of truths', in *Theology and Dialogue: Essays in Conversation with George Lindbeck*, edited by Bruce D. Marshall (Notre Dame, Indiana: University of Notre Dame, 1990), pp. 69–102) argues that 'assimilative

tested through time, as it engages with new facts and ideas. The testing does not conclude 'until the disappearance of the last communities of believers or, if the faith survives, until the end of history'.[109] On this account, apologetics can only be *ad hoc*, and the Church advances the reasonableness of its faith through its preaching and practice, inviting the outsider to come inside and learn its language and way of life: to become a catechumen. The 'logic of coming to believe, because it is like that of learning a language, has little room for argument, but once one has learned to speak the language of faith, argument becomes possible.'[110] The model is Christ's call to the disciples.

At this point it may help to look at the work of another person who, like Lindbeck and before him Newman, has often been accused of irrationalism and fideism. In his essay 'Religious Belief and Language Games' (1970), D. Z. Phillips argues that religious beliefs can be usefully characterised as Wittgensteinian language-games.[111] He acknowledges that

power' – the ability of a 'text' to redescribe the world in its own terms – is a 'significant test for criteria of truth' (p. 79). For Marshall, '"assimilative power" is always the assimilative power of a specific web of belief and practice and its associated criteria of truth' (p. 82). Marshall's argument is not perspicuous, but there is some reason to suspect assimilation as a test either of the truth of the Christian 'web' or of its criteria of truth. For a 'web of belief and practice' may have great assimilative power, and yet remain entirely dubious. Freudianism is an example. Assimilative power may warrant rationality – because internally consistent – but hardly truth, when the latter is taken as 'correspondence' between the 'web' and something that is not the 'web'. (At this point in his argument, Lindbeck is concerned only with the 'reasonableness' of religion, not its 'truth'.) Assimilative power does not *justify* in any final sense 'the primacy of Christian criteria of truth' (p. 89).

109 Lindbeck, *Nature of Doctrine*, p. 131.

110 Lindbeck, *Nature of Doctrine*, p. 132.

111 D. Z. Phillips, 'Religious beliefs and language games', in *Faith and Philosophical Enquiry* (London: Routledge and Kegan Paul, 1970), pp. 77–110 (p. 78). Frei himself seems to misidentify Phillips as a fideist (*Types*, p. 4). 'Seems' because Frei's narratorial distance and tentativeness suggests that he might not have wished to press the description (see *Types*, pp. 46–55). But it is bizarre to suggest that for Phillips the theologian cannot offer 'responsible redescription of biblical and traditional beliefs', but only 'total silence' when not parroting biblical and traditional formulae (p. 55). See further Fergus Kerr, 'Frei's Types', *New Blackfriars* 75 (1994), 184–93. As Kerr suggests, Phillips is much closer to Frei than the latter seemed to suppose (pp. 192–3).

this can give rise to the suspicion that, as he notes, 'religious beliefs are being placed outside the reach of any possible criticism'. This suspicion arises because Phillips holds that the criteria by which we decide whether something is meaningful or not is internal to religion (intratextual). But the rationalist insists that criteria of meaningfulness or rationality must apply both within and without religion. That by which we judge the worth of any statement must be applicable in all contexts. Phillips questions this assumption: not that rationality applies both within and without religion, but that the same *criteria* of rationality apply within religion as elsewhere, that what is to count as reasonable is the same in all contexts. In order to suggest that the criteria of rationality may be different within religion, Phillips considers the specific logic that applies in theological discourse. It is specific because God is not like the things we otherwise talk about.

> God's reality is not one of a kind; he is not a being among beings. The word 'God' is not the name of a thing. Thus, the reality of God cannot be assessed by a common measure which also applies to things other than God.[112]

It is important to note that Phillips is not denying God's reality, only that God's reality is the same as that of things. To say that God is not a thing is not to say that God is nothing.[113] It is the difference between no-thing and nothing that gives rise to the specific logic of theology. That the same criteria do not apply is suggested by the fact that it makes no sense to ask

[112] Phillips, 'Religious beliefs', p. 85.

[113] Indeed, Phillips finds this confusion in Lindbeck (D. Z. Phillips, *Faith After Foundationalism* (London: Routledge, 1988), pp. 203–6). 'To be prepared to jettison talk of an independent reality, as Lindbeck seems to be, is to fall back into the grammatical trap which led one astray in the first place. It is to assume that the notion of an independent reality only has application where talk of physical objects is concerned. Yet, when a believer strays from the ways of God, he clearly thinks of himself as departing from a reality which is independent of himself' (p. 203). 'Lindbeck, while half-realising that theological doctrines are not descriptions of an object given independently of them, cannot free himself from the tempting and prestigious grammar of that relation, a grammar drawn, in the main, from our talk of physical objects' (p. 205).

the same questions of God as of physical things. For example, it makes no sense to ask when God began or will cease to exist. This is not because we do not know when God began or will end, or if God always has and will exist; it is because these questions are inappropriate to the reality named 'God'. They are 'ungrammatical' because they construe God as a thing whose existence and properties we could materially investigate as we could a putative object in the world. 'That would be complete nonsense.'[114]

The rationalist holds that we should not believe without good evidence or ground for our belief. But what sort of evidence is required for belief in God? Do we need the same sort of evidence as for believing the weather to be inclement? Must we ground belief in God and belief in the state of the weather upon sensory experience?

Phillips suggests that we rationally come to belief in God not by looking at the world, but by learning certain stories, and that believing in God is like believing in these stories. In Lindbeck's terms it is a matter of learning a language, assimilating a culture, entering a textual world. It is not a matter of 'weighing evidence or reasoning to a conclusion',[115] but of interrogating our hearts.

> It is in the life of the spirit, in the 'interrogation of our hearts', in the practice of loving obedience, that we are brought to a 'real apprehension' of those symbols of transcendence which serve, analogously to sense experience, as the 'starting points' for Christian reflection. The mode of rationality appropriate to such apprehension is – in its concreteness and irreducible complexity – closer to 'personal knowledge', or to literary and aesthetic cognition, than it is to the 'linear' rationality characteristic of theoretical deduction.[116]

Is this irrational? Phillips thinks not. It is merely an illustration of the fact that criteria of rationality, intelligibility and

114 Phillips, *Faith After Foundationalism*, p. 203.
115 Phillips, 'Religious beliefs', p. 89.
116 Lash, 'Introduction' to Newman, *Essay in Aid of a Grammar of Assent*, p. 10.

meaningfulness are not universal. If this is not understood then neither will the nature of religious belief. The rationalist who claims that the same sort of evidence applies in relation to God as to the weather, will think that believing in God is like believing in the existence of some thing like the weather. Here Phillips wants to resist any 'craving for generality, the insistence that what constitutes an intelligible move in one context must constitute an intelligible move in all contexts.'[117] Words are used differently in different contexts, and in different contexts there are different criteria of reasonableness.

What criteria apply within religion? Phillips suggests that they are simply the basic beliefs of the religion in question, Lindbeck's normative and authoritative doctrines. 'The absolute beliefs are the criteria, not the object of assessment'.[118] The basic beliefs or doctrines, the religious language-games that are played and which constitute the religion as such, provide the framework in which questions of right and wrong, appropriateness and inappropriateness, can be asked and answered; but they are not themselves subject to assessment. And here, of course, the rationalist will detect the claim that religion is immune to criticism. Is Phillips not in fact saying that 'religious believers can say what they like'?[119]

In responding to this question Phillips begins by reminding us that religious beliefs are not cut off from our other beliefs; they jostle with the other language-games we play, and if this were not so religion would not have the importance it does have for us. We have to play other language-games if we are also to play religious ones. For example, we could not understand the religious claim that the Kingdom of God is not of this world if we did not understand what it is to speak of the world. Indeed, the sense of the Kingdom of God is in part constituted by contrast with our profane knowledge. Thus there must be credible relations between what we say in religious discourse and what we say elsewhere. Put more

[117] Phillips, 'Religious beliefs', p. 87.
[118] Phillips, 'Religious beliefs', p. 90.
[119] Phillips, 'Religious beliefs', p. 92.

strongly, religious beliefs must not 'ignore or distort what we already know.'[120]

The beliefs we hold – religious and non-religious – are held in place by those which surround them.[121] Thus we look for consistency between beliefs. When tensions arise between profane and sacred beliefs, however, we should give initial priority to the latter, for it may well be that what we thought we knew was mistaken. But just as profane facts may challenge religious beliefs, so may religious beliefs challenge profane knowledge. The apparent finality of death challenges the claim that after death we continue to exist as disembodied minds; but the claim that when we die, we die not into darkness but into God's eternal light challenges the belief and fear that death has the last word.[122]

The charges often brought against D. Z. Phillips – that he denies the reality of God and the cognitive status of religious beliefs while affirming the inviolability of the religious worldview – are those often brought against narrativist theology. They are brought, as we have seen, against George Lindbeck as they were brought against Newman in the last century. What all these thinkers have in common is a conviction that religious belief and practice is a response to, and not an inference from, a word spoken, a hand held out, a story shared, experienced as a gracious act: as pure gift.[123]

120 Phillips, 'Religious beliefs', p. 98.

121 'There have to be "points of contact", and they are not "arbitrary". On the contrary, the contexts in which we need to look for hints in exploring the meaning of specifically Christian beliefs and practices would include: "conscience, nature, birth, death, relations between men and women" (Phillips, *Faith After Foundationalism*, p. 112).' (Kerr, 'Frei's Types', p. 193.)

122 For a similar argument see Marshall, 'Absorbing the world', pp. 93–7. Taking coherence with the 'plain' sense of Scripture as the criterion of Christian truth, and adopting 'Aquinas' rule that nothing should be identified as the plain sense of scripture which is obviously false' (p. 94 – see *Summa Theologiæ*, 1, 1, 10, ad 3 and chapters 4 and 5 below), Marshall argues that 'Christians should seek the plain sense in ways which maximise the number of well-supported beliefs they can hold true without prejudice to the way the words go. Thomas formulates a nice summary . . . : "Every truth which can be adapted (*aptari*) to divine Scripture, while agreeing with the way the words go, is the sense of Scripture."' (pp. 96–7; Aquinas, *Quaestiones Disputatae de Pontentia*, 4, 1, r.)

123 See further chapter 8.

CONSUMING TEXT

This and the preceding chapter have explored aspects of narrativist theology's chief conceit, that the Bible is an all-consuming text. For Erich Auerbach it is a tyrant, demanding the absolute commitment of its readers; for Hans Frei and George Lindbeck it overcomes reality and absorbs the world. We are to be written into its story, which is the true story of the world, containing the antitype of all types.

As a number of narrativist theologians stress, this understanding of the Bible is ancient in the Church; for example, the absorption of Platonism and Aristotelianism in the reading of Augustine and Aquinas. But it is also the medieval idea of the Book: the idea of the world, its nature and history, as a totality that can be read as a book, the plot of which is given in God's other book, the Bible. The medievals conceived the Bible as the book 'that revealed or made present God's transcendent and absolute will, law, and wisdom, a container of the divine plan and itself a sign of the totality of that plan in the world.'[124] Thomas of Celano said that the Revelation of St John 'is the book in which the total is contained',[125] and that is how the medieval Church came to understand the entire Bible: as the text of totality.[126]

For Jacques Derrida, the medieval idea of the Book is yet another synonym for logocentrism, for the belief that meaning, value and truth, are founded and legitimated by an

[124] Jesse M. Gellrich, *The Idea of the Book in the Middle Ages: Language Theory, Mythology, and Fiction* (Ithaca and London: Cornell University Press, 1985), p. 32. See also E. R. Curtius, *European Literature and the Latin Middle Ages*, translated by W. R. Trask (London: Routledge and Kegan Paul, 1953), chapter 16 'The book as symbol'.

[125] Thomas of Celano, *Dies irae* in *Hymns of the Roman Liturgy*, edited by Joseph Connelly (Westminster, Maryland: Newman Press, 1957), p. 254, lines 13–15.

[126] The encyclopaedia is the inheritor of this medieval conception. For d'Alembert, the *Encyclopédie* places the philosopher above the vast labyrinth of the arts and sciences, enabling him to 'view with a single glance his object of speculation and those operations which he can perform on those objects to distinguish the general branches of human knowledge and the points dividing it and uniting it and even to detect at times the secret paths which unite it.' Quoted in Umberto Eco, *Semiotics and the Philosophy of Language* (London: Macmillan, 1984), p. 83.

authoring presence, a self-same and purely independent signified. Things (signifiers) depend upon it, but it does not depend upon them.[127]

> The idea of the book is the idea of a totality, finite or infinite, of the signifier; this totality of the signifier cannot be a totality, unless a totality constituted by the signified pre-exists it, supervises its inscriptions and its signs, and is independent of it in its ideality . . . It is the encyclopaedic protection of theology and of logocentrism against the disruption of writing, against its aphoristic energy, and . . . against difference in general.[128]

Derrida opposes the idea of writing (*écriture*) or text to that of the book. 'The idea of the book, which always refers to a natural totality, is profoundly alien to the sense of writing.'[129] Indeed, Derrida will insist that there are no books, only texts or textuality; for, as Kevin Hart puts it, text is the 'condition of possibility for both "text" and "book".'[130] This conclusion results from generalising Derrida's deconstruction of the 'sign'.

The sign is comported of signifier and signified, with the meaning of the first dependent on the presence of the second: the second being the meaning of the first. For logocentrism the signified (meaning) is not itself a signifier, but that which the signifier expresses, its ideality.[131] The signifier is thus

[127] Things can be signifiers in an appropriate, sufficiently generalised semiotics, as in Aquinas.

[128] Jacques Derrida, *Of Grammatology*, translated by Gayatri Chakravorty Spivak (Baltimore and London: Johns Hopkins University Press, [1967] 1976), p. 18. For Derrida, the desire for totality is 'theological'. 'The word "theological" pertains, then, to the use of any vocabulary in which meaning or being is said to be wholly resolved by reference to an origin, end, centre or ground . . . We do not need "God" in a discourse for it to be "theological" in Derrida's sense; all we need is something which functions as an agent of totalisation, and that can be "man", "Being", "substance", "impression", "Form", "logical atom", and so forth.' Kevin Hart *The Trespass of the Sign: Deconstruction, Theology and Philosophy* (Cambridge: Cambridge University Press, 1989), p. 32.

[129] Derrida, *Of Grammatology*, p. 18.

[130] Hart, *Trespass*, p. 25.

[131] 'It is possible to use the Saussurian vocabulary of signifier and signified without being wholeheartedly committed to metaphysics, yet if one uses "signified" to mean a concept that is present to consciousness then one is complicit with

different from, and a deferral of, that which it expresses, its signified. The signifier 'stands in' for the signified; present when the latter is absent. It also repeats. The signifier repeats its signified, and is itself repeatable; and it is this second repetition which jeopardises the first. For when a signifier (sign) is repeated in different contexts it may no longer repeat its signified (meaning). A person may sign their name repeatedly, the signature 'repeating' the signer; but when someone else signs her name – a forger – the signature will no longer represent (repeat) her in her absence.[132] 'No context can circumscribe a sign's meaning; the sign's meaning will alter if repeated in a different context; but the sign is structurally open to repetition: therefore, alterity is a structural feature of the sign.'[133] And if alterity is structural in the sign – if the signifier is always open to being different from its signified – how can we suppose the signifier to have its own, 'proper' signified; the sign its own 'proper' meaning? Surely the most we can suppose is that the sign marks the trace of a presence; the signifier the trace of a signified? And if 'presence' turns out to be the trace of a 'presence which has never presented itself', must we not speak of a trace of a trace?[134]

It is this argument that Derrida generalises into a deconstructive critique of any thought that seeks to establish a 'text' as a 'book', as the proper repetition of a presence. The latter is always an illusion, dependent on the textuality it is supposed to support. It is not presence, but the repetition of the differential system that comes first.

metaphysics. A discourse is metaphysical, then, if the concept is fashioned as a moment of pure presence, and the sign is representing the concept in its absence.' Hart, *Trespass*, p. 12. For the purpose of my exposition I am deploying 'signifier' and 'signified' in this metaphysical sense; but one could as well deploy 'sign' and 'presence' or 'sensible' and 'intelligible', as does Hart. The point is the logic of logocentrism, which Derrida espies everywhere.

132 See Jacques Derrida, 'Signature Event Context', in *Limited Inc* (Evanston, Illinois: Northwestern University Press, 1988), pp. 1–23; Hart, *Trespass*, p. 13.

133 Hart, *Trespass*, p. 13.

134 Hart, *Trespass*, p. 14.

The deconstruction of 'sign' leaves us not with a presence but with the trace of a trace; and, by the same token, the deconstruction of any signifying system – a consciousness, a society, an epoch, or whatever – leaves us with a text, 'a differential network, a fabric of traces referring endlessly to something other than itself, to other differential traces'.[135]

The medievals were themselves aware of difficulties in supposing the 'author' the ground and guarantee of proper meaning. This was expressed in anxiety about the unity and stability of biblical meaning. The seemingly endless proliferation of commentaries threatened the idea of a single unitary reading, a true and right interpretation.

Exegesis, itself another text, can never exhaust the possibilities for meaning, never reach closure, never represent, once and for all, the unity which is logos. Exegesis and commentary are never-ending, forever attempting to lay bare in another discourse that which was suppressed or unexpressed in the object text. For the early medieval exegetes, the biblical text is a vast field of signs so constituted by its rhetoric to be forever indicating its own insufficiency as the univocal statement of the Logos. The biblical text is polysemous and therefore necessitates multiple interpretations in many supplementary texts; the unity of truth and of the Logos is dispersed into polysemy.[136]

Michael Irvine argues that the medievals, realising the polysemic nature of the biblical text, sought authoritative interpretation in the 'authority of textual community, in the discourse that invests the texts with authority, and not in the texts themselves.' But that opened up new areas of indeterminacy: 'signs require interpretation, but according to which ideologically encoded discourse?'[137]

At the end of *De trinitate*, and before God, Augustine ponders

[135] Hart, *Trespass*, p. 25; quoting Derrida, 'Living on', in *Deconstruction and Criticism*, edited by Harold Bloom *et al.* (London: Routledge and Kegan Paul, 1979), p. 84.

[136] Martin Irvine, *The Making of Textual Culture: 'Grammatica' and Literary Theory, 350–1100*, Cambridge Studies in Medieval Literature 19 (Cambridge: Cambridge University Press, 1994), p. 265. See also Gellrich, *Idea of the Book*, pp. 21–8.

[137] Irvine, *Textual Culture*, p. 266.

his many words on the holy triad: 'I know that it is written, *In much speaking you will not avoid sin.*[138] If only I spoke when preaching your word and praising you!'[139] He wishes to say only one Word, but finds he must speak many. 'A wise man was speaking of you in his book which is now called Sirach as its proper name, and he said, *We say many things and do not attain, and the sum of our words is, he is all things* (Sirach 43.27).'[140]

Augustine recognises that it is impossible to say only one thing because humankind is circumscribed by language and signs, and, therefore, by temporality: meaning comes only through interpretation, not verbatim repetition, and we therefore multiply words and texts, interpret signs by other signs. Augustine registers an anxiety caused by the continual deferral of meaning generated by signs: the interpreter cannot capture, once and for all, the Being who is beyond signs. God is not a sign, yet language provides only the mediation of signs.[141]

As Irvine notes, the medievals knew that commentary promises and defers closure and the resolution of ambiguity. For in presenting the plain meaning of the biblical text, it delivers only another text which must register its difference and secondariness to the original. If commentary is the truth of its source, it must efface itself or otherwise unsettle the originariness of its origin. 'Commentary has a peculiar mode of being – it is, and is not, "the text". It collapses the opposing terms – literal/figurative, source/derivation – into a process – semiosis.'[142]

Thus the medieval idea of the book is not just the idea of totality; it is also the idea of its impossibility: of a text that promises and defers self-present meaning, that involves its readers in an endless process of interpretation.

[138] Proverbs 10.19.

[139] Augustine, *The Trinity*, translated by Edmund Hill OP, The Works of Saint Augustine 5 (Brooklyn, New York: New City Press, 1991), p. 436 (Book xv).

[140] Augustine, *The Trinity*, p. 437.

[141] Irvine, *Textual Culture*, p. 268. See Augustine, *Confessions*, translated by R. S. Pine-Coffin (Harmondsworth: Penguin Books, 1961), book 12.

[142] Irvine, *Textual Culture*, p. 271.

Scripture was the supreme Text, a variegated fabric of multiple discourses, some manifest, but many hidden. This Text can never signify its totality – the sum of its productivity of meaning – in one temporally instantiated act of interpretation, but continuously promises and postpones this totality through dissemination in a limitless chain of interpretations in supplementary texts. This model of textuality implies that a variorum commentary on the Scriptures compiled at the end of the world would still be incomplete, even though the chain of interpretations would be temporally closed, superseded by a signless, transcendental grammar.[143]

Irvine thus finds in the medievals typically Derridean themes: difference, deferral and supplementarity. If for Derrida the book is finally impossible because it can never bring to closure the play of difference, but can only be a temporary enclosure of the textuality from which it is constituted, so also for the medieval theologians. At the end of *De trinitate*, Augustine prays for the totality he knows to be impossible in human language. 'So when we do attain to you [God], there will be an end to these many things which we say and do not attain, and you will remain one, yet all in all, and we shall say one thing praising you in unison, even ourselves being also made one in you.'[144] The attempt to say the divine unity results in the endless multiplication of human discourse.

The Revelation of Saint John provides a figure for this state of human discourse before the divine mystery, and for our earlier conclusion that the Scripture is an all-consuming text only insofar as it itself is consumed. It is the figure of John eating the little scroll or book.

Then the voice that I had heard from heaven spoke to me again, saying, 'Go, take the scroll that is open in the hand of the angel who is standing on the sea and on the land.' So I went to the angel and told him to give me the little scroll; and he said to me, 'Take it, and eat; it will be bitter to your stomach, but sweet as honey in your mouth.' So I took the little scroll from the hand of the angel and ate

143 Irvine, *Textual Culture*, p. 271.

144 Augustine, *The Trinity*, p. 437. See also Augustine, *Confessions*, book 12, sections 31–2.

it; it was sweet as honey in my mouth, but when I had eaten it, my stomach was made bitter.[145]

The little scroll or book is the scriptural word that saves and judges (sweet and bitter). Just as John eats, so must the Church if it is to grow into the shape and strength of Christ, if it is to embody his word. Everyone who eats and is nourished by the scriptural word is him or herself a living commentary on that word, a supplementary telling or performance of the story which is both additional to, and necessary for, its telling. As John and the Church eat, so the words of the Scripture are endlessly assimilated and disseminated; containing as they do 'every truth that we can deduce from them and others beside that we cannot, or cannot yet, find in them but are nevertheless there to be found. Thus we are fed from the hand of God.'[146] Here it is not a matter of comprehending a totality, but of digesting a text,[147] of allowing it to become a part of the Church and the Church a part of it so that finally there is only the text: the textuality of the Word.

145 Revelation 10.8–10.
146 Augustine, *Confessions*, book 12, chapter 32 (p. 309).
147 Gellrich, *Idea of the Book*, p. 21.

PART II

Reading and writing

Blessed is the one who reads . . .

Revelation 1.3

CHAPTER 4

Making it plain

In recent years the Bible has increasingly been read as literature rather than as Scripture, as a text of pleasure rather than of edification: a site for the exercise of literary skill rather than 'for training in righteousness'.[1] It has come to be read as one would read 'any other book'.[2] This literary interest is not new,[3] but it has only recently become possible for libraries to catalogue the Bible as world poetry rather than as sacred Scripture.[4]

Prior to the interest of literary critics, historians had long taken the Bible as they would any other document. For them the Bible is to be read as they would Tacitus or Cicero. It is but a trace of the past. Indeed, the problems of historical criticism

1 'All Scripture is inspired by God and is useful for teaching, for reproof, for correction, and for training in righteousness, so that everyone who belongs to God may be proficient, equipped for every good work' (II Timothy 3.16,17).

2 John B. Gabel and Charles B. Wheeler, *The Bible as Literature: An Introduction* (New York and Oxford: OUP, 1986), p. 3. For literary approaches to the Bible see: Robert Alter and Frank Kermode (eds), *The Literary Guide to the Bible* (London: Collins, 1987); Northrop Frye, *The Great Code: The Bible and Literature* (London: Routledge, 1982); Wesley A. Kort, *Story, Text and Scripture: Literary Interests in Biblical Narrative* (University Park and London: The Pennsylvania State University Press, 1988); Gabriel Josipovici, *The Book of God: A Response to the Bible* (New Haven and London: Yale University Press, 1988); Regina M. Schwartz (ed.), *The Book and the Text: The Bible and Literary Theory* (Oxford: Basil Blackwell, 1989); T. R. Wright, *Theology and Literature* (Oxford: Basil Blackwell, 1987).

3 See David Norton, *A History of the Bible as Literature*, 2 vols. (Cambridge: Cambridge University Press, 1993). He notes that 'modern critics . . . have created a myth . . . that respectable literary criticism of the Bible is a modern invention' (Vol. II, p. 357).

4 Colin Falck, *Myth, Truth and Literature: Towards a True Post-Modernism* (Cambridge: Cambridge University Press, 1989), p. 134. See Norton, *History of the Bible*, Vol. II, pp. 363–88.

– especially in regard to the Bible – are very largely literary ones; questions of imaginative reading.[5] Faced with the levelling of the Bible in the nineteenth century, Cardinal John Henry Newman felt it needful to point out that for the Church, the Bible 'cannot be put on the level of other books'. He insisted that the 'Catholic scholar or man of science' must never 'forget that what he is handling is the Word of God, which, by reason of the difficulty of always drawing the line between what is human and what is divine, cannot be put on the level of other books, as it is now the fashion to do, but has the nature of a Sacrament, which is outward and inward, and a channel of supernatural grace.'[6]

As the distinction between 'what is human and what is divine' and the idea of Scripture as Sacrament indicate, Newman felt the difficulty as well as the necessity of saying how for the Church the Bible is and is not like 'any other book'. The Bible is like any other book in that it is the product of particular circumstances, written by particular people for specific communities, historically situated. It is unlike any other book, however, in that it has been and is used as the textual matrix of a tradition which at the same time constitutes the Bible as Scripture through and in that usage. Newman was concerned to maintain the Church's traditional use of the Bible and thereby its usefulness for the Church; in short, he was concerned to maintain the Bible as the living word of God. This is not to argue against historical and literary criticism, but that they should serve rather than rule the Church's reading of Scripture.

Newman rightly feared that if the Bible is read only as one would any other book, as expressive of universal verities or as

[5] This point is made by Norton (*History of the Bible*, Vol. II, pp. 349–57), who notes that what Albert Schweitzer called 'the historical imagination is no different from the imagination employed by readers of fiction, bringing the more or less complete information of the text into an imaginative whole' (p. 351). For example, the 'synoptic problem' is first and last a literary question, the exploration of which tells us much about the reading of the gospels and little about their writing.

[6] John Henry Newman, *On the Inspiration of Scripture*, edited by J. Derek Holmes and Robert Murray SJ (London: Geoffrey Chapman, 1967), p. 114.

traces of the past – and so read within the Church – it can no longer be a word of promise to us, or a word of judgement upon us. For its use will no longer be such that it is at the same time God's use of the Church for the use of the world.[7] It will no longer be a telling of the story that shapes the teller; no longer a sacrament of God's Word.

How the Bible is understood as God's address to the Church – the Word in the words of Scripture – is the concern of this and the following chapter. The next chapter will show how it is possible that the Word incarnate in Jesus of Nazareth is given to us more truly in the scriptural story than in any conceivable historical reconstruction. It will also consider how easily the Church may, and has, failed to hear God's address in that story: how what is sweet in the mouth becomes bitter in the belly. First however I turn to consider the doctrine of inspiration as serving to remind the Church how to read its sacred texts, before proceeding to consider how reading for the literal sense of Scripture is a reading for the Word.

GOD IS HIS OWN INTERPRETER AND HE WILL MAKE IT PLAIN

As Austin Farrer (1904–1968) shows, this couplet from William Cowper's hymn, 'Light shining out of darkness',[8] expresses what is central in the Church's reading of Scripture, the essence of its biblical hermeneutic. It is possible to construct a properly postmodern account of biblical inspiration upon it; one that is not in hock to the foundationalism of modernist historical criticism. Postmodern because, with Farrer, it looks to the pre-modern thought of the ancient Church,[9] and yet comes after the labours of modernism; not so much in the

7 On the Church's use to God, and God's uselessness to the Church see Robert W. Jenson, 'The Christian Doctrine of God', in *Keeping the Faith: Essays to Mark the Centenary of Lux Mundi*, edited by Geoffrey Wainwright (London: SPCK, 1989), 25–53 (pp. 27–30).

8 *The Poems of William Cowper*, edited by J. C. Bailey (London: Methuen and Company), pp. 56–7.

9 Austin Farrer, *The Glass of Vision* (Westminster: Dacre Press, 1948), p. 36.

sense of accepting the latter's 'assured results' – which are minimal – but in recognising the textuality of the scriptural writings: their being wrought by human hands.

Austin Farrer taught that the criticism 'of most use for getting to the bottom of the New Testament is often more like the criticism we apply to poetry than we might incline to expect.'[10] It was thus that he sought to show the 'poetical inevitability' of ending Mark's Gospel at chapter 16.8. 'So they went out and fled from the tomb, for terror and amazement had seized them, and they said nothing to anyone, for they were afraid.'[11] Tracing a complex pattern of allusion and repetition in the Gospel, Farrer shows that Mark's 'words are shaped by a play of images and allusions of the subtle and elusive kind which belongs to imagination rather than to rational construction', and that being such it requires an appropriate criticism.[12] He thus saw the need to demarcate the scope of an over-rational historical criticism and the limitation of its methods.

Historical criticism is a net with its own sort of meshes let down into the ocean of total fact and gathering whatever harvest of fishes that sort of net will catch. No net will catch all the living matter in the water and no historical method will fish up the whole of live historical reality, unless we give to 'historical reality' the tautological sense of 'what our historical method fishes up.' [13]

[10] Farrer, *Glass*, p. 136.

[11] Farrer, *Glass*, p. 139. Farrer brought a similar poetic sensibility to the book of Revelation in *A Rebirth of Images: The Making of St John's Apocalypse* (Westminster: Dacre Press, 1949).

[12] Farrer, *Glass*, pp. 145–6.

[13] Austin Farrer, *Interpretation and Belief*, edited by C. C. Conti (London: SPCK, 1976), p. 12. Consider the fishy 'discovery' of Q, the source document of the early Church, long since lost, that provided the writers of Matthew and Luke with the material common to them both. Farrer was a notable writer 'On dispensing with Q' (in *Studies in the Gospels*, edited by D. E. Nineham (Oxford: Basil Blackwell, 1955), pp. 55–88), arguing that it was more sensible to suppose that Luke read Matthew than that both read Q. Michael Goulder is surely right in judging that even if the supposition of Q is yet to be falsified, 'Farrer's achievement is the not inconsiderable one of reducing Q from a fact to a hypothesis.' (Goulder quoted in Philip Curtis, *A Hawk Among Sparrows: A Biography of Austin Farrer* (London: SPCK, 1985), p. 198.)

It is with such tautologies, however, that historical science works. Once the biblical scholar has taken the Bible apart in order to show how it was put together, there seems little room for ideas of inspiration, divine or otherwise. We have before us a text like any other, a wholly human work. The doctrine of inspiration, however, does not deny that Scripture is a wholly human work; it simply adds that it is also a wholly divine one. In order to see how Scripture is both wholly human and divine, we have to take seriously the maxim that 'God is his own interpreter'; that he reads his own writing.

If one takes Cowper's maxim seriously – as a theological axiom – with regard to the relation between the testimony of Scripture and that to which it testifies, one must construe the relation as more intimate than that of record to event. One cannot suppose that Scripture is just the record of what someone saw and heard and said to others. 'It is what St Luke couldn't help fancying someone's having said that he thought he remembered St Peter's having told him: or it is the way St Paul felt about what Christ meant to him.'[14] Such a view leaves little if any room for a notion of inspiration, and calls in question the role of Scripture as matrix and criterion of the Christian life.

If God reads Scripture, then Scripture, as testimony to God's revelation, is itself part of that revelation, part of God's intimate self-disclosure, part of God's incarnation. As Farrer puts it, 'God speaks without and within; he reveals himself both through the situation with which he presents the recipients of revelation, and through the imagination, in terms of which he leads them to see and hear the voices and sights surrounding them.'[15] The doctrine of biblical inspiration serves to remind the Church of this double aspect of divine disclosure – God both within and without.

Scripture is in part constitutive of the events it discloses, as they are of it. The relation between situation and imagination, event and text, is inter-constitutive of both. Describing the events of revelation and the testimony of Scripture as

[14] Farrer, *Glass*, p. 37. [15] Farrer, *Interpretation*, p. 44.

inter-constitutive reminds us that the Church is at least in part a socio-textual reality, shaping the texts by which it is shaped.

Thus it has always been. There never was, at the first, a non-textual event of which the text is but the record or to which it is but a response. For all events within the life of the people of God – which is always a traditioned and traditioning life, forming the future as it is formed by the past – are traditioned or textualized events. They are always-already interpreted, always-already a reading of what has gone before, in part constituted by a preceding textual reality.

Jesus of Nazareth – whose life, death and resurrection are the historical origin of Christian faith – comes after the words of God in the Hebrew Scriptures, both as their continuation and, as the Church believes, their fulfilment. Precisely as the one who is figured in the gospels, Jesus the Christ is already prefigured in the Hebrew Scriptures. Jesus is in part a textually constituted reality. As Farrer reminds us, the advent of John the Baptist is written out of the text of Isaiah, 'but it is an imperceptive reader . . . who supposes that the Christ of the blessed message springs out of Scripture any less evidently than his messenger does'.[16]

For Farrer, Christ self-consciously constituted himself through his own reading of the Hebrew Scriptures, a constitution continued by the Church. 'Christ both performed the primary action and gave the primary interpretation: the Apostles, supernaturalized by the Spirit of Pentecost, worked out both the saving action and the revealing interpretation by Christ.'[17] Christ clothed himself in scriptural images, and in the clothing constituted the character and identity of God's Messiah. The inter-constitution of man and image – an existential-textual reality and event – was and is the self-disclosure of God. For Farrer, the 'great images interpreted the events of Christ's ministry, death and resurrection, and the events interpreted the images; the interplay of the two is revelation.'[18]

[16] Farrer, *Interpretation*, p. 64.
[17] Farrer, *Glass*, p. 41.
[18] Farrer, *Glass*, p. 43.

If Christ is the revelation of God, and if Christ and the community he inaugurates are socio-textual realities, irreducibly bound to Scripture, then Scripture is inevitably part of God's revelation. Person and text are interconstitutive: the Word and words of God. The one is necessary for the meaning of the other. Christ and the Church are understood properly only in the light of Scripture, and Scripture is understood properly only in the light of Christ and the Church.

Nevertheless, it remains the case that the 'primary revelation is Jesus Christ himself', and not Scripture.[19] Hence Scripture is not itself revelation but interconstitutive of revelation, and only thus said to be inspired. Scripture in itself, abstracted from the life of the community in which it lives, is not and cannot be inspired. It is then but an ancient text, a curiosity. To speak of Scripture as inspired is to speak of it enjoying that life in which it is taken up as interconstitutive of its users. For to be inspired is to be in the Spirit, and that is to be in the community to whom the Spirit is given.[20]

It is part of the mystery of the incarnation that it is disclosed or mediated to us in the reading and refiguring (appropriation) of four canonical gospels, whose agreements and disagreements are irreducibly part of the event they present.[21] The text is a dead thing until it is taken up and performed in the Church. It is then that the Scriptures, read together as the canonical story of God, open up a world in which the reader can live, construing his or her life, past, present and future, as a continuing part of the biblical story. To enter the world of the Scripture, to become a part of its story, is to enter the community that reads the Scripture as that which delineates the world of the community; it is to become a part of the

19 Farrer, *Glass*, p. 39.

20 This may seem to contradict Scripture: 'All Scripture is inspired by God' (II Timothy 3.16). However: 'no prophecy of Scripture is a matter of one's own interpretation, because no prophecy ever came by human will, but men and women moved by the Holy Spirit spoke from God' (II Peter 1.20–1). Scripture is inspired because of its placing within the people 'moved by the Holy Spirit'.

21 This is further discussed in chapter 7 with regard to the resurrection of Jesus Christ.

community's own story. There is a dynamic to communal reading, which is always interanimative and socio-textual.

The location of biblical inspiration is not the text itself, but the life of the community in which the text is read and celebrated. As John Henry Newman noted, the books of Scripture 'are inspired, because the writers were inspired to write them. They are not inspired books, unless they came from inspired men.'[22] To speak of biblical inspiration is to speak of a Church charism, a gift of God's grace to the Church. It is people not things who are inspired, for to be inspired is to be made alive.

Understanding biblical inspiration as a gift of the Spirit – a charism of the Church, a practice and usage of the community – allows us to present an account of biblical inspiration as the writing and reading of Scripture in the Church, for inspiration attends both. 'We', as Farrer reminds us, 'may be inspired to embrace what St Paul revealed; he was inspired to reveal it. We may be inspired to expound what he taught; but he was inspired to teach it.'[23]

WRITING AND READING

The writers of Scripture were inspired. This does not mean that the biblical writers were, as Farrer puts it, 'out of their ordinary senses when they composed. God did not suspend their normal consciousness and wag their tongues and hands for them as a showman does his puppets.'[24] The writers of the gospel narratives were not any less themselves; they were just themselves. But they were themselves as people writing for their fellow Christians. They were writing accounts of the life, death and resurrection of Jesus, attending to the mystery of his life. Their inspiration was different from that of others in the Church only in that they were doing something different from them. The point is St Paul's, who notes that the one Spirit given to the Church issues in diverse practices. 'There

22 Newman, *Inspiration of Scripture*, p. 115.

23 Farrer, *Interpretation*, p. 10.

24 Farrer, *Interpretation*, p. 10.

are varieties of gifts, but the same Spirit; and there are varieties of services, but the same Lord; and there are varieties of activities, but it is the same God who activates all of them in everyone.'[25]

Farrer teaches that when God inspires a good action it is the action itself that is inspired.[26] This is the matter precisely. God inspires the action, the doing, the writing of the evangelists and the reading of believers. There is no whispered voice; no inspirational mechanism. God's inspiration is not a further determinate in addition to all the others and in competition with them. Rather God's inspiration is the relation that the Church's writing and reading of Scripture bears to the Creator. Inspiration is not additional to the writing of the evangelist, it is the evangelist writing; it is not additional to the reading of the Church, it is the Church reading.

God's inspiration is not a whispering in the writer's ear, a divine dictation or verbal inspiration.[27] It is rather the relation between the eternal God and the biblical writers, concretely established through their life in the community of God's people.[28] However, in order to make evident the force of this claim it is necessary to turn to the other pole on which an account of biblical inspiration can be thematised, the reading of Scripture. In doing so it becomes evident that the two poles of writing and reading cannot be held apart, but must be understood as two moments in the one dynamic of the Church's life.

If God inspired St Paul to reveal further the mystery of God,

[25] I Corinthians 12.4–6. Newman uses this text to support his argument that while the Spirit is wholly given to the biblical writers, it does not inform the whole of their writing. *Inspiration of Scripture*, pp. 135–6.

[26] Farrer, *Interpretation*, p. 12.

[27] On verbal inspiration see Robert Gnuse, *The Authority of the Bible: Theories of Inspiration, Revelation and the Canon of Scripture* (New York: Paulist Press, 1985), pp. 22–41.

[28] The doctrine of biblical inspiration advocated in this chapter best fits the fourth of Robert Gnuse's four categories of biblical inspiration: (1) strict verbal inspiration; (2) limited verbal inspiration; (3) non-textual inspiration and (4) social inspiration: a charism of the community of believers. Gnuse, *Authority of the Bible*, p. 21.

to teach what he taught about Christ – about Christ's life and death and our own in relation to Christ – then equally, as Farrer suggests, God inspires us insofar as we discern in Paul what is to be read there of God's mystery. 'If we do not believe that the same God who moved St Paul can move us to understand what he moved St Paul to say, then . . . it isn't much use our bothering about St Paul's writings.'[29]

THE WORD IN THE WORDS

Maurice Wiles looks forward to a time when Scripture will be seen as an 'indispensable resource rather than as a binding authority'. He desires an 'abandonment of the idea of the Bible as authoritative', and since, as he admits, 'the notion of authority is implicit in the notion of Scripture, the abandonment of the Bible as Scripture'.[30] For Wiles there is no room for biblical inspiration. This is because, as he puts it, 'critical study of the Bible has enabled us to see things about the nature of scriptural texts . . . whose general truth cannot seriously be questioned'.[31] These unquestionable things include the social conditioning of the texts, the diversity of opinions within them, and the historical unreliability of their witness.[32] Farrer raises the same question with regard to St Paul. 'If God inspires St Paul to speak, how are we to strain out St Paul, so as to be left with the pure Word of God? We do not want St Paul's national prejudices or personal limitations, which, good man as he was, he could not wholly escape.' Farrer answers that 'no one can, it is like trying to jump off one's own shadow.'[33]

29 Farrer, *Interpretation*, p. 11. It may be noted that on this account of God's reading of Scripture in and by the Church, the translation of the Bible is also a matter of inspiration. Indeed if it were not, the idea of biblical inspiration would be of little use, the original autographs being long gone. On the inspiration of the King James Version of the Bible see Norton, *History of the Bible*, Vol. II, pp. 189–91.

30 Maurice Wiles, 'Scriptural authority and theological construction: the limitations of narrative interpretation', in *Scriptural Authority and Narrative Interpretation*, edited by Garrett Green (Philadelphia: Fortress Press, 1987), pp. 50–1.

31 Wiles, 'Scriptural authority', p. 43.

32 Wiles, 'Scriptural authority', pp. 43–4.

33 Farrer, *Interpretation*, pp. 10–11.

The Bible contains many inaccuracies and errors. For example, as Farrer notes, 'St Paul's astronomy is (as astronomy) no good to us at all. St Luke appears to have made one or two slips in dating, and St John was often content with a very broad or general historical effect, and concentrated more on what things meant than just the way they happened.'[34]

More problematically the Bible also contains many monstrosities, 'texts of terror' that we today would not have thought to write and certainly don't want to privilege.[35] Can these disquieting texts, along with the more comforting, really be the word of God, the site of divine disclosure?

We cannot iron out the contradictions of Scripture, nor simply forget those parts that counter our most cherished beliefs and sentiments. This was a problem that long troubled Augustine, and it delayed his entry into the Church. It was not until he learned from Ambrose how to read for the hidden, allegorical meaning that he could accept the 'absurdities' of Scripture as the word of God.[36] Recourse to allegory is not so plausible today, and what Augustine found so difficult no longer troubles us, but other matters do.[37] It would seem that we must admit the Bible is what it appears to be: the fallible production of an erring humanity.

In order to see how inspiration and scriptural incongruity can be reconciled it is necessary to explore the way in which the writing of Scripture is a moment within its reading. We have seen how Jesus meets us in the gospels as himself an interpretation of Scripture, a person who in his action and teaching constitutes a living reading of the Prophets.

[34] Farrer, *Interpretation*, p. 12.

[35] See Phyllis Trible, *Texts of Terror: Literary-Feminist Readings of Biblical Narratives*, Overtures to Biblical Theology 13 (Philadelphia: Fortress Press, 1984).

[36] Augustine, *Confessions*, Bk VI.6 (p. 116).

[37] The stories of Hagar – wounded for our transgressions, bruised for our iniquities (Genesis 16.1–16, 21.9–21); Tamar – a woman of sorrows acquainted with grief (2 Samuel 13.1–22); the raped, murdered and dismembered concubine – her body broken and given to many (Judges 19.1–30); and the daughter of Jephthah – forsaken by God (Judges 11.29–40), may not have concerned Augustine as they do Phyllis Trible; yet he may have recognised her use of Scripture to interpret Scripture, refiguring these women as types of Christ.

He stood up to read, and the scroll of the prophet Isaiah was given to him. He unrolled the scroll and found the place where it was written: 'The Spirit of the Lord is upon me, because he has anointed me to bring good news to the poor. He has sent me to proclaim release to the captives and recovery of sight to the blind, to let the oppressed go free, to proclaim the year of the Lord's favour.' And he rolled up the scroll, gave it back to the attendant, and sat down. The eyes of all in the synagogue were fixed on him. Then he began to say to them, 'Today this Scripture has been fulfilled in your hearing.'[38]

Jesus is God's *midrash* on the Law and the Prophets; God's embodied reading of his own writing. The writing of the gospels, letters and vision, is the Church's inspired reading – and therefore God's reading – of God's own writing. Precisely because it came after, the writing of (Christian) Scripture is constituted as a moment in the Church's reading of (Hebrew) Scripture;[39] a moment in God's reading of his own story.

It is because and not despite the fact that God reads his own writing – reads the story of his dealings with the world, with kings and prophets, saints and fools, with Sarah and Abraham, Mary and the Apostles – that the Bible is errant and requires discernment. This will seem less paradoxical when it is remembered that the God who reads is the one who became incarnate in Jesus of Nazareth. The eternal reality of God, so Christian faith affirms, is given over to the contingent history of one man and the community he gathered for the sake of the world. Here we must take with full seriousness what Ronald Gregor Smith called 'the wholeness of God's condescension in Christ, his complete entering into the world through his Word'.[40] With equal seriousness we must take the wholeness of Christ's work, which, as Farrer writes, is 'the work of the mystical Christ, who embraces both Head and members'.[41]

38 Luke 4.17–21.

39 Though of course many Christian writings are also readings of other Christian writings. With the formation of the Church's canon of Scripture, intertextuality becomes intratextuality.

40 Ronald Gregor Smith, *J. G. Hamann 1730–1788: A Study in Christian Existence* (London: Collins, 1960), p. 20.

41 Farrer, *Glass*, p. 41.

The wholeness of God's condescension includes the Church, and thus its reading of Scripture.[42] The idea of biblical inerrancy results from a failure to take with full seriousness the wholeness of God's work in Christ; the incarnation of the Word in words.

God is his own interpreter, but his interpretation is incarnate, concrete and human. The mystery of God's self-interpretation, God's reading of his own story, is that in being given over to human contingency, that contingency is taken up into the mystery of God's triune life. When Scripture as inspired writing is understood in this way its all too human production is expected rather than surprising. What does surprise is that human finitude should be 'taken up' into the triune life of God through God's condescension in Christ. What confounds human expectation is that God should give his Word over to our reading; that he should love us so much.

Insofar as Scripture is inter-constitutive of the Church as a socio-textual reality, inspired by the love and power of the incarnate God, it cannot be treated as a text dropped from heaven, but must be read with discernment, struggling for its sense and reference. For the reading of Scripture by and in the Church is the continuing incarnation of God's own self-interpretation and, precisely as such, is a wholly human work just as Jesus was a wholly human man.

Christ is the rule for the Church's reading of Scripture. He is the norm by which the text is judged; the reading context in which the sense of God's writing is discerned. But Christ himself is given in the text; given in the Church's reading or performance of the text. Christ, as the norm of Christian reading, is realised only in the practice of faithful reading. He is not given apart from that for which he is normative. The Church is better able to read Scripture the more the Scripture lives in the Church; the more the Scripture is faithfully read and performed.

[42] In the sense that the Church's reading of Scripture is part of God's whole work, we can say that revelation has not come to an end with the last apostle, only the writing of which it is a reading.

BIBLE READING

I now turn to consider how the Church struggles for the sense and reference – the meaning and truth – of Scripture. The Church has always understood its Scripture to have many meanings. For Origen, Augustine and Aquinas, the scriptural sense was multiple. One thing signified another, one sense led to the next. From the literal one was led to the allegorical, anagogical and tropological; from the earthly to the spiritual, the heavenly and the moral.[43] But always the literal sense mattered most. It was the one upon which all the others rested. For Hugh of St Victor it was like the foundation of a house.[44] Today, however, the literal sense seems the most problematic. Like Hugh of St Victor we take the literal to be the historical, but unlike Hugh we find the historical incredible. The Bible refers us to the past only falteringly. Today we look to metaphor for our meaning. But for narrative theology meaning and truth are still to be found in the literal sense, when Scripture is followed to the letter.

AVOIDING THE LITERAL

Liberal theologians provide many examples of what can happen when one does not attend to the literal sense of Scripture. In particular liberal bishops provide a rich source, Bishop John Shelby Spong being a good example. In his book *Born of a Woman* (1992), Bishop Spong attempts to rescue women from the dire effects of a 'literalised' reading of the gospel narratives: 'literalisation guarantees death'.[45]

[43] G. R. Evans, *The Language and Logic of the Bible: The Earlier Middle Ages* (Cambridge: Cambridge University Press, 1984), pp. 114–22.

[44] *The Didascalicon of Hugh of St Victor: A Medieval Guide to the Arts*, translated by Jerome Taylor, Records of Western Civilization (New York: Columbia University Press, [1961] 1991), Bk VI, Ch 3, pp. 135–9; Evans, *Language*, pp. 67–71.

[45] John Shelby Spong, *Born of a Woman: A Bishop Rethinks the Birth of Jesus* (San Francisco: Harper Collins, 1992), p. 176. Bishop Spong's book is something of a period piece. It is redolent of 60s Bultmannism, as suggested by the now quaint contrast between the 'three-tiered universe' of first century people and the cosmology of 'space-age people' (p. 10). Compare John A. T. Robinson, *Honest to God* (London: SCM Press, 1963), pp. 11–18.

However, in failing to attend to the letter of the text, Spong renders women more securely dependent upon men. He does not take the gospel texts literally and therefore he does not take their stories of independent women seriously; stories of women whose primary relations are not with men, in particular with husbands, but with God.

Spong finds the idea that a man was not responsible for the birth of Jesus so problematic that he departs from the letter of the text and speculates that Jesus was the issue of a rape. The narrative of Jesus's conception – a conception chosen by Mary and without male agency – is then a cover-up for the actual story: conception by male force – 'an illegitimate baby born through the aggressive and selfish act of a man sexually violating a teenage girl'.[46] Spong thinks that if we take the story as it is written we will have to speculate about 'parthenogenesis, or postulate a spirit with sexual organs and fluids'.[47] Rather than this, Spong re-writes the story, violating the letter of the text and inserting a man where no man was previously to be found.[48]

It has been said that early tradition obscured the role of women in the Church; but Spong suggests that the Church 'has done Joseph a disservice by relegating him to near obscurity'. Spong suspects that Joseph was far more important in the early life of Jesus than we have been led to believe.[49] If we follow the letter of the text we are led to Mary; but Spong would have us find our way to Joseph.

In Spong's world women must be attached to men; they cannot be allowed to do their own thing. He tells us that in first-century Jewish society, a 'group of women who followed a male band of disciples had to be wives, mothers or prostitutes'.

46 Spong, *Born of a Woman*, p. 185.

47 Spong, *Born of a Woman*, p. 127.

48 Of course the choice is not between parthenogenesis or rape; it is between the story we have, which mentions neither, or some other story.

49 Spong, *Born of a Woman*, pp. 181–2. 'I think we must entertain the possibility that Joseph, whatever his physical ties were with his son Jesus, did in fact give Jesus a relationship of such substance and beauty that it shaped his very understanding of God' (p. 184).

Consequently, Spong marries Mary Magdalene to Jesus. This speculation is said to reverse the calumny of the early Church, which quickly developed the need to remove the 'flesh and blood woman who was at Jesus's side in life and in death, and to replace her with a sexless woman, the virgin mother'.[50] Rather than having Mary Magdalene a disciple in her own right – a woman who chooses to follow Jesus as much as the men have done, and who follows him more faithfully – Spong makes her a sexual chattel; part of the group that follows the band rather than part of the band itself.

Bishop Spong, of course, wants the Church to have a balanced view of sexuality and of relationships between the sexes; he wants to overcome the 'historic negativity toward women that has been a major gift of the Christian Church to the world'.[51] But in not reading the Bible literally he falls short of achieving his intention. Because he does not follow the letter of the text he does not find stories about women who are first of all independent women, whose relationships with God are not dependent on men, but who are themselves disciples, the prime exemplars of Christian faith.[52] He makes up a story about a woman who was raped, rather than follow the gospel story about a woman who chose to conceive and didn't need a man to do so;[53] and he makes up a story about a woman who followed Jesus because she was married to him, rather than the story we have about a woman who chose to follow Jesus because she loved him as a disciple.

Bishop Spong's reading of the Bible may be called 'allegorical' in the sense that it takes the biblical text as pointing

[50] Spong, *Born of a Woman*, pp. 191 and 197.

[51] Spong, *Born of a Woman*, p. 198.

[52] 'In Luke we find a woman [Mary] who is not only in charge of her own destiny . . . but also the destiny of humanity . . . the perfect radical model of Christian discipleship.' Deborah F. Middleton, 'The story of Mary: Luke's version', *New Blackfriars* 70 (1989), 555–64 (p. 563).

[53] It is interesting to note that for Spong, Mary's faithful obedience to God in Luke's Gospel (1.35) is the action of a 'compliant Jewish peasant girl' in the face of 'divine sexual aggression', while her son's faithful obedience to God (Luke 22.42) is an action of intense human integrity, of self-giving and life-giving love (p. 179). It is not Luke who so belittles the mother's part.

towards a second text – that of historical speculation – where the truth is to be found.[54] Spong's 'allegorical' approach is instructive of a general diremption of the literal sense in the modern period: between the literal-as-written and the literal-as-historical. This diremption is no doubt irretrievable, and can now be signified only in writings such as this. Here it is signified by the idea of the letteral sense.[55] The letteral is the literal proper, the literal-as-written. The idea of the literal can then be used, as it is used, in the (improper) modern sense: the literal-as-historical. That the latter is a modern use can be indicated by attending to the discussion of Scripture's several senses in the *Summa Theologiæ* of St Thomas Aquinas (1224–1274).

LITERAL FIGURES

In the modern period we have been taught to contrast the literal with the metaphorical. Thus Spong argues that there is only one literal phrase in the historic creeds, one 'literal fact of history': 'He suffered under Pontius Pilate, was crucified,

54 Spong argues that attempts to 'reconcile or to harmonise the differences between Matthew and Luke are based on the false premise that some historical, factual truth lies behind these birth narratives.' (p. 60) Yet Spong's entire book is concerned with speculating about the 'historical, factual truth' that lies behind the gospel stories. For an account of similar 'allegorising' in other liberal theologians see my articles, 'On telling the story of Jesus', *Theology*, 87 (1984), 323–9; and 'Myths, signs and significations', *Theology*, 89 (1986), 268–75.

55 The 'letteral' is a term borrowed from Rachel Salmon and Gerda Elata-Alster. There are interesting similarities between the textual attention I intend by the term and the midrashic reading outlined in their article, 'Retracing a writerly text: in the footsteps of a midrashic sequence on the creation of the male and female', in *Hermeneutics, the Bible and Literary Criticism*, edited by Ann Loades and Michael McLain (London: Macmillan, 1992), pp. 177–97. Indeed, Hans Frei suggests that *midrash* (and *peshat*) is 'the nearest Jewish equivalent to Christian literal reading.' (Hans Frei, *Theology and Narrative: Selected Essays*, edited by George Hunsinger and William C. Placher (New York and Oxford: Oxford University Press, 1993), p. 149.) For further on *midrash* see Gerald L. Bruns, *Hermeneutics Ancient and Modern* (New Haven and London: Yale University Press, 1992), pp. 104–23; and on *peshat* see Raphael Loewe, 'The "plain" meaning of Scripture in early Jewish exegesis', *Papers of the Institute of Jewish Studies in London*, 1 (1964), 140–85.

died and was buried.'[56] By contrast, the credal phrase 'He sitteth on the right hand of God' is not to be understood literally but figuratively. It is then very odd for the modern mind to find Aquinas making no such distinction between the literal and the figurative.

It is not that Aquinas would not recognise 'He sitteth on the right hand of God' as a figure of speech. On the contrary, he teaches that in holy Scripture 'spiritual things' are delivered to us 'beneath metaphors taken from bodily things'. This is because Scripture is to be used 'in common without distinction of persons'. The uneducated may also lay hold of spiritual things. For the same reason, holy teaching (theology) finds the use of metaphors indispensable.[57] The use of metaphors is also important because it reminds us that God cannot be directly signified.[58]

But for Aquinas, unlike Spong, metaphors and other figures of speech are found at the level of the literal sense.[59] As Fr Thomas Gilby notes, in Aquinas there is 'no depreciation of the literal sense as though it expressed just the flat and unimaginative significance of the words as they stand'.[60] For Aquinas the metaphorical or figural is a disposition of the literal.

Aquinas draws a basic distinction between the literal and the spiritual senses of Scripture. Under the heading of the literal sense he places history, etiology and analogy. 'You have history when any matter is straightforwardly recorded; etiology when its cause is indicated . . . analogy when the truth of one Scriptural passage is shown not to clash with the

56 Spong, *Born of a Woman*, p. 177.

57 St Thomas Aquinas, *Summa Theologiæ*, vol. 1: Christian Theology (1a.1), translated by Thomas Gilby OP (London: Blackfriars, Eyre and Spottiswoode, 1964), p. 35.

58 The use of 'figures of base bodies' reminds us that no figure can be 'taken in the proper sense of their words and be crudely ascribed to divine things', for what God is not is clearer to us than what God is (*Summa Theologiæ*, p. 35).

59 Aquinas, *Summa Theologiæ*, vol. 1, p. 41. For a succinct statement of Thomas' teaching see Beryl Smalley, *The Study of the Bible in the Middle Ages* (Oxford: Clarendon Press, 1941), p. 234.

60 Thomas Gilby OP, 'The senses of Scripture', Appendix 12 in Aquinas, *Summa Theologiæ*, vol. 1, 140–1 (p. 140).

truth of another'. Under the heading of the spiritual or allegorical sense he places the tropological, the moral and the anagogical. The tropological sense 'is brought into play when the things of the Old Law signify the things of the New Law; the moral sense when the things done in Christ and in those who prefigured him are signs of what we should carry out; and the anagogical sense when the things that lie ahead in eternal glory are signified'.[61]

Aquinas discusses metaphor and figure in discussing the parabolic sense which he says is contained in the literal sense. He writes that 'words can signify something properly and something figuratively; in the last case the literal sense is not the figure of speech itself, but the object it figures'.[62] This is because things as well as words signify.

> That God is the author of holy Scripture should be acknowledged, and he has the power, not only of adapting words to convey meanings (which men also can do), but also of adapting things themselves. In every branch of knowledge words have meaning, but what is special here is that the things meant by the words also themselves mean something.[63]

An example of this is provided by Hugh of St Victor in his *Didascalicon* of the late 1130s.

> The Scripture says: 'Watch, because your adversary the Devil goeth about as a roaring lion.'[64] Here, if we should say that the lion stands for the Devil, we should mean by 'lion' not the word but the thing. For if the two words 'devil' and 'lion' mean one and the same thing, the likeness of that same thing to itself is not adequate. It remains, therefore, that the word 'lion' signifies the animal, but that the animal in turn designates the Devil.[65]

Aquinas was heir to this way of thinking, to a tradition of commentary that had, as Beryl Smalley puts it, 'groped' its

[61] Aquinas, *Summa Theologiæ*, vol. 1, p. 39.
[62] Aquinas, *Summa Theologiæ*, vol. 1, p. 41.
[63] Aquinas, *Summa Theologiæ*, vol. 1, p. 37. [64] 1 Peter 5.8.
[65] Hugh of St Victor, *Didascalicon*, Bk v Ch 4, p. 122.

way to the position 'that figures and metaphors belonged to the literal interpretation without quite understanding why.'[66] For Aquinas, figures and metaphors belong to the literal sense because the latter is the intention of the inspired writer. Thus the figural takes place at the level of the letteral, the literal-as-written, and points beyond itself.

> When Scripture speaks of the arm of God, the literal sense is not that he has a physical limb, but that he has what it signifies, namely the power of doing and making. This example brings out how nothing false can underlie the literal sense of Scripture.[67]

Thus, to use Spong's example, when it is said that Christ sits on the right hand of God, the literal sense is not that he sits to the right of God or, as Spong's joke has it, on God's right hand – so that God can use only his left hand – but that Christ is what it signifies, namely that Christ is one with God. And this is the literal sense of the phrase.

It is important to note that for Aquinas the literal sense is 'that which the author intends, and the author of holy Scripture is God who comprehends everything all at once in his understanding'. From this it follows, for Aquinas, that 'many meanings are present even in the literal sense of one passage of Scripture'.[68] The difference between Aquinas and Spong on the literal sense of Scripture is the difference between supposing the historical to be but one part of the literal and supposing the historical to be all of it.

[66] Smalley, *Study of the Bible*, p. 234.

[67] Aquinas, *Summa Theologiæ*, vol. 1, p. 41. Aquinas is concerned to establish the truthfulness of Scripture against any suggestion of its falsity. Clearly this is what concerns Spong: that at the literal level certain passages of Scripture are false. Allegory has often been understood as avoiding such a suggestion. Thus David Norton writes that in the ancient world, allegory 'is a primary road of escape from the literal text'. (Norton, *A History of the Bible*, vol. 1, p. 55.) But here Norton reveals as much about the modern as about the ancient world, for he understands the figurative as an 'escape' from the literal. This is not what Aquinas understands, for whom the figurative takes us deeper into the literal sense of the text.

[68] Aquinas, *Summa Theologiæ*, vol. 1, p. 39.

THE DIREMPTION OF THE LITERAL

During the early medieval period the literal sense of Scripture was often described as historical, in the sense of telling a story: *historia*. Hugh of St Victor (1096–1141) notes in his *Didascalicon*, that 'it is not unfitting that we call by the name "history" not only the recounting of actual deeds but also the first meaning of any narrative which uses words according to their proper nature.'[69] However, as Gillian Evans notes, by the twelfth century there existed 'the germ of a distinction' between *littera* and *historia*, and by the middle of the century, Gerhoch of Reichersberg could use *littera* and *historia* in distinct senses.[70] However, the diremption of the literal did not really take place until the rise of modern biblical criticism, beginning as early as the seventeenth century with Benedict de Spinoza (1634–1677).[71]

For modern biblical criticism the historical sense is found only when a second step is taken. First, one steps not from the biblical story to history, but from the story to a critically constructed narrative, which in turn leads to the past. The historical sense is found not in the biblical stories, but in the narratives of critical historians. If you want to know who Jesus was and what he was like you go, not to the Bible, but to an historian's critical narrative about him; not to a gospel, but to a life of Jesus; not to Matthew, Mark, Luke and John, but to Strauss or Schweitzer, Crossan or Sanders.[72]

According to Hans Frei, this development was due to a

[69] Hugh of St Victor, *Didascalicon*, p. 137.

[70] Evans, *Language*, p. 68.

[71] For an account of the interdependency of literary and biblical criticism in the early modern period, focused upon Isaac La Peyrère (1596–1676) and Richard Simon (1638–1712), see Françoise Deconinck-Brossard, 'England and France in the Eighteenth Century', in *Reading the Text: Biblical Criticism and Literary Theory*, edited by Stephen Prickett (Oxford: Basil Blackwell, 1991), pp. 136–81.

[72] David F. Strauss, *The Life of Jesus Critically Examined* (London: SCM Press, [1835] 1973); Albert Schweitzer, *The Quest of the Historical Jesus: A Critical Study of Its Progress from Reimarus to Wrede* (New York: Macmillan, [1906] 1968); John Dominic Crossan, *The Historical Jesus: The Life of a Mediterranean Jewish Peasant* (Edinburgh: T. and T. Clark, 1991); E. P. Sanders, *The Historical Figure of Jesus* (London: Allen Lane/ Penguin Press, 1993).

number of related disjunctions or uncouplings: of the literal from the historical and of both from the figural; of history-likeness from history; of narrative from reality; and of meaning from truth.[73] All these disjunctions follow from the severance of the literal and the historical. 'When the identity of literal sense and historical reference is severed, literal and figurative likewise no longer belong together'.[74] In the modern period history becomes an autonomous domain, accessible by routes other than the biblical. It can be narrated otherwise, by stories which are not merely history-like but historical-critical, scientific.[75]

> The real events of history constitute an autonomous temporal framework of their own under God's providential design. Instead of rendering them accessible, the [biblical] narratives, heretofore indispensable as means of access to the events, now simply verify them, thus affirming their autonomy and the fact that they are in principle accessible through any kind of description that can manage to be accurate either predictively or after the event.[76]

For Frei the biblical stories are characteristically realistic or history-like narratives. 'The distinctiveness is simply indelible and a significant feature the synoptic gospels share with large sections of the Old Testament'.[77] Frei contends that while this characteristic was widely recognised in the eighteenth century, it could be understood only in terms of historical reference.

> Commentators, especially those influenced by historical criticism, virtually to a man failed to understand what they had seen when they had recognised the realistic character of biblical narratives, because everytime they acknowledged it they thought this was identical with affirming not only the history-likeness but also a degree of historical likelihood of the stories.[78]

[73] Hans Frei, *The Eclipse of Biblical Narrative: A Study in Eighteenth and Nineteenth Century Hermeneutics* (New Haven and London: Yale University Press, 1974), p. 12.
[74] Frei, *Eclipse*, p. 37.
[75] Frei, *Eclipse*, p. 52.
[76] Frei, *Eclipse*, p. 4.
[77] Frei, *Eclipse*, pp. 12–13.
[78] Frei, *Eclipse*, pp. 11–12.

When the literal and historical are conjoined, when what Frei calls the explicative sense and the historical reference are one, so also are the literal and the figurative.[79] For the most part, Frei takes the figurative to be that of type and antitype. An historical event is rendered by a story, and this story-event figures another storied-event. This reading strategy permits the relation, both literally and historically, of otherwise separate stories and events, which are then both related and separate. They retain their own identities and yet at the same time partake in the larger identity of the temporal succession rendered by the figural coding. The separate stories become part of a larger narrative. 'Figural interpretation . . . sets forth the unity of the canon as a single cumulative and complex pattern of meaning'.[80]

But when the literal is dirempted – between, on the one hand, the letteral, and on the other hand, the literal construed as the historical – the figural is required to relate actual events rather than written narratives; histories rather than stories. It then becomes difficult to see how one event can be the type of another. The figural pattern appears more like artifice than transcription. If the Bible has a unity it is only because the history it relates has one also, and if history does have a unity it must display it to historical science. Thus was developed the idea of a special history: *Heilsgeschichte* – salvation history – the idea that 'the unitary meaning of Scripture is its reference to one special sequence of real events, from creation to the end of history, with their centre in Christ's incarnation, the whole sequence ambiguously related to other historical events'.[81]

As story and history unravelled, so also meaning and truth. Once upon a time the meaning of the Bible was the truth of the world. The biblical narrative rendered the significance of the world's history. But in the seventeenth and eighteenth centuries people increasingly began to look elsewhere for the

[79] Frei, *Eclipse*, p. 28.
[80] Frei, *Eclipse*, p. 33. [81] Frei, *Eclipse*, p. 46.

truth of their condition. The Bible told stories, but Reason rendered truth.

Universal reason teaches true religion, a divine law common to all. As Spinoza wrote in his *Tractatus Theologico-Politicus* (1670), Reason teaches 'that there exists a God, that is, a Supreme Being, Who loves justice and charity, and Who must be obeyed by whomsoever would be saved; that the worship of this Being consists in the practice of justice and love towards one's neighbour'.[82] This is the Bible's truth also, but not necessarily its meaning. For the purpose of the Bible is to move people to the practice of neighbourly love and justice, and to this end it tells stories which may not always, or not in all their parts, be true.

> Scripture does not explain things by their secondary causes, but only narrates them in the order and the style which has most power to move men, and especially uneducated men, to devotion; and therefore it speaks inaccurately of God and of events, seeing that its object is not to convince the reason, but to attract and lay hold of the imagination.[83]

Consequently one must distinguish between the meaning of the biblical stories and their religious significance. Biblical interpretation is concerned only with the first. As Spinoza taught, 'we are to work not on the truth of passages, but solely on their meaning'.[84] This limitation of the exegetical task, and the distinction on which it is based, further buttresses the dissociation of history from story.

We now have three accounts of meaning: literal, historical and religious. Firstly, there is the story; secondly, the history, to which the story wholly or partly refers; and thirdly, religious truth, which the story may or may not accurately portray. Only the third really matters, and increasingly it cannot be thought to depend on the other two.

[82] Benedict de Spinoza, *The Chief Works of Benedict de Spinoza*, translated by R. H. M. Elwes, 2 vols (New York: Dover Publications, 1951), vol. 1, p. 186.
[83] Spinoza, *Chief Works*, vol. 1, p. 40.
[84] Spinoza, *Chief Works*, vol. 1, p. 101.

In the work of the English Deist, Anthony Collins (1676–1729), Frei finds a moment in which the literal ceases to be the written as such, and becomes merely a modality of the actual, as the written form of the historical; merely and only representation. 'A proposition is literal if it describes and refers to a state of affairs known or assumed on independent probable grounds to agree or disagree with the stated proposition'.[85] In this Collins predates the positivists, for whom the meaning of a statement is the method of its verification.[86] The literal-as-written or letteral no longer presents but merely re-presents the actual. It is no longer the place of truth, but rather the sign of where such a place is to be found: the historical-empirical rendered by (scientific) processes of verification.

As the historical reliability of the biblical narrative became increasingly doubtful, there emerged what Frei describes as 'mediating' theology. This located the religious significance of the biblical narratives in their relation to general human experience; a universal human condition. The biblical story is to be fitted into the story of the world, rather than the world into the story of the Bible.[87] With this development the modern world of John Spong comes into view.

Following Frei's story into the twentieth century, we find that the significance of the biblical text is now thought to lie either behind or in front of it. The Bible's truth is to be found either in the history it possibly re-presents; or in the truths of human self-consciousness, which are accessible by universal reason or phenomenological hermeneutics, and which the Bible quaintly discloses and expresses. Above all, the significance of the Bible is not to be found in the actual biblical stories themselves. It is Frei's project, in both *The Eclipse of Biblical Narrative* (1974) and *The Identity of Jesus Christ* (1975), to steer a course between the behinders and the in-fronters –

[85] Frei, *Eclipse*, p. 76. For further on Collins see Henning Graf Reventlow, *The Authority of the Bible and the Rise of the Modern World*, translated by John Bowden (London: SCM Press, [1980] 1984), pp. 354–60.

[86] Frei, *Eclipse*, p. 77.

[87] Frei, *Eclipse*, p. 130.

between the critical historians and the 'proponents of the "second naiveté" of "restorative" hermeneutics' – to the written text itself, the letteral.[88]

USING THE BIBLE LITERALLY

My earlier reference to Aquinas and his view of the literal sense of holy Scripture as that intended by its divine author, should not be taken as endorsing a strictly recognitive hermeneutic, so that Scripture means what it meant to its writers. Strictly speaking it is people, not texts, who mean things. Texts mean something only when they are used in some way by someone. When texts are used they become occasions of meaning, usually the meanings of their authors but also of their readers. A text may be used by its readers as its author would use it or would have it used; but a reader may use it differently from how its author intended or imagined.

Clearly, then, a text can be used in more than one way. However, this does not mean that a text can be used in just any way. For usage is always particular to a time and place; context conditions and constrains usage. There is little doubt that the Church now uses the Bible somewhat differently from how it was used in the past, especially past use of the 'Old Testament'.[89] Equally, different Christians have used and use Scripture differently, and make scriptural uses the bases of their differences.

On this Wittgensteinian account of scriptural meaning as (churchly) use, the question of the *sensus literalis* becomes a question of literal usage. How does one use the Bible literally? By using it as it is commonly used within the Christian community. This answer renders in terms of usage the idea that the literal sense is the plain sense; the sense it is normally held to have within the Church. This is a purely formal

[88] Hans Frei, *Theology and Narrative*, p. 139.

[89] See John F. A. Sawyer, 'Combating prejudices about the Bible and Judaism', *Theology*, 94 (1991), 269–278; and in reply, Walter Moberly, '"Old Testament" and "New Testament": the propriety of the terms for Christian theology', *Theology*, 95 (1992), 26–32.

answer, since it tells us little about the 'material character' of the scriptural sense. Kathryn Tanner notes that when 'participants in a practice of appealing to texts talk about the plain sense, they need not . . . mean by that the sense that commands general agreement. They may mean instead . . . "the sense the author intended", "the verbal or grammatical sense", "the sense for the writer's public", "the sense that God intends"'.[90] This comment returns us to the idea of Godly intention, and suggests, as an answer to our question, that to use Scripture literally is to use it as God would have the Church use it.

A question about the literal sense of Scripture will then take the form: How does God, as the true author of Scripture, intend us to use this text in our present circumstances? The question has to be put in contextual terms because Scripture – as co-constitutive of God's revelation – is addressed not only to the time of its writers, but to all times and places; but not all times and places are the same. As Aquinas, after Augustine, noted, divine authorship suggests multiple usage: 'it comes not amiss . . . if many meanings are present even in the literal sense of one passage of Scripture'.[91]

Frei locates the significance of the scriptural narrative in its depiction of Jesus of Nazareth; its rendition of his identity. That identity is such that those who follow after him are invited to find their own identities in his. The scriptural text is used literally when the Church seeks, in the circumstances of its time and place, to be conformed to the one whom the Scripture depicts. A literal reading of the text is one that follows it to the letter; not in the sense of trying to discern the frailties of its historical reference; nor in seeking for the disclosure of the human condition within its interstices; but in the sense of making oneself over to its narrative in order to be made anew.

[90] Kathryn E. Tanner, 'Theology and the plain sense', in *Scriptural Authority and Narrative Interpretation*, edited by Garret Green (Philadelphia: Fortress Press, 1987), 59–78 (p. 65).

[91] Aquinas, *Summa Theologiæ*, vol. 1, p. 39.

This making over in order to be made anew is a way of enacting or performing the Scripture.[92] As Rowan Williams has suggested, it is a telling or reading of the Scripture in which the tellers or readers take a part in the story so that it becomes their story and they become characters in its narrative.

> Christian interpretation is unavoidably engaged in 'dramatic' modes of reading: we are invited to identify ourselves in the story being contemplated, to reappropriate who we are now, and whom we shall or can be, in terms of the story. Its movements, transactions, transformations, become ours; we take responsibility for this or that position within the narrative . . . our appropriation of the story . . . is an active working through of the story's movement in our own time.[93]

As Williams notes, the most obvious example of such dramatic reading in Christian life is the 'scriptural lectionary bound to the festal cycle', above all the paschal celebration which is 'evidently designed to bring our time and the time of the canonical narrative together'.[94] In such celebration the Church's story clearly retells the story of Jesus as one and the same story.

Living the Christian life within the ecclesial community involves more than just liturgical enactments; it involves radically reimagining and resituating one's entire life within the story of Jesus, seeking to remove once and for all the line between acting and play-acting. This is why even the figure of play-acting, of performance, fails to grasp the risk and radical contingency, the open-endedness, of the play being enacted, the performance being given. The players 'are invited to "create" themselves in finding a place within . . . [the] drama – an improvisation in the theatre workshop, but one that purports to be about a comprehensive truth affecting one's

92 See Nicholas Lash, 'Performing the Scriptures', in *Theology on the Way to Emmaus* (London: SCM Press, 1986), pp. 37–46.

93 Rowan Williams, 'The literal sense of Scripture', *Modern Theology*, 7 (1991), 121–34 (p. 125).

94 Williams, 'Literal sense', p. 126.

identity and future . . . In Paul's terms, all may find themselves both prisoners of disobedience and recipients of grace (Romans 11.32).'[95]

READING TIME

According to Rowan Williams the literal sense of Scripture is to be read diachronically. He makes central to his understanding of the *sensus literalis* the narrativity or temporality of the text, the time of its telling. To attend to the literal sense of Scripture is to insist upon 'there being some controlling force in the fact that meaning comes to light in a process of learning to perceive'.[96] This 'process of learning to perceive' is a matter of following through a written text in a 'single-time continuum, reading it as a sequence of changes, a pattern of transformations'.[97]

Williams sets a literal, diachronic reading of Scripture over against a non-literal, synchronic viewing of the text as a '"field" of linguistic material, of signs that refer backwards and forwards to each other in a system of interaction more like the surface of a picture than a performance of drama or music'.[98] When such a structuralist mode of reading is adopted, the text is situated, as it were, in space rather than in time; it is viewed at a glance, read all at once. For Williams this way of reading is decidedly unfruitful, and he argues for the primacy of the diachronic over against the synchronic; of time over space. The primary fact of the literal form of attention is that the reader takes time, living with or in the text.

Concern with the literal, the diachronic, is a way of resisting the premature unities and harmonies of a non-literal reading (whether allegorical, existentialist, structuralist or deconstructionist), in

[95] Rowan Williams, 'Postmodern theology and the judgement of the world', in *Postmodern Theology: Christian Faith in a Pluralist World*, edited by Frederic B. Burnham (San Francisco: Harper Collins, 1989), pp. 92–112 (p. 97).

[96] Williams, 'Literal sense', p. 123.

[97] Williams, 'Literal sense', p. 121.

[98] Williams, 'Literal sense', pp. 121–2.

> which the time that matters is only the present of the reader faced with the 'spatial' expanse of a text cut off from its own inner processes and the history of its production.[99]

The non-literal, synchronic or spatial reading of text is unsatisfactory, Williams suggests, because it ignores the basic fact that for human life meaning is not something that comes all at once, but is unfolded over time, slowly discovered, explored and assimilated. 'So long as our humanity remains unintelligible except as a life of material change, irreversible movement, it is unlikely – to say the least – that we could establish non-diachronic modes of reading as primary.'[100]

Williams suggests that synchronic or spatial modes of reading which, as he rightly notes, are notoriously idealist, run up against the basic materiality of human existence. Thus it is that Christianity, itself unable to avoid human materiality, takes for granted the fact that, as Williams puts it, 'meanings are learned and produced, not given in iconic, ahistorical form'.[101]

Williams argues that a literal reading of Scripture requires a point of focus if it is to have any sort of unity. He finds this point of focus in the story of Jesus and his cross. He suggests that all Christian communities have found their corporate symbolic life centred in the death and resurrection of Jesus, such that they construe and enact their own lives, through Baptism and Eucharist, as participating in his death and its meaning.

> Reading Scripture in faith is reading it as moving towards or around a unifying narrative moment, the story of the work of Jesus: how it does so, how we are to carry through such a reading in points of detail, is constantly elusive; we know only that, as a matter of fact, the movement that is portrayed by the texts of Scripture had produced the identifiable and distinctive meanings of the Church.[102]

99 Williams, 'Literal sense', p. 123.
100 Williams, 'Literal sense', p. 124.
101 Williams, 'Literal sense', p. 125.
102 Williams, 'Literal sense', p. 131.

However, it is perhaps necessary to reinstate synchronic modes of reading as inter-constitutive with diachronic ones of literal reading. In setting the literal against the non-literal, the diachronic against the synchronic, time against space, Williams is in danger of distorting the diachronic character of the reading he seeks to delineate. For any (diachronic) reading must consist, at least in part, of successive synchronies, some of which will remain and some of which will give way to others.

Reading is in part constituted by a number of passing provisional patterns, through which both the shape and movement of the text is apprehended in a process of invention and discovery. The synchronic or spatial moment – when, as it were, the forward movement of the narrative is twisted out of time's flight and pinned flat upon the earth – is no more than the projection-perception of patterns in the text. This moment is repeated in time as the text is read. The patterns are both vertical and linear, in space and in time. We know them as projected expectations that enable us to grasp the movement of the story, to understand what has been by what we expect to come.

As we read a text in time we imagine how it will turn out. We look for patterns or synchronies. Often the excitement of a text in time is constituted by the defeat of our expectations, of the patterns we project upon it in advance of its completion. Thus the thrill of the book, play or film that subverts the genres it at first appears to encode. Simple pleasure is to be had by the confirmation of our expectations, as when the child insists upon the retelling of the tale he or she already knows by heart, word for word. The child is comforted by the repeated pattern of the text. A syntagmatic succession of patterns is constitutive for any diachronic reading attentive to the time of the text, and productive of meaning.

When the Church enacts the story of Christ's passion in yearly celebration, it lives both in the diachronic moment and in the synchronic pattern. The pattern of the passion gives meaning to Easter week and informs its performance. But performing the pattern takes time, and this duration, with its enacted expectations and confusions, its desperation and horror, its numbed silence and dawning hope, gives meaning to and informs the pattern. Consuming the text takes time; but through feeding on the words the 'Christ of the passion' comes to us: 'it is the words we must taste and meditate.'[103]

[103] Farrer, *Glass*, p. 146.

CHAPTER 5

True stories

Narrativist theology sets the Scripture before us as a consuming text; or better, as a text to consume in order that we might grow in the strength and shape of Christ. We are not so much enjoined to get inside the text, as to let the text get inside us, so that we are nourished by its word and enabled to perform its story. However, the story of the text is about a particular person – Jesus of Nazareth – and about God incarnate in that person. Thus the story has both an historical and a transcendent reference, and it is the possibility of such reference that many think narrativist theology calls in question, with its stress on the story against anything behind or in front of it. How does the Bible refer to God in Christ? How is it a true story?

NARRATIVE WORK

Narrative, for the philosopher Paul Ricoeur (born 1913), is that work which renders experience significant, humanly meaningful. Without the work of narrative, experience would be only successive occurrence, one thing after another. Through the work of narrative it is given structure and form. As the term 'work' suggests, narrative here is not a thing but a process, not so much a noun as a verb. It is dynamic rather than static; a movement that transforms its elements into a unity or whole. Ricoeur's terms for this work of narrative are 'emplotment' and 'configuration', and they mark what Kevin

J. Vanhoozer has called 'Ricoeur's great discovery about narrative, its configurative dimension'.[1]

Aristotle's *Poetics* provides Ricoeur with his concept of narrative as emplotment.[2] The Aristotelian notion of *muthos* contains the ideas of both fable and plot, imaginary tale and well-constructed story. It is the latter idea which Ricoeur uses for his account of narrative-work as the synthesising of 'heterogeneous elements'.[3]

Ricoeur delineates three ways in which narrative as emplotment synthesises its elements. Firstly, it works to make one story out of many incidents or events. The events of a story are not simply related one to another, but also to the whole story.[4] They are related to the story's beginning, middle and end. This, of course, recalls Aristotle's conception of the well-structured plot.

[1] Kevin J. Vanhoozer, 'Philosophical antecedents to Ricoeur's *Time and Narrative*', in *On Paul Ricoeur: Narrative and Interpretation*, edited by David Wood (London and New York: Routledge 1991), pp. 34–54 (p. 39).

[2] Paul Ricoeur ('Life in quest of narrative', in *On Paul Ricoeur: Narrative and Interpretation*, edited by David Wood (London and New York: Routledge 1991), pp. 20–33) notes that he could have employed a 'more modern model of thought' than Aristotle's, such as Kant's account of the productive imagination with its schematism and categories, in *The Critique of Pure Reason*: 'Just as in Kant the schematism designates the creative centre of the categories, and in the categories the principle of the order of the understanding, in the same way emplotment constitutes the creative centre of the narrative and narratology constitutes the rational reconstruction of the rules underlying poetical activity' (pp. 23–4). Kevin J. Vanhoozer provides an illuminating discussion of this possibility, arguing that Ricoeur's narratology stands on Kant's 'shoulders' and completes his project (Vanhoozer, 'Philosophical antecedents', p. 39). Vanhoozer also explores Ricoeur's completion of Heidegger's project in *Being and Time*, suggesting *Time and Telling* as an alternative title for Ricoeur's *Time and Narrative* (*Temps et Récit*): 'In Ricoeur's work, telling mediates being and time.' (Vanhoozer, 'Philosophical antecedents', p. 43.) For further on Ricoeur's use of Kant see Pamela Sue Anderson, *Ricoeur and Kant: Philosophy of the Will*, AAR Studies in Religion 66 (Atlanta, Georgia: Scholars Press, 1993). I am indebted to Pamela Anderson for her careful reading of the present chapter; needless to say remaining infelicities are my own.

[3] Ricoeur, 'Life in quest of narrative', p. 21.

[4] 'A text is a whole, a totality. The relation between whole and parts – as in a work of art or in an animal – requires a specific kind of "judgement" for which Kant gives the theory in the third Critique.' Paul Ricoeur, *Hermeneutics and the Human Sciences: Essays on Language, Action and Interpretation*, edited and translated by John B. Thompson (Cambridge: Cambridge University Press, 1981), p. 211.

Now a whole is that which has a beginning, a middle, and an end. A beginning is that which does not necessarily come after something else, although something else exists or comes about after it. An end, on the contrary, is that which naturally follows something else either as a necessary or as a usual consequence, and is not itself followed by anything. A middle is that which follows something else, and is itself followed by something. Thus well-constructed plots must neither begin nor end in a haphazard way, but must conform to the pattern I have been describing.[5]

Secondly, emplotment synthesises character, action and circumstance. It emplots together different sorts of incident and event, in particular the intentional with the accidental. Narrative relates both natural occurrences and human actions, as well as their consequences, both intended and unintended. Thus Ricoeur describes plot as both concordant and discordant. A character may strive for resolution, harmony or peace which circumstances thwart or other characters wantonly destroy.

Thirdly, narrative works to produce a sense of time. Ricoeur suggests that there are two sorts of time in every story. Firstly, there is the time of succession, which is open and indefinite. It can always be asked what happened before the story began and after it ended. But the time between the opening and ending of the story constitutes a second sort of time: the synthetic time of the story itself. Ricoeur describes the temporal work of emplotment as the drawing of 'a configuration out of a succession'.[6] Thus there is a successive and a configured time; a time which 'passes and flows away' and a time which 'endures and remains'. The latter is the temporal totality and identity of a story, which cuts across and challenges the former, the perpetual passing away of succession.

[5] Aristotle, 'On the Art of Poetry', in *Classical Literary Criticism*, translated by T. S. Dorsch (Harmondsworth: Penguin Books, 1965), pp. 31–75 (p. 41).

[6] Ricoeur, 'Life in quest of narrative', p. 22. Ricoeur stresses the 'kinship' between configuration as 'grasping together' and Kant's account of judging. See Paul Ricoeur, *Time and Narrative*, 3 vols., translated by Kathleen McLaughlin/Blamey and David Pellauer (Chicago and London: University of Chicago Press, 1984–1988), vol. 1, p. 66.

Ricoeur summarises the threefold work of emplotment as mediation between 'multiple incidents and unified story', the 'primacy of concordance over discordance', and the 'competition between succession and configuration'.[7] Thus one can say that narrative or emplotment is that work which draws out of multiplicity, discordance and succession, a configured and concordant unity: a story. It is the means by which life is rendered humanly significant.[8]

While narrative works to transform or configure its elements into a concordant whole, that work is already underway in the prefiguring of occurrences as events or actions. Prefiguration precedes configuration. Even before we start to tell stories, that of which we tell has been storied or emplotted. Life is always-already narrative, in advance of our narration. Or at least it is virtual narrative, demanding to be narrated.[9] It is the demand of experience to be told that anchors narrative in life, as something more than optional.

Ricoeur distinguishes three related ways in which life solicits narrative. The first is human action, which is always-already an interpretation, worked over by a semantics which renders intentional or purposive what would otherwise be merely movement or behaviour. The event is entangled within a network of concepts, figured as an action even before it is narrated in a larger story. This network of concepts carries out the same work as narrative when it synthesises the heterogeneous.

> Our familiarity with the conceptual network of human acting is of the same order as the familiarity we have with the plots of stories that are known to us; it is the same phronetic understanding which presides over the understanding of action (and of passion) and over that of narrative.[10]

[7] Ricoeur, 'Life in quest of narrative', p. 22.

[8] 'Time becomes human to the extent that it is articulated through a narrative mode, and narrative attains its full meaning when it becomes a condition of temporal existence.' Ricoeur, *Time and Narrative*, vol. 1, p. 52.

[9] Ricoeur, 'Life in quest of narrative', p. 29.

[10] Ricoeur, 'Life in quest of narrative', p. 28.

In addition to the semantics of action there is also an implicit or immanent symbolic system which informs action in its social context. A particular action depends for its meaning on a socially instituted system of 'signs, norms and rules'.[11] The symbolic system 'gives an initial readability to action.' It is by a 'given symbolic convention that we can interpret a particular gesture as signifying this or that: the same gesture of raising one's arm can, depending on the context, be understood as a way of saying hello, of hailing a taxi, or of voting.'[12]

The third anchorage point for 'narrative in life' is what Ricoeur calls the 'pre-narrative quality of human experience.' This 'quality' is something other than the semantics and symbolism of action, and it leads to the idea that life is a nascent story, an 'activity and a passion in search of a narrative.'[13] However, while Ricoeur insists that life has this desire of narrativity, he finds it difficult to demarcate its character beyond indicating situations where there is a 'genuine demand for narrative.'[14]

> The patient who addresses the psychoanalyst brings him the scattered fragments of lived stories, dreams, 'primal scenes', conflictual episodes. One can legitimately say with respect to analytic sessions that their aim and effect is to allow the analysand to draw out of these story-fragments a narrative which would be at once more bearable and more intelligible. This narrative interpretation of psychoanalytic theory implies that the story of a life grows out of stories that have not been recounted and have been repressed in the direction of actual stories which the subject could take charge of and consider to be constitutive of his personal identity. It is the quest of personal identity that assures the continuity between the potential or virtual story and the explicit story for which we assume responsibility.[15]

[11] Ricoeur, 'Life in quest of narrative', p. 28.
[12] Ricoeur, 'Life in quest of narrative', p. 29.
[13] Ricoeur, 'Life in quest of narrative', p. 29.
[14] Ricoeur, 'Life in quest of narrative', p. 29.
[15] Ricoeur, 'Life in quest of narrative', p. 30.

In seeking to describe situations where experience demands narrative fulfilment, Ricoeur wants to show that it is not only a matter of our living within a society where stories as well as symbols are always-already at play, always-already interpreting our experience, but that human life itself demands such interpretation. Even if there were a society where symbol and story were not always ready to hand, life would demand their finding. For Ricoeur, as his psychoanalytic example suggests, story-telling is making manifest the latent stories within. Narrating is a 'secondary process grafted upon our "being-entangled in stories".'[16]

Narrative-work or configuration, which we now see is always-already underway even before we begin to tell stories, prefigured in the experiences of life which demand narrative fulfilment, is not complete until a moment of refiguration in the listener or reader of the story. Ricoeur's narratology thus sets before us a threefold narrative movement or dynamic, three mimetic stages, that takes us from prefiguration, through configuration to refiguration. It is to this last moment of the narrative-work that I now attend. It brings us to the question of truth in narrative.

NARRATIVE TRUTH

Poetry, for Aristotle, teaches truth, and is defined by the sort of truth it teaches. It is defined not in terms of its form, but in terms of its subject matter. Poetry can be prose narrative, but unlike history, which can also be prose or verse, and which 'tells of what has happened', poetry tells of 'the kind of things that might happen.'[17] It teaches universal possibilities or truths. This is why, for Aristotle, poetry is more 'philosophical and more worthy of serious attention than history', which tells only of 'particular facts.'[18] Equally, a poet is defined not as someone who makes verses, but as someone who makes

[16] Ricoeur, 'Life in quest of narrative', p. 30.
[17] Aristotle, *On the Art of Poetry*, p. 43.
[18] Aristotle, *On the Art of Poetry*, pp. 43–4.

representations of possible actions.[19] A poet is a maker of plots.[20]

Ricoeur takes from Aristotle the idea of poetry as emplotted possibility and uses it to suggest that narrative is more concerned with practical wisdom than anything else. Through story we learn about the possibilities of human action, fulfilment and happiness.

It is the function of poetry in its narrative and dramatic form, to propose to the imagination and to its mediation various figures that constitute so many thought experiments by which we learn to link together the ethical aspects of human conduct and happiness and misfortune. By means of poetry we learn how reversals of fortune result from this or that conduct, as this is constructed by the plot in the narrative.[21]

Aristotle named practical wisdom *phronesis* (in Latin *prudentia*), and Ricoeur suggests that the meaning and truth of narrative is primarily phronetic. Ricoeur's idea of narrative as the representation of phronetic possibility is related to his idea of the 'world of the text'; for the latter is a space of possibility. Each narrative projects a possible world we can enter, a way of living we can entertain, through imagination.

To speak of a world of the text is to stress the feature belonging to every literary work of opening before it a horizon of possible experience, a world in which it would be possible to live. A text is not something closed in upon itself, it is the projection of a new universe . . . which includes the actions, the characters and the events of the story told.[22]

19 'And even if he writes about things that have actually happened, that does not make him any the less a poet, for there is nothing to prevent some of the things that have happened from being in accordance with the laws of possibility and probability, and thus he will be a poet in writing about them.' (Aristotle, *On the Art of Poetry*, p. 44.)

20 Aristotle, 'On the Art of Poetry', p. 44.

21 Ricoeur, 'Life in quest of narrative', p. 23.

22 Ricoeur, 'Life in quest of narrative', p. 26.

The world of the text has its own 'horizon', and a reader who enters the text, merges its horizon with that of his or her own world. In the reader's imagination the two horizons become one. In this Ricoeur recalls Gadamer's idea of the 'fusion of horizons',[23] but his own term for the process is 'refiguration'. In the fusing of horizons, the configured world of the text refigures the world of the reader. Or rather, refiguration is a work carried out by the reader. It is the reader's completion of the narrative-work.

For Ricoeur reading is the act of following after or reimagining the process of configuration. 'Following a narrative is reactualizing the configuring act which gives it its form.'[24] It is because this reactualizing or reimagining of a narrative is at work in the reader as a reliving of the story, that Ricoeur can say that a story is not merely recounted or told but lived. Reading is living in the 'mode of the imaginary'.

The ability of narrative to open possible worlds which we may enter, entertain and refigure in our own lives, constitutes the unique power of narrative for Ricoeur. From his early work on *Freedom and Nature*[25] onward, Ricoeur has been concerned with possibility as the condition of the 'project', the intending of a future which is not an identical repetition of the past. It is narrative which gives us such possibility, showing us what is humanly possible.[26]

> Fiction has the power to 'remake' reality and, within the framework of narrative fiction in particular, to remake real praxis to the extent that the text intentionally aims at a horizon of new reality which we may call a world. It is this world of the text which intervenes in the world of action in order to give it a new configuration or, as we might say, in order to transfigure it.[27]

23 Hans Georg Gadamer, *Truth and Method* (London: Sheed and Ward, 1975); Ricoeur, *Time and Narrative*, vol. 1, p. 77.

24 Ricoeur, 'Life in quest of narrative', p. 27.

25 Paul Ricoeur, *Freedom and Nature: The Voluntary and the Involuntary* (Evanston: Northwestern University Press, [1950] 1966).

26 Vanhoozer, 'Philosophical antecedents', p. 48.

27 Paul Ricoeur, 'On interpretation', in *Philosophy in France Today*, edited by Alan Montefiore (Cambridge: Cambridge University Press, 1983), pp. 175–97 (p. 185); quoted in Vanhoozer, 'Philosophical antecedents', p. 49.

Having sketched Ricoeur's theory of narrative, which presents story-telling as the means by which human life is rendered significant, a narrative significance demanded by life itself, we can perhaps see how such a theory would serve a theological understanding of biblical narrative. The gospels in particular can be seen as configurations of both earlier and nascent stories, which open before us a possible world that may serve to refigure our own. The truth of the gospels would then be the truth of Aristotelian poetry: the presentation of a possible world for our dwelling, a possible way of re-making our world. Such an idea is not of course without its difficulties. How can we think together what the gospels seem to require us to think: story as both history and as poetic possibility or fiction?

TRUE NARRATIVE

What is truth? Pontius Pilate famously asked this question of Jesus, and did not wait for an answer.[28] For many truth is fact, and biblical truth is historical fact, and fact and fiction do not go together. For the historian Robin Lane Fox the Bible is largely fiction, with few historical facts, and no matter how wonderful the former, the absence of the latter renders the whole untruthful.[29]

For Ricoeur, both history and fiction are narrative configurations of time. History configures lived or phenomenological time as historical time by inscribing it upon world or calendar time, upon a 'single spatial-temporal network constitutive of chronological time.' Fiction, on the other hand, is not bound by calendar or cosmic time; it configures time according to its own rules. The 'time of fictional narrative has been freed from the constraints requiring it to be referred back to the time of the universe.' Each fiction is different. 'Each fictive temporal

[28] John 18.38.

[29] Robin Lane Fox, *The Unauthorized Version: Truth and Fiction in the Bible* (London: Viking, 1991).

experience unfolds its world, and each of these worlds is singular, incomparable, unique.'[30]

It is in the distinction between calendar or clock time and lived or experienced time, that Ricoeur notes a first difference between history and fiction. For the latter does not refer to calendar time. While a fiction may mention actual dates, and several fictions the same date, in such cases, Ricoeur argues, we do not have a 'common reference' to historical time, but an 'identical quotation within temporal universes that cannot be superimposed upon one another, that cannot communicate with one another.'[31]

One may think this a rather tenuous distinction. Why are discrete histories not also 'temporal universes' that cannot communicate with one another? Is it because they share the same characters as have shared our temporal universe? But what then of historical novels, many of them peopled with characters who have also shared our world? The difference between history and fiction seems to depend on no more than the distinction between referring and mentioning. How slight this distinction is becomes apparent when we reflect on those fictions whose discrete 'universes' are thought by many to infringe upon their own. Many took *Monty Python's Life of Brian* (1980) to refer to the life of Jesus; as many took Martin Scorcese's *The Last Temptation of Christ* (1988) to be a superimposition upon the gospel story; and many others took Salman Rushdie's *The Satanic Verses* (1988) as referring to the Prophet Mohammed and his wives. It is possible to be prosecuted for defamation of character, if one is thought to have portrayed a living person in a fictional work. The law does not seem to recognise Ricoeur's distinction.

The Gospel of Luke repeatedly seeks to locate itself in historical time, in the time of ruling successions: 'In the days of King Herod of Judea . . . ';[32] 'Now at this time Caesar

[30] Ricoeur, *Time and Narrative*, vol. 3, p. 128.
[31] Ricoeur, *Time and Narrative*, vol. 3, p. 129.
[32] Luke 1.5.

Augustus issued a decree for a census . . . ';[33] 'In the fifteenth year of Tiberius Caesar's reign . . . '.[34] Are these examples of referring or of mentioning, of history or of fiction? The Gospel of Matthew also seeks historical location, telling us that Jesus was born 'during the reign of King Herod'.[35] But it opens with a 'genealogy of Jesus Christ, son of David, son of Abraham',[36] which is not biological, unless we assume Joseph to be the biological father of Jesus, but ancestral and apparently mythical. This seems to indicate that the Gospel is both history and fiction.

One of the problems with distinguishing history and fiction at a theoretical level is that both are narrative works; they are both made by people. Michel de Certeau, in his sociology of history-writing, reminds us of this and of its concealment by some historians, who in desiring to be scientific often claim the goal of objectivity, of writing as if from nowhere.[37] But if history-writing always proceeds from somewhere, as it must, one can go on to question its privileged status as alone representing the past. Indeed one can question, as have many historians, the idea of 'representation' itself. For whatever else may be said of historical narrative it is different from that which it narrates. It is not a reduplication of past reality, but a present construction.

Ricoeur suggests that all good historians will want to say that their work is not just a construction, but a reconstruction. But beyond noting the desire on the part of history to reconstruct or represent the past, it seems almost impossible to clarify the distinction between construction and reconstruction in such a way that it will permit a hard distinction between history and fiction. The difference between history and fiction cannot be given in a strong sense, at a formal level. For it is not possible to isolate a 'fact' in distinction from its fictive form. The idea of facts outside of fiction or rhetoric, that is outside of language, is an illusion of language itself.

[33] Luke 2.1. [34] Luke 3.1.
[35] Matthew 2.1. [36] Matthew 1.1.
[37] Ricoeur, *Time and Narrative*, vol. 3, p. 150.

How might it be said that facts are fictional or rhetorical? Toward the end of his chapter on 'The Reality of the Past', Paul Ricoeur turns his attention to what he calls the 'subtle but often obscure analyses' of Hayden White.[38] Yet White's argument seems clear enough, and is, as Ricoeur himself notes, akin to the latter's idea of prefiguration. When an historian starts to write a history, she has first to sift the traces of the past, deciding what is relevant and what is not. And moreover, even before the historian begins to figure these traces into an historical narrative, she must have prefigured the events of which they are said to be traces. The historian must already have begun to tell stories.

> Before a given domain can be interpreted, it must be construed as a ground inhabited by discernible figures . . . In order to figure out 'what really happened' in the past, therefore, the historian must first prefigure as a possible object of knowledge the whole set of events reported in the documents.[39]

On this view, history-writing is the writing of plotted narratives about the past. Ricoeur argues that attempts to write plotless histories always fail as soon as human agents enter the story.[40] However, before the historian can write her history she must imagine the events of which she believes she has traces, as themselves part of a plotted story. The historian who sifts the birth narratives of Jesus for historical facts, for traces of what really happened, can do so only because she already imagines the possible stories of which they will be the traces. The 'fact', as a trace of past events, is always-already figured within the rhetoric of the narrative imagination.

Ricoeur insists that there is no formal or stylistic difference between history and fiction, since both are emplotted stories.

[38] Ricoeur, *Time and Narrative*, vol. 3, p. 154.

[39] Hayden White, *Metahistory: The Historical Imagination in Nineteenth-Century Europe* (Baltimore: Johns Hopkins University Press, 1973), p. 30.

[40] Ricoeur, *Time and Narrative*, vol. 1, pp. 206–25; Hayden White, 'The metaphysics of narrativity: time and symbol in Ricoeur's philosophy of history', in *On Paul Ricoeur: Narrative and Interpretation*, edited by David Wood (London and New York: Routledge 1991), pp. 140–59 (pp. 145–6).

Nor can they be clearly distinguished at the level of content, by saying that historical narratives are about 'real' events, while fictional narratives are about imaginary events. As we have seen, fictions can also be about 'real' events.

Ricoeur is most successful in his attempt to demarcate history from fiction when he writes of the 'intention that gives soul' to his analysis of history-writing.[41] This 'soul' is the intention of rendering a debt to the dead.

> Unlike novels, historians' constructions do aim at being reconstructions of the past. Through document and their critical examination of documents, historians are subject to what once was. They owe a debt to the past, a debt of recognition to the dead, that makes them insolvent debtors.[42]

It is this sense of a debt, of a need to 'render its due' to what once was,[43] that Ricoeur seeks to 'articulate conceptually' in his work.[44] Yet even the idea of rendering a debt does not wholly succeed in distinguishing history from fiction, for a poet or novelist may equally aim at the recognition of the dead. It may be said that the gospels, whether history or fiction, aim to render a 'debt of recognition' to the death of a man, which for them makes all people 'insolvent debtors'.

Ricoeur sets the debt which the historian renders to the dead against the debt that the writer of fiction owes to her imagined world. The historian must remain faithful to the documents; the fictionist to the coherence of the imagined world. The historian aims at what has happened, the fictionist at what is possible.[45]

Reading Ricoeur teaches that it is not possible to theorise the difference between history and fiction, such that one could tell them apart simply by their form. With Hayden White we have to acknowledge that fiction and history are indiscernible

[41] Ricoeur, *Time and Narrative*, vol. 3, p. 152.
[42] Ricoeur, *Time and Narrative*, vol. 3, pp. 142–3.
[43] Ricoeur, *Time and Narrative*, vol. 3, p. 152.
[44] Ricoeur, *Time and Narrative*, vol. 3, p. 143.
[45] Vanhoozer, 'Philosophical antecedents', p. 49.

as verbal artefacts; that 'history is not less a form of fiction than the novel is a form of historical representation'.[46] We can then see how it might be possible for the Bible to be, as Hans Frei claims, 'at once intensely serious and historical in intent and fictional in form'.[47] We might say that the Bible has a double intention of recognition and of possibility; it is doubly aimed at what has happened and what is to come.

The difference between history and fiction shows only in the intention or aim, in the debt to render the past, and in the use people make of the narrative. Intention and use go together, for the perception of the former in a text is always a construction of its readers or users. If one perceives a text as aiming at the past, as seeking to render its reality, one will use it accordingly. And where text and users are understood as standing within a tradition, the users may be more confident of the perceived intention.[48]

As we have seen in the previous chapter, the Church has traditionally perceived the intention of the Bible to be God's intention. As St Thomas Aquinas said of the Bible's literal sense, it is 'that which the author intends, and the author of holy Scripture is God who comprehends everything all at once in his understanding'. From this it follows, for Aquinas, that 'many meanings are present even in the literal sense of one passage of Scripture'.[49]

The idea of Godly intention directs us away from seeking to understand the biblical stories as traces of past thoughts or itineraries, and toward taking them as showing forth truths we could not otherwise know; as showing us the true identities of the Bible's characters and readers. For their identities are fully knowable only to God, who knows the whole story. That the Bible renders such identities, though in a hidden way, is in part what it means to speak of the Bible as inspired.

[46] Hayden White, *Tropics of Discourse: Essays in Cultural Criticism* (Baltimore and London: Johns Hopkins University Press, 1978), p. 122.

[47] Hans Frei, *The Identity of Jesus Christ* (Philadelphia: Fortress Press, 1975), p. 145.

[48] Stanley Fish, *Doing What Comes Naturally: Change, Rhetoric, and the Practice of Theory in Literary and Legal Studies* (Oxford: Clarendon Press, 1989), p. 99.

[49] Aquinas, *Summa Theologiæ*, vol. 1, p. 39.

FAITHFUL NARRATIVES

Having seen that histories are historical not so much in virtue of their form as of their intent to render a debt of recognition to the past, an intent they share with some narratives we may otherwise class as fiction, we are in a position to understand the suggestion that the biblical narratives are historical not despite but in virtue of their fictionality; in a position to understand why Hans Frei believes that the Church is fortunate in having accounts of Jesus that are 'more nearly fictional than historical in narration'.[50] We are in a position to understand how the biblical stories might be both history and poetry, remembrance and possibility, testaments of both past and future: faithful fictions.[51]

The biblical narratives may be considered faithful in the sense that while they employ the skills of the fictive imagination, they aim to faithfully render the identity of the characters to which the stories are ascribed, and in them our own possible identities. While not everything in the biblical narratives may refer to historical events, the stories may yet serve to render the truth of the historical events to which they do refer. It may be that Jesus was not born at Bethlehem, in a manger, attended by angels, shepherds and wise men. Yet it may be that he was born, and that the stories about his birth both faithfully render his identity and open for us the possibility of affirming that identity along with the shepherds and the wise; an identity that cannot be given by treating these stories as traces of some other story.

This understanding of the Bible as faithful narrative is not new; but it shows what is perhaps so touching about the historical labours of someone like Robin Lane Fox: that they so spectacularly miss the point. And that point, as Austin Farrer tried to show, is that the biblical narratives more clearly belong to the genre of poetry than to any other, and

[50] Frei, *Identity*, p. 144.
[51] See also Anderson, *Ricoeur and Kant*, pp. 63–8.

must be read accordingly.[52] It is only a modern prejudice to suppose that poetry cannot faithfully render the truth of past, present or future.

If the Bible's poetical rendering of the past is a Godly intention, then it is more faithful to that which is rendered than any historical account could be; even more faithful than the account of an eyewitness. But this supposition is clearly dependent upon the belief of a community. Thus it can be said that we will not understand the possibilities of biblical meaning and truth without looking at the use and users of the Bible. Hans Frei located the question of the Bible's meaning and truth in the Church's faithfulness to its Godly intended fiction.

For Frei the Bible is not to be judged by its adequation to history, but history by its adequation to the Bible. As we have seen, Frei follows Eric Auerbach's suggestion that the biblical narratives 'seek to overcome our reality'.[53]

> We are to fit our life into its world, feel ourselves to be elements in its structure of universal history . . . Everything else that happens in the world can only be conceived as an element in this sequence; into it everything that is known about the world . . . must be fitted as an ingredient of the divine plan.[54]

In his important essay of 1986, 'The "Literal Reading" of Biblical Narrative in the Christian Tradition', Frei notes the similarity between his view of the biblical story and the standing of the autonomous literary text in Anglo-American 'New Criticism'.

> Both claim that the text is a normative and pure 'meaning' world of its own which, quite apart from any factual reference it may have, and apart from its author's intention or its reader's

52 Austin Farrer, *The Glass of Vision* (Westminster: Dacre Press, 1948), p. 145.

53 See above chapter 2.

54 Hans Frei, *The Eclipse of Biblical Narrative: A Study in Eighteenth and Nineteenth Century Hermeneutics* (New Haven and London: Yale University Press, 1974), p. 3.

reception, stands on its own with the authority of self-evident intelligibility.[55]

However, as we have already seen (see above chapter 3), Frei argues that his understanding of the biblical narrative is not an instance of a more general, New Critical theory; but that the latter is a generalisation of a specifically theological understanding of the gospel narratives, which is dependent upon the doctrine of the incarnation. For it is belief in the incarnation that is the basis in faith for understanding the biblical narratives as the locus and cohesion of meaning and truth. This understanding of the autonomous biblical text is 'strictly in the mode of faith seeking understanding'.[56]

'The irony of the New Criticism', Frei writes, 'is to have taken this specific case and rule and to have turned them instead into a general theory of meaning, literature, and even culture, in their own right'.[57] The idea of the autonomous text makes sense in the Christian tradition in a way that it does not in a general literary theory.

In that [Christian] tradition, the ascriptive literalism of the story, the history-likeness if you will, of the singular agent enacting the unity of human finitude and divine infinity, Jesus of Nazareth, is taken to be itself the ground, guarantee, and conveyance of the truth of the depicted enactment, its *historicity* if you will.[58]

Frei's stress on the ruled reading of the Bible within the Christian community – which community is itself predicated upon its reading of the Bible – goes some way to meeting a criticism that has been directed at his account of the biblical text as subsuming world, and which he himself directs at the autonomous texts of the New Criticism: namely, that it is 'artificial and dubious to claim a purely external relation of

[55] Hans Frei, 'The "Literal Reading" of Biblical Narrative in the Christian Tradition: Does It Stretch or Will It Break?' (1986), in *Theology and Narrative: Selected Essays*, edited by George Hunsinger and William C. Placher (New York and Oxford: Oxford University Press, 1993), pp. 117–52 (p. 140).

[56] Frei, 'Literal Reading', p. 141.

[57] Frei, 'Literal Reading', p. 142.

[58] Frei, 'Literal Reading', p. 143.

text and reading, which in effect sets aside the mutual implication of interpretation and textual meaning . . . or of reading and the textuality of the text'.[59] In other words, texts are never truly autonomous, for they exist only when they are read. Texts and readers are mutually constitutive.

Thus, while we may, perhaps, understand how the biblical narratives may be both fictive and historical, and how their meaning and truth may be one; that they really are faithful narratives or true stories is a judgement that can be made only from inside the community that takes them to be so.

TRUTH AND REALITY

The foregoing account of the scriptural story's historicity may seem meagre. The narratives may not, or not in all their parts, be literally descriptive of past events – almost certainly many of them are not. They do however render the true identity of an actual person – Jesus of Nazareth. They show us what no merely descriptive story can show us, that he was and is the Christ of God. In this sense they are more profoundly referential than any historian's account, which is always hypothetical. The gospels are not hypotheses but poetic and faithful narratives.

Before proceeding in the latter half of this chapter to consider the Church's failure to faithfully tell God's story, it may help to further clarify the conception of truth that narrativist theology develops, to consider some of the criticisms that have been made of both Frei and Lindbeck regarding their positions in this matter.

Mark Wallace, in a study of Karl Barth, Paul Ricoeur and the 'new Yale theology', argues for the sort of 'realism' to be found in Barth's biblical hermeneutics. The biblical world is not just intrasystematically true – real within its own confines – but extrasystematically true of the real world beyond its pages. The Bible is true not because it tells a good story, but because it rightly corresponds with God's actual world.

[59] Frei, 'Literal Reading', p. 141.

Christian beliefs and doctrines are true to the degree that they are adequate in disclosing the order of things revealed by God. Graham White makes this point well: 'Barth's position clearly involves assuming that theological assertions, if true, are true because there is some sort of objective order that they conform to, independently of our ability to recognise them as true; this sort of position is known as realism.'[60]

The Yale theologians claim to follow Barth, but according to Wallace they abandon his realism in favour of a relativism which makes the idea of the Bible absorbing the world 'platitudinous at best and impossible at worst.'[61] I want to suggest that Wallace is correct in what he affirms and mistaken in what he rejects. The Bible is true because the world is as it says it is. But the narrativist theology of Frei and Lindbeck is wholly congruent with such a view.

According to Wallace, the Yale theologians teach that a 'theological statement is true not because of a correspondence between words and things but because the statement coheres with the literary world of Scripture.'[62] Frei, on Wallace's reading, ascribes the biblical stories about Jesus to the 'character' of Jesus in the stories, and not to an actual historical person. Against this, Wallace insists that the 'Scripture witnesses to something more than a character in a story (*pace* Frei). It witnesses as well to a historical occurrence and the Christ alive now in the community's proclamation.'[63] Frei, however, would agree; or rather he would say more – not just an 'historical occurrence', and not just alive in the Church's proclamation, but alive in the power of God: gone on ahead but coming to meet us.

It is possible to read Frei as Wallace suggests. Frei was so concerned to stress that the identity of Christ is to be found in the literal meaning of the narratives and nowhere else, that

[60] Mark I. Wallace, *The Second Naiveté: Barth, Ricoeur, and the New Yale Theology* (Macon, GA: Mercer University Press, 1990), p. 109; Graham White, 'Karl Barth's theological realism', *Neue Zeitschrift für systematische Theologie und Religionsphilosophie*, 26 (1984), 54–70 (p. 57).

[61] Wallace, *Second Naiveté*, p. 110.

[62] Wallace, *Second Naiveté*, p. 104.

[63] Wallace, *Second Naiveté*, p. 109.

the emphasis falls very strongly on the story. But Frei also made it clear – perhaps clearer in some places than in others – that the 'character' whose identity is truly given in the stories is none other than that of an actual historical person. This after all is the point of the identity so narrated: that God's Christ is this particular person and no other.

> I cannot take the biblical story, the gospel story especially, in separation from its being the identification, the literal identification of someone identified as Jesus of Nazareth. It's not about something else, not about somebody else. And it's not about nobody in particular, nor is it a story or an allegory about a mode-of-being in the world or something of that sort, although it may include that kind of dimension.[64]

Wallace's criticisms of Lindbeck are more searching. Because the meaning of a statement is dependent upon the system of relations in which it is embedded, Lindbeck appears to think the truth of a statement is likewise dependent upon its location within the semantic system, rather than upon its reference to reality beyond the system. 'Lindbeck has confused notions of truth and reference in theological language with notions of meaning and use.'[65] Lindbeck thus mistakenly concludes that 'believers do not make ontological "assertions" about the order of reality, but simply "utterances" that are only intrasystematically coherent with their particular religious vision.'[66] As Wallace rightly insists, such relativism counters the narrativist claim that the biblical story narrates the world, absorbing all other claims to render reality. The meaning of a theological statement may be intrasystematically dependent, but its truth is a matter of ontological reference.

However – and this is the point that narrativist theology seeks to stress – the truth of a theological statement cannot be

64 Frei, *Theology and Narrative*, pp. 208–9.
65 Wallace, *Second Naiveté*, p. 106.
66 Wallace, *Second Naiveté*, p. 107. For similar argument see Colman E. O'Neill, 'The rule theory of doctrine and propositional truth', *The Thomist*, 49 (1985), 422.

given other than in the system from which it also derives its meaning. In this sense theological truth, as well as meaning, is intrasystematic. Lindbeck's cultural-linguistic account of religious meaning and truth does not deny the possibility of ontological reference. It merely asserts that because meaning and truth can be displayed only within the religious system, 'intrasystematic truth is a necessary but not sufficient condition for ontological truth.'[67] As Lindbeck clearly states, a religion can be understood as 'containing ontologically true affirmations, not only in cognitivist theories but also in cultural-linguistic ones.'

> There is nothing in the cultural-linguistic approach that requires the rejection (or acceptance) of the epistemological realism and correspondence theory of truth which, according to most of the theological tradition, is implicit in the conviction of believers that when they rightly use a sentence such as 'Christ is Lord' they are uttering a true first-order proposition.[68]

Lindbeck's account of truth is further complicated – and opened to misinterpretation – by his insistence that religious propositions are finally performances, or as he prefers to say, forms of life. Truth in religion therefore is not so much a matter of correspondence between propositions and reality as between reality and patterns of behaviour. Thus for Lindbeck, believing that 'Christ is Lord' is not so much a matter of conforming one's mind to reality, as one's behaviour.

> The crusader's battle cry '*Christus est Dominus*', for example, is false when used to authorise cleaving the skull of the infidel (even though the same words in other contexts may be a true utterance). When thus employed, it contradicts the Christian understanding of Lordship as embodying, for example, suffering servanthood.[69]

[67] George A. Lindbeck, *The Nature of Doctrine: Religion and Theology in a Postliberal Age* (London: SPCK, 1984), p. 65.
[68] Lindbeck, *Nature of Doctrine*, pp. 68–9.
[69] Lindbeck, *Nature of Doctrine*, p. 64.

Wallace takes offence at this statement, insisting that 'Christ is Lord' can be true (ontologically referential) irrespective of the crusader's behaviour. Its truth is not dependent upon the form of life in which it is uttered. However, this is to forget how closely bound together are a statement's truth and meaning, and that a statement is not just the utterance of words, but words uttered in a particular context – the language game in a form of life. Thus the truth of the crusader's cry is dependent on its meaning and that is dependent, at least in part, on his actions. What does it mean to say that 'Christ is Lord' while cleaving someone's head? And could such a meaning be true within the Christian story? Could it have the same meaning and truth as when a person confesses Christ's Lordship while tending the sick and dying, when confession is such tending? Bruce Marshall has the measure of what is at stake in Lindbeck's position.

The problem with the crusader's use of the sentence, '*Christus est Dominus*', is simply that, uttered as a warrant for splitting people's heads open, it lacks the meaning which the religion insists it must have if it is to be a true proposition, one which corresponds to reality. By using '*Dominus*' in this context, the crusader shows that what he means by the term is a medieval knight errant, much like himself. But according to the normative patterns of Christian speech and action, Christ is not that kind of Lord; when the predicate '*Dominus*' has that meaning, it is not applicable to the subject '*Christus*', that is, '*Christus est Dominus*' becomes intrasystematically false.[70]

As Marshall goes on to note, if the crusader's cry is intrasystematically false it is also ontologically false. For where the

[70] Bruce D. Marshall, 'Aquinas as postliberal theologian', *The Thomist*, 53 (1989), 353–402 (pp. 364–5). The main force of Marshall's argument is the demonstration of congruence between Aquinas and Lindbeck on matters of truth in theology. In 'Response to Bruce Marshall' (*The Thomist*, 53 (1989), 403–6), Lindbeck concurs with his reading, noting that the issue turns on holding together a correspondence theory of truth with coherentist and pragmatist criteria of justification (the crusader's cry is untrue because incoherent with Christian practice). See further Bruce D. Marshall, *Christology in Conflict: The Identity of a Saviour in Rahner and Barth* (Oxford: Basil Blackwell, 1987), pp. 176–89.

categories of a system are true (ontologically referential), a statement that contradicts them must be ontologically false as well as intrasystematically incoherent. But how do we assess the truth of the system as a whole? This is to raise a question the answer to which can be determined only by testing the system through living the story. There are those, and Marshall cites David Tracy and James Gustafson, who argue that the truth of the Christian story must be ascertainable by a measure external to the story.[71] It is this, however, that Frei, Lindbeck and narrativist theology in general denies. The Christian story comes first. It is the measure of all other stories. Deciding on its truthfulness is a matter of judging how good a story it is, and that – as our discussion of Lindbeck's crusader suggests – is at least a matter of judging how well the tale is told by its tellers.

TRAGEDY AND THE TEST OF TRUTH

George Steiner tells us that tragedy is in essence a 'questioning and an enacted testing of theodicy'.[72] If we understand by 'theodicy' the Christian story of the world redeemed in Christ, then 'tragedy' is the name of its telling and testing, its performance and validation. But why speak of 'tragedy' in relation to the gospel story?

It is not evident that the gospel story has much to do with tragedy. If one adopts as a definition of the difference between tragedy and comedy, the difference between stories of decline and ascendancy, of disaster and triumph – stories, as Dante observed, moving in 'precisely contrary directions' – the gospel story will almost certainly appear a comedy, the very form of Dante's *commedia*; the story of 'a soul ascending from shadow to

71 See David Tracy, 'Lindbeck's new program for theology: a reflection', *The Thomist*, 49 (1985), 460–72; James M. Gustafson, 'The sectarian temptation: reflections on theology, the Church, and the university', *Proceedings of the Catholic Theological Society*, 40 (1985), 83–94.

72 George Steiner, 'A note on absolute tragedy', *Literature and Theology*, 4 (1990), 147–56 (p. 153).

starlight, from fearful doubt to the joy and certitude of grace.'[73] The gospel is 'good news' after all.

Jesus of Nazareth . . . was crucified and killed by the hands of lawless men. But God raised him up, having loosed the pangs of death, for it was not possible for him to be held by it . . . Being therefore exalted at the right hand of God, and having received from the Father the promise of the Holy Spirit, he has poured out this which you see and hear.[74]

It is, Stewart Sutherland tells us, a '*prima facie* presumption that although there is Christian drama, Christian poetry and perhaps even Christian philosophy, there is no sensible use of the expression "Christian tragedy".'[75] Sutherland cites Richard Sewell: 'Christianity reverses the tragic view and makes tragedy impossible.'[76] The movement of the gospel story is upward not downward, toward a happy not an unhappy ending. It thus denies and subverts the very form of tragedy, for as George Steiner succinctly tells us, all tragedies 'end badly'.[77] Tragedies are irreparable. This, for Steiner, is the mark of the Greek tragic drama. Death, in the gospel story, is destroyed, undone, its pangs loosed; the Christ is set free and raised to the Father. Steiner tells us that tragedy is alien to the Judaic sense of the world, it being 'vehement in its conviction that the order of the universe and of man's estate is accessible to reason. The ways of the Lord are neither wanton nor absurd.'[78] The story of Job is not a counter instance to this observation, for the 'Lord blessed the latter days of Job more than his beginning';[79] and so he should, for in Steiner's view, 'God has enacted upon him a parable of justice'.[80] It is this Jewish sense of propriety and justice that is continued in the

[73] George Steiner, *The Death of Tragedy* (London: Faber and Faber, 1961), p. 11.
[74] Acts 2.22, 23–4, 33.
[75] Stewart R. Sutherland, 'Christianity and tragedy', *Literature and Theology*, 4 (1990), 157–68 (p. 157).
[76] Richard Sewell, *The Vision of Tragedy* (New Haven: Yale University Press, 1959), p. 50.
[77] Steiner, *Death of Tragedy*, p. 8. [78] Steiner, *Death of Tragedy*, p. 4.
[79] Job 42.12. [80] Steiner, *Death of Tragedy*, p. 8.

Christian tradition, in the divine vindication of the Christ and his followers. For Steiner, both Christianity and Marxism are continuations, religious and secular, of Judaic messianic eschatology, and neither will 'generate tragedy'.[81]

It would seem that the resurrection of Christ must render the gospel story a comedy, for it furnishes the tale with a happy ending which, moreover, is not confined to Christ but extended to all who have faith in him.[82] Yet the condition of this happy ending is the agony of Jesus on the cross, the ending of his life in torture and bloody execution. His suffering is not undone by his resurrection; it remains, like all suffering, for all time. The resurrection does not go back on what has gone before; it comes after and moves on. When Cleopas and his fellow disciple listen to the stranger whom they meet on their way to Emmaus, they do not learn that what had happened in Jerusalem had not, but rather the meaning of what had happened; that it was 'necessary that the Messiah should suffer'.[83] They learn that one ending is the condition of the other; no happy ending without an unhappy one; no comedy without tragedy. This point is made by Stewart Sutherland when, having characterised tragedy and the tragic vision as dislocation, a world 'out of joint',[84] and having affirmed Christianity's commitment to an ultimate reconciliation, he insists that the point of such reconnection or redemption, 'can only be grasped following the depths of the experience of disconnection and discontinuity'.[85] That disconnection precedes reconnection, and that tragedy precedes comedy, as the very condition of the latter's possibility, is perhaps sufficient reason to describe the gospel story as a comedy. That comedy has tragedy as its condition is perhaps reason enough to speak, with Donald MacKinnon of a 'deeply tragic quality' in the gospel story,[86] of a 'tragic element in the

81 Steiner, 'A note on absolute tragedy', p. 155.
82 See below chapter 7. 83 Luke 24.26.
84 Sutherland, 'Christianity and tragedy', p. 161.
85 Sutherland, 'Christianity and tragedy', p. 164.
86 Donald MacKinnon, *The Problem of Metaphysics* (Cambridge: Cambridge University Press, 1974), p. 125.

Christian vision'.[87] It is the nature of this irreducible 'quality' or 'element' that I now want to explore by turning to Hegel.

THE TRAGIC HERO

In his lectures on aesthetics (delivered in the 1820s) G. W. F. Hegel (1770–1831) drew a distinction between epic, lyric and dramatic poetry. He found the central significance of the dramatic in the 'collisions between characters and between their aims, as well as the necessary resolution of this battle'.[88] The different forms of dramatic poetry, which display such schism and resolution, are determined by the relation of the individuals to their purposes and natures. Thus Hegel distinguishes between tragedy and comedy, with drama the middle term.

In tragedy, individuals have to do with those substantive forces which, as Hegel puts it, are 'independently justified'.

> Family love between husband and wife, parents and children, brothers and sisters; political life also, the patriotism of the citizens, the will of the ruler; and religion existent, not as a piety that renounces action and not as a divine judgement in man's heart about the good or evil of his actions, but on the contrary, as an active grasp and furtherance of actual interests and circumstances.[89]

Only individuals permeated by such forces and thoroughly consonant with them, may be described as tragical. It is only at such an elevation that the 'mere accidents of the individual's purely personal life disappear' and one finds the 'tragic heroes of dramatic art' standing forth like 'works of sculpture'.[90]

It is because tragic characters are, as it were, the embodiment of spiritual forces, divine substantives in their purity,

[87] MacKinnon, *Metaphysics*, p. 131.

[88] G. W. F. Hegel, *Lectures on Fine Art*, translated by T. M. Knox, 2 vols. (Oxford: Clarendon Press, 1975), vol. 2, p. 1193.

[89] Hegel, *Lectures on Fine Art*, vol. 2, p. 1194.

[90] Hegel, *Lectures on Fine Art*, vol. 2, p. 1195.

that, in the world they find themselves in conflict with other such powers of equal force and divinity. One attains to the original essence of tragedy where both sides of the conflict are justified; yet in seeking the absolute fulfilment of their end, the tragic characters negate and violate one another, and thus plunged into the mess and misery of ethical life, are led, 'despite all their justification, to guilt and wrong'.[91] Thus, as A. C. Bradley puts it, 'the essentially tragic fact is the self-division and intestinal warfare of the ethical substance, not so much the war of good with evil as the war of good with good.'[92]

Tragedy occurs when an 'ensemble of *different* relations and powers' moves from abstract ideality to reality, 'appearing in the mundane sphere'.[93] It is when one tries to live out the totality of differing values of 'imagination and religious ideas', that conflicts, blame and wrong become inevitable; when the ideal becomes actual, when one tries absolutely to live by the values one says one lives by.

Hegel holds that such conflict can be resolved, but only at the cost of the character who causes such a collision of substantives and the disruption of totality. 'Eternal justice', Hegel writes, 'is exercised . . . in the sense that it restores the substance and unity of ethical life with the downfall of the individual who has disturbed its peace'.[94] For the 'truly substantial thing' is the 'reconciliation in which the specific individuals and their aims work together harmoniously without opposition and without infringing on one another'.[95] In tragedy, Hegel tells us, the 'eternal substance of things emerges victorious' by simply removing the 'false one-sidedness' which is the tragic hero, and, in so doing, exhibiting the 'positive elements' which are both the support and object

91 Hegel, *Lectures on Fine Art*, vol. 2, p. 1196.
92 A. C. Bradley, 'Hegel's theory of tragedy', in *Oxford Lectures on Poetry* (London, 1950), pp. 69–95.
93 Hegel, *Lectures on Fine Art*, vol. 2, p. 1196.
94 Hegel, *Lectures on Fine Art*, vol. 2, p. 1197.
95 Hegel, *Lectures on Fine Art*, vol. 2, p. 1197.

of the hero's volition.[96] Bradley explains that for Hegel the end of tragic conflict is not the work of 'chance or blank fate' but the 'act of ethical substance itself, asserting its absoluteness against the excessive pretensions of its particular powers'.[97]

Thus the tragic hero is someone who can neither succeed in accommodating himself to ethical harmony, nor resign himself to the compromise of his ideals, and being thus situated, must perish. 'It is the nature of the tragic hero', Bradley tells us, 'that he knows no shrinking or half-heartedness, but identifies himself wholly with the power that moves him, and will admit the justification of no other power'.[98]

Such a tragic character is the occasion of fear, not simply as emotion, but as a proper response to the 'external power' of the 'ethical order' which is at one and the same time a determinant of the hero's 'free reason' and 'that eternal and inviolable something which he summons up against himself if once he turns against it'.[99]

The tragic character is also the occasion of sympathy, not simply as fellow-feeling, but as recognition of an essential responsibility. 'A truly tragic suffering', Hegel writes, 'is only inflicted on the individual agents as a consequence of their own deed which is both legitimate and, owing to the resulting collision, blameworthy, and for which their whole self is answerable'.[100] Through an intense and absolute attachment to his ideals, the tragic character brings upon himself tribulation and thus invites sympathy as the one who is responsible for his own suffering. The tragic hero suffers from an obstinacy of purpose.

Thus from Hegel we take the idea that tragedy is the embodied conflict, in the lives of actual men and women, of values that, in ideality, are harmoniously related, but which when enacted with an absolute fidelity are irreducibly and

96 Hegel, *Lectures on Fine Art*, vol. 2, p. 1199.
97 Bradley, 'Hegel's theory of tragedy', p. 72.
98 Bradley, 'Hegel's theory of tragedy', p. 72.
99 Hegel, *Lectures on Fine Art*, vol. 2, p. 1198.
100 Hegel, *Lectures on Fine Art*, vol. 2, p. 1198.

violently antithetical. If the Christian gospel is tragedy in this sense, it is a story of a conflict the resolution of which must involve the destruction of its hero and the affirmation of a harmony not of this world. Can this be said of Christ's story?

THE TRAGEDY OF CHRIST?

Ulrich Simon judges that Christ is not a tragic hero. Christ sets his sight upon the Kingdom of God, and though tempted to look elsewhere, his vision, to the last, is always set on God's heavenly rule. Jesus cannot be tragic in the Shakespearean sense, because he is without sin. His suffering is not senseless but significant for all time, his death not waste but a sacrifice that saves. All that happens, happens according to the will of God.[101]

Yet there are tragic elements in the story of Christ, not least the pain and suffering he undergoes, both anguish of mind and agony of body. Hegel is surely right when he tells us that to live in the world, to become involved in the 'contradictions of the broken and confused medley of earthly existence', is to find oneself unable to withdraw from the 'ill fortune and ill health that cling to finite existence'. Even the 'immortal gods of polytheism' find themselves involved in 'mighty conflicts wherein contending passions and interest are roused', and so also, Hegel notes, Christ and those with whom he is involved, the other characters in his story. They are equally enmeshed in a world, not only of joys and pleasures, but of fearsome woes and terrible tribulations.

> Even the God of the Christians was not exempt from passing to the humiliation of suffering, yes, to the ignominy of death, nor was he spared the grief of soul in which he had to cry: 'My God, my God, why hast thou forsaken me?' His mother suffers a similar agonizing pain, and human life as such is a life of strife, struggles, and sorrows.[102]

[101] Ulrich Simon, *Pity and Terror: Christianity and Tragedy* (London: Macmillan, 1989), p. 43.

[102] Hegel, *Lectures on Fine Art*, vol. 1, p. 178.

Yet in themselves, misfortune and suffering do not make a tragic hero; they must, as Bradley reminds us, 'spring in great part from human agency, and in some degree from the agency of the sufferer', as well as being borne with 'noble endurance'.[103] Certainly the first and last of these requirements are characteristic of Christ's passion: it is engineered by the malice of others and received, not in rage or with self-pity, but in a manner of sober submission, a strange combination of fortitude and resignation that is a giving of himself to others. But Christ is also, at least in part, the agent of his pain. There is no question, as Jesus sets his face toward Jerusalem, that he is not aware that what he does precipitates the actions of others. Judas goes out into the night of his own volition, but Jesus has already told him to do quickly what he is going to do.[104] Thus in a sense the Christ brings his sufferings upon himself, and insofar as he could not have done otherwise without betraying his very being, partakes of tragic suffering and excites our deepest, most awe-stricken sympathies.

However, for Hegel the tragic hero is one who contests for an absolute power against other such powers and whose triumph of will is the signal for destruction and defeat, not by an opposed malignancy but by justice itself, by the ideal of ethical harmony. The story of Christ is indeed that of a contest, between God's champion and the forces of Satan, and, as St John surreptitiously relates, Christ is both brought down and raised up, by and because of his obstinacy of purpose, his absolute commitment and fidelity and compassion for and to the disciples in whom he has placed his trust. Though Christ's love of both God and people is beyond dissuasion, and his giving of himself over to the world the concrete grasp of an ideal he will not let go or compromise, every bit as strongly held as by any tragic character dreamt by Hegel, Christ's contestation is not, surely, with other powers that in heaven are consonant with such a fierce devotion, but which on earth must find themselves in contention, collision and conflict?

103 Bradley, 'Hegel's theory of tragedy', pp. 81–2. 104 John 13.27.

And yet if we were to take the story of Christ's temptation in the wilderness as disclosing the very values with which Christ was in conflict, and by which he was ultimately destroyed at the hands of Roman soldiers, would we not find values for which one might seek a unified harmony, if indeed they were truly temptations for the Christ of God? Many in the Church have thought so since. Christ chooses one way but might he not have chosen another, could not God have worked out his purposes by the very means Satan suggests: that he should, in the words of Donald MacKinnon, 'by a dramatic descent from the pinnacle of the temple, at once establish beyond question in his own mind the reality of the powers at his disposal and by their exercise in this overwhelmingly self-assertive act establish himself as a force to be reckoned with where the destiny of his people was concerned.'[105] MacKinnon slants the temptation in a particular direction, by developing the notions of self-assertion and imposition, but the temptation is to establish the Kingdom at once, without pain, a 'bloodless victory' whereby, as MacKinnon puts it, Christ would become the leader of a 'great spiritual revival'. And what is wrong with that? Is it not that for which Church leaders are always praying? It may be, as MacKinnon notes, that in choosing as he did, Christ kept himself 'free to be the open associate of tax-gatherers and harlots, of all on the very fringes of respectable society or beyond its boundaries', but could they not equally be brought into the Kingdom by more direct means? It may be that Christ had to choose one way or the other, but is it so obvious that he could choose only one way? He accepts the cup of suffering handed him by his Father, but might not the alternative manifestation of his power and glory, not on the cross but on the pinnacle of the temple, have been equally, if not a better means to attain God's final purpose for his people?

These questions have force just insofar as they are questions that Christians face in the decisions of their own lives, and that the Church has itself answered differently from its Lord.

[105] MacKinnon, *Metaphysics*, p. 131.

Christian bishops have long sat amongst the princes of the world. To preach a Kingdom not of this world inevitably involves the preacher, whether Christ or his disciple, in the ambiguities of the ethical life, of having, so it seems, to choose between good and good, and when the choice leads to destruction, of confronting the tragedy of a good life bearing evil fruit. And Christ's own life has borne such fruit, not simply in the history of his followers – whose actions in his name have not only been for good but also for so much evil that the balance is not to be judged – but from even before his birth, it being attended by the slaughter of innocents as well as the ministry of angels.

If Christ himself – in virtue of resurrection rather than defeat, of being lifted up on to the right hand of God – is not the tragic hero of the Christian story, then what issues from him most certainly is: the tragedy of the Church.

THE TRAGEDY OF THE CHURCH

Ulrich Simon insists that the 'Christian tradition is not opposed to the tragic sense of life',[106] that 'Christianity is tragic because of the Cross'.[107] Though the sense in which Christianity is tragic and not comic – because of the resurrection – remains unclear in Simon's work, he is surely correct in locating the place at which tragedy enters into Christianity and Christianity becomes tragic: the conflict of power subsequent upon Christ's entry into the world. Christ's power is not of this world and those who follow him are not to confuse worldly power with the power of the Kingdom. Yet even before the death of Christ, as Simon reminds us, the disciples are arguing among themselves as to who is to be first in the Kingdom of God. 'The seed of further contention is sown and it sprouts with threatening force in the Church . . . This struggle for power can never die and it remains the core of Christian tragedy'.[108]

[106] Simon, *Pity and Terror*, p. 143.
[107] Simon, *Pity and Terror*, p. 145.
[108] Simon, *Pity and Terror*, pp. 45–6.

The Church – as the sacramental continuation of the incarnation in history – is forever between powers; between the power of this world and the power of God's coming Kingdom. The stark choice is always before it: God or Caesar? The choice of Christ was clear and fixed, from all time and for all time, and yet made definitive in a passing moment; having resisted all temptations he 'bowed his head and gave up his spirit',[109] passing from life to death. But the Church's choice is always before it, even now and after having so often chosen in the past, one way or the other. It is in the history of the Church as a history of choice between powers and, at the same time, the proclamation and performance of the gospel, that the Church's telling of the gospel becomes tragic.

There is a fundamental distinction and disparity between that which is told and its telling, between that which is performed and its performance. The history of the Church, which should be the history of a concrete grace bringing both freedom and joy, a time of growth and blessing, has proved itself to be at least equally a history of destruction and all manner of physical and spiritual dominion; a history that mocks the gospel and brings despair to those to whom the gospel is preached.

The gospel is played on a stage that is, as Steiner reminds us, a 'platform extending precariously between heaven and hell. Those who walk on it may encounter at any turn ministers of grace or damnation'.[110] The players are between possibilities, between damnation or salvation, a world lost or a world redeemed; stretched between absolute tragedy and glorious comedy, just as Christ on the cross was stretched between glory and despair, heaven and hell.[111]

[109] John 19.30.

[110] Steiner, *Death of Tragedy*, p. 194.

[111] It is the darker possibility that the modern world seeks to deny. The 'end of history' is also the 'end' of tragedy. See above chapter 1.

JUDGEMENT, HEAVEN AND HELL

Steiner, in *The Death of Tragedy*, has little good to say of twentieth century attempts to revive the tragic tradition, describing the 'tragic poets' of our own time as 'grave robbers and conjurors of ghosts out of ancient glory'.[112] By invoking the past glories of ancient myths, modern tragedians may sound the tragic note and produce a work 'momentarily arresting', but they cannot escape the 'staleness which falls upon any fancy-dress party at break of day'.[113] Thus defeated are the likes of W. B. Yeats, Jean Cocteau and T. S. Eliot; only Bertolt Brecht and Paul Claudel survive in their respective plays, *Mother Courage* (*Mutter Courage*) and *Le soulier de satin*. Their success is surprising, for according to Steiner, both were handicapped by their essential commitment and loyalty to Western mythologies of optimism, Brecht to Marxism and Claudel to Christianity. But their ideologies were subverted, and thus their poetry able to attain to the truly tragic, because, Steiner tells us, 'Brecht lacked hope' and 'Claudel lacked charity'.[114] It is Steiner's judgement on Claudel that is here pertinent to the theme of Christian tragedy, for he locates Claudel's want of charity in his being a 'terrifying kind of Roman Catholic . . . of the age of Gregory rather than of the modern Church'.[115] Steiner writes: 'The glow of hell-fire seemed to evoke in him a stern approval, nearly a delight in the vengeful grandeur of God's ways'.[116]

Claudel's notion of tragedy, like Brecht's, is one of 'waste rather than predestined or inevitable disaster',[117] his characters entangling themselves in tragedy 'because they turn their backs on the redemptive power of God', and thus their suffering, though real, rendered 'metaphysically absurd'.[118] But in looking to the 'glow of hell-fire', Claudel's world has a place for judgement and damnation, and thus for the possibility of

[112] Steiner, *Death of Tragedy*, p. 304.
[113] Steiner, *Death of Tragedy*, p. 326.
[114] Steiner, *Death of Tragedy*, p. 344.
[115] Steiner, *Death of Tragedy*, p. 340.
[116] Steiner, *Death of Tragedy*, p. 341.
[117] Steiner, *Death of Tragedy*, p. 341.
[118] Steiner, *Death of Tragedy*, p. 345.

Christian tragedy. The 'death of tragedy', Christian or otherwise, is intimately related to the demise of a world in which judgement and its outcome in heaven or hell are no longer possibilities.

Steiner locates the point at which tragedy ceases to be a possibility for the West in the rise of Romanticism at the end of the eighteenth century, when fear of hell gave way to the necessity of heaven, and the feeling of remorse replaced judgement to damnation. 'In authentic tragedy the gates of hell stand open and damnation is real. The tragic personage cannot evade responsibility'.[119] Romanticism is the evasion of such responsibility and thus of tragedy.[120] The tragic hero of romantic 'near-tragedy', Steiner tells us, 'has committed a terrible, perhaps nameless, crime.'

> He is tormented by his conscience and roams the earth, hiding an inward fire which reveals itself by his feverish aspect and glittering eye. We know him as the Ancient Mariner, Cain, the Flying Dutchman, Manfred, or the Wandering Jew. . . . At the hour of mortal crisis or approaching death, the soul of the romantic hero is 'wrenched with a woeful agony'. Suddenly, there is a flowering of remorse . . . Salvation descends on the bruised spirit, and the hero steps toward grace out of the shadow of damnation.[121]

The powerful rise of romantic optimism and its attendant displacement of judgement and damnation is well known to anyone who has studied the rise of liberal Christianity at the end of the eighteenth century. It is not just that tragedy, as a dramatic form, ceased to be a possibility with Romanticism, but that Western culture and civilization, and in particular Christian thought and practice, lost its ability to confront and contend with the intractabilities of fallen humanity.

It is perhaps possible to say that tragedy ceased to be a possibility because, with the rise of the romantic state, the tension between individual conscience and external economy, which for Hegel is essential for the possibility of tragedy,

119 Steiner, *Death of Tragedy*, p. 128.

120 Steiner, *Death of Tragedy*, p. 133.

121 Steiner, *Death of Tragedy*, p. 130.

was dissolved in the process whereby individuality internalised the constraints of heteronomy, accepting what Terry Eagleton has called the bourgeois burden of 'internalised governance'.

> Like the work of art as defined by the discourse of aesthetics, the bourgeois subject is autonomous and self-determining, acknowledges no merely extrinsic law but instead, in some mysterious fashion, gives the law to itself. In doing so, the law becomes the form which shapes into harmonious unity the turbulent content of the subject's appetites and inclinations. The compulsion of autocratic power is replaced by the more gratifying compulsion of the subject's self-identity.[122]

Thus the turbulence that gave rise to the possibility of tragedy is displaced by a 'harmonious unity' in which comedy can flourish.

But with the advent of the individual's constitution by Romanticism, it is not the reality of power that vanishes within the subject's self-identity, when law is transformed to custom and second-nature; rather, it is the subject as responsible agent that is dissipated in the endless incitement of its desire. Precisely because the State and its powers become identical with the wants and interests of the subject, the possibility of tragedy recedes, as also the possibility of recognising oppressions and the space in which one might give obstinate loyalty to that which is outside of oneself, located at the point of the 'other', and not merely as one more turn within the labyrinth of the self.

It would thus seem that if the Church is not to deny its own tragic character, or rather, the possibility of its transformation, it must keep open the possibility of judgement and damnation, not simply as internal moments of the guilty conscience, but as the very destruction of the body. It must resist those romantic tendencies which, given force in liberal theology, would enact the foreclosure of heaven and hell as

122 Terry Eagleton, *The Ideology of the Aesthetic* (Oxford: Basil Blackwell, 1990), p. 23.

radical possibilities for the responsible and properly autonomous spirit, the possibilities of bodily death and resurrection. It must eat the word that is both sweet in the mouth and bitter in the belly.

PART III

Linkages

I saw no temple in the city, for its temple is the Lord God the Almighty and the Lamb. And the city has no need of sun or moon to shine on it, for the glory of God is its light, and its lamp is the Lamb. The nations will walk by its light, and the kings of the earth will bring their glory into it. Its gates will never be shut by day – and there will be no night there. People will bring into it the glory and the honour of the nations. But nothing unclean will enter it, not anyone who practices abomination or falsehood, but only those who are written in the Lamb's book of life.

Revelation 21.22–7

CHAPTER 6

The event of God

For Christian faith God is known only as that which happens: not as a being or as a thing, but as an event. The 'I am' to Moses; the 'It is the Lord who speaks' to the prophets; the 'I am the way, the truth and the life' to the apostles; the rabbi eating fish with his friends by the lake shore; the eucharistic celebration of the gathered community.[1] Here, the event of God is the fact that 'something happens' after which nothing is the same again. The event disrupts our world, interrupts our narratives, dislodges our stories – the tales we tell without thinking. It is the 'it happens' rather than the 'what happens' that constitutes the eventhood of the event. Here it is God who happens; and in this happening a universe is given, a site for the beginning of a story.[2]

That God is not a thing – not a being or even Being itself – is the knowledge lost and found in the history of modernity. It was lost when God became all too comprehensible, an object of the speculative intelligence, grasped by reason. It was found again, when the God of the rationalists died, proving

[1] 'The divine is precisely what manifests itself and is recognizable outside of all knowledge about its "being". God does not propose himself as a new type of being – or of absence of being – for us to know. He proposes himself, that is all'. Jean-Luc Nancy, *The Inoperative Community*, edited by Peter Connor, Theory and History of Literature 76 (Minneapolis and Oxford: University of Minnesota Press, 1991), pp. 115–16.

[2] 'God's humanity introduces itself into the world as a story to be told.' See Eberhard Jüngel, *God as the Mystery of the World: On the Foundation of the Theology of the Crucified One in the Dispute Between Theism and Atheism*, translated by Darrell L. Guder (Grand Rapids, Michigan: William B. Eerdmans Publishing Company, 1983), pp. 299–314 (p. 302).

unnecessary for the needs of modern man, who could order the world, conceptually and practically, without need of deity. The weakening of modernity does not return us to the reasonable God of the philosophers, but it does allow us to think again the radical incomprehensibility of God's event.

The idea of God's event has a history like any other. It does not convey divine alterity of itself, but only as deployed in response to certain conceptualities, and then only poorly. It has its attractions and its limitations. Francis Watson notes that the concept lets God act 'now' as well as 'then', avoids turning encounter with God into the entertainment of propositions, and allows God to crack open our complacent certainties.[3] But he also finds the idea wanting. 'It does not in itself signify an occurrence of a kind that can only take place between two personal agents, an I and a Thou.'[4] It renders language secondary, with a gap 'between the ineffable moment of disclosure-encounter and subsequent attempts to make linguistic sense of it in the language of faith and theology.'[5] It misleadingly suggests that we can avoid propositional knowledge. 'We cannot know God without knowing about God; knowing about God is a necessary although not sufficient condition for knowing God.'[6] The idea of the event is a static rather than dynamic notion, for in 'breaking in' and 'overturning', it refuses narrative integration and continuation. It must be repeated again and again.[7] Further, the event not only punctures linear time, but in so doing it isolates the people it confronts. 'The event singles out and isolates individuals from their communal contexts. At least for a time, their own being appears to stem not so much from those broad communal contexts as from the event itself.'[8] Thus the 'event-model suppresses or downplays both the informational-

[3] Francis Watson, 'Is revelation an "event"?', *Modern Theology*, 10 (1994), 383–99 (p. 383).
[4] Watson, 'Is revelation an "event"?', p. 384.
[5] Watson, 'Is revelation an "event"?', p. 387.
[6] Watson, 'Is revelation an "event"?', p. 388.
[7] Watson, 'Is revelation an "event"?', pp. 389–90.
[8] Watson, 'Is revelation an "event"?', p. 391.

cognitive and the diachronic aspects of self-revelation within interpersonal relations, and it implies an immediacy of presence that isolates the recipient of revelation from community.'[9]

The following sketch of an eventful theology may not meet all or any of Watson's concerns, but it does suggest that while the emphasis must fall on the 'it happens' rather than the 'what happens', the latter remains unavoidable, the cognitive dimension unsuppressable; and that while the event of God 'falls on us from above',[10] it is nevertheless constituted and constitutive of story. The event of God is a mediated immediacy.[11] It can be this if we think of it as a narrative phrase.

PHRASING THE EVENT

The philosopher Jean-François Lyotard has developed a 'philosophy of phrases' in a number of his works, especially in *The Differend*.[12] It is his idea of the phrase, suitably bent to theological pursuit, that informs my account of God's event. In the following I will briefly sketch the range, nature, and dependent primordiality of the phrase, which together give it a flexibility appropriate for theological use.

For Lyotard phrases are many things. They are not just spoken or written sentences, grammatically and semantically complete. Phrases are words and gestures, signals and notes of music, as well as silences. Extrapolating further, we may say

9 Watson, 'Is revelation an "event"?', p. 392.

10 Watson, 'Is revelation an "event"?', p. 390.

11 Otherwise stated, the point is to show that the alterity of God is not opposed to the world. The divine 'other' is not a difference *within* the world, so not in competition with the world, or anything in it. Since there is nothing that can exclude God, mediation cannot get in the way of God or stand in for God. See further Walter Lowe, *Theology and Difference: The Wound of Reason* (Bloomington and Indianapolis: Indiana University Press, 1993), pp. 33–47.

12 Jean-François Lyotard, *The Differend: Phrases in Dispute*, translated by Georges van Den Abbeele (Manchester: Manchester University Press, 1988). On Lyotard see Geoffrey Bennington, *Lyotard: Writing the Event* (Manchester: Manchester University Press, 1988) and Bill Readings, *Introducing Lyotard: Art and Politics* (London: Routledge, 1991).

that phrases are also persons or narratives, life-stories. The range of the phrase is indeterminate.

A phrase presents a universe which positions four poles or instants. These are addressor and addressee, referent and meaning, and their situation, their relation to one another.[13] 'I am the light of the world. Whoever follows me will never walk in darkness but will have the light of life'[14] positions Jesus (addressor) and the people (addressees) in relation to himself (referent) as the one who enlightens their darkness (meaning). It is the constitution of the phrase, as an interrelated whole, that is important. None of the poles or instants exists of itself, separate from the others, or from the situation that binds them together and makes them to be.

It should be said that addressor and addressee are instances, either marked or unmarked, presented by a phrase. The latter is not a message passing from an addressor to an addressee both of whom are independent of it. They are situated in the universe the phrase presents, as are its referent and its sense.[15]

The phrase comes first, and it is indubitable. '*There is no phrase* is a phrase.'[16] This is why Geoffrey Bennington describes Lyotard's philosophy of phrases as a 'sort of Cartesianism without the subject.'[17] There is a phrase, therefore we are.

Simply that there is a phrase is indubitable. That there is a phrase is presupposed in saying anything at all. In this conception, neither reality nor the subject stands prior to and in principle independent of a phrase. Reality is attributed by a phrase to a referent positioned by a phrase, and a subject is also positioned by a phrase. A phrase which declares that a thinking subject or transcendental ego stands outside the phrase positions that subject as the referent of a phrase, and describes that subject as standing outside phrases in general.[18]

We do not give phrases to one another, we are given by phrases. The addressor does not give a phrase to the

[13] Bennington, *Lyotard*, p. 126. [14] John 8.12.
[15] Lyotard, *Differend*, p. 11. [16] Lyotard, *Differend*, p. 65.
[17] Bennington, *Lyotard*, p. 123. [18] Bennington, *Lyotard*, p. 125.

addressee, the speaker to the listener. Rather it is the phrase that gives them to one another. It is the story that constitutes both story-teller and hearer. The language of religion is paradigmatic in this regard, for it is not possessed by those who seek to use it. It uses them, or better, they are positioned by it.

Language, for Lyotard, is not a simple reflection of events in the world, nor events the products of language, of a 'narrating agency'.[19] Yet events take place in language and nowhere else. The world is given in narrative-phrases, and we live within them. *Il n'y a pas de hors-texte*.[20]

Consider the reality of death. 'Death is a matter of archives. You are dead when stories are told about you, and when only stories are told about you.'[21] When people are dead they live only in the stories of others. When they are alive they live in the stories that they tell themselves.

> They are acting out scenarios that are running through their heads or that they have been told about. They are galvanised into action by the constant interplay between the agency of the narratee (narrataire), or the agency where the story is heard, and that of the narrated (narré), where it is acted out . . . they become witnesses to the fact that the stories they are acting out are the best stories, simply because they testify to their accuracy.[22]

A phrase presents, but it cannot present that it presents. The occurrence of the phrase is not itself presented by the

[19] Bennington, *Lyotard*, p. 107.

[20] The interlocutor in Lyotard's essay 'Lessons in Paganism' (in *The Lyotard Reader*, edited by Andrew Benjamin (Oxford: Basil Blackwell, 1989), pp. 122–54) is incredulous when told that there are only stories, that narratives refer only to other narratives; that 'outside' is always staged 'inside'. This, however, is what Bennington calls the 'disconcerting simplicity' of Lyotard's answer to the 'vexed question of reference and reality': the reference of narrative is always simply another narrative (Bennington, *Lyotard*, p. 111). 'Reality is never given, but always situated by particular narratives as referents: just as story-teller and addressee do not precede the story told but are positioned by it' (Bennington, *Lyotard*, p. 112). On Derrida's version of this view see above chapter 1.

[21] Lyotard, 'Lessons in paganism', p. 126.

[22] Lyotard, 'Lessons in paganism', p. 127. On Alasdair MacIntyre's version of our narrative constitution see below chapter 7.

phrase. For that is required another phrase whose referent is the first phrase. But in referring, the second phrase forgets its own presenting or event of presentation. 'The presentation entailed by a phrase is forgotten by it, plunged into the river Lethe. Another phrase pulls it back out and presents it, oblivious to the presentation that it itself entails.'[23] Bennington notes that this sounds Heideggerian: 'Being (which is not an entity and which therefore is not) is inevitably forgotten in the entities the Being "of" which it "is". Presentation (which is not a phrase) is inevitably forgotten in the phrase presentation presents.'[24]

Narrative phrases do not come singly. If there is one phrase, as there is indubitably, there is a totality of phrases. The one phrase presupposes all the others. A phrase is not an entity because it is always constitutively linked to other phrases. The illusion that a phrase is an entity is due to the possibility of treating a phrase as the referent of another phrase.

After a phrase it is inevitable that another follows, but what phrase follows is contingent. Genres limit that contingency, directing the necessity of linking. 'A genre of discourse determines what is at stake in linking phrases: to persuade, to convince, to vanquish, to make laugh, to make cry, etc. . . . Teleology begins with genres of discourse, not with phrases. Insofar, though, as they are linked together, phrases are always caught up in one (or at least one) genre of discourse.'[25]

The foregoing is sufficient for us to understand the phrase as that event which gives addressor and addressee to one another, both constituting and constitutive of their relation.

[23] Lyotard, *Differend*, p. 77.

[24] Bennington, *Lyotard*, p. 128.

[25] Lyotard, *Differend*, p. 84. There are, perhaps, three broad genres of divine discourse: revelation, prayer, theology. 'I the Lord your God am a jealous God' would be a phrase from the genre of revelation. 'In thee, O Lord, do I take refuge; let me never be put to shame' would be a phrase from the genre of prayer; and from theology: 'All things are dealt with in holy teaching in terms of God, either because they are God himself or because they are relative to him as their origin and end' (St Thomas Aquinas, *Summa Theologiæ*, vol. 1, translated by Thomas Gilby (London: Blackfriars Eyre and Spottiswoode, 1964), 1a 1, 7, responsio). However, one may have to allow for the collapse of genre in that theology is finally prayer, and prayer the passivity that hears the Word.

The burning bush presents a universe in which Moses is given to the 'I am' by which he is addressed, as also the 'I am' to Moses. Indeed Lyotard's account of phrases includes such an example. He notes the similarities between revelatory phrases and phrases of moral injunction. The latter are understood as Kantian imperatives, falling upon the obligee as a command from an obligor who is not known, an addressor who is missing. The phrase of divine address is similar, coming as it does from an addressor who is 'absent'.

Is the order Abraham receives to sacrifice his son any more intelligible than a memorandum directing round-ups, convoys, concentratings, and either slow or quick death? . . . Abraham hears: That Isaac die, that is my law, and he obeys. The Lord speaks at this moment only to Abraham, and Abraham is answerable only to the Lord. Since the reality, if not of the Lord, then at least of the phrase imputed to Him, cannot be established, how can it be known that Abraham isn't a paranoiac subject to homicidal (infanticidal) urges? Or a fake?[26]

The phrases of obligation and divine address dispossess the ego, forcing the 'I' into the 'you' pole of the phrase. In the phrase of obligation the 'I' is 'stripped of the illusion of being an addressor of phrases, grabbed hold of upon the addressee instance, incomprehensibly'. One is commanded without knowing by whom or why, without knowing that there is one who commands or a reason for the command. 'I hear: *Hail*, and I am the angel's obligee, the you of the other.'[27] For Lyotard, the command or injunction that issues from an absent other is a phrase universe in which the ego is denied, and thus also the possibility of its experience, for 'experience and cognition take place in the first person, or at least as a self'.

What you judge to be the Lord's call is the situation of you when I is deprived of experience, 'estranged', 'alienated', disauthorized. You

[26] Lyotard, *Differend*, p. 107. *The Differend* is also a book about the Shoah. See further Jean-François Lyotard, *Heidegger and 'the Jews'*, translated by Andreas Michel and Mark S. Roberts (Minneapolis: University of Minnesota Press, 1990).

[27] Lyotard, *Differend*, p. 111.

> do not therefore have the experience of the Lord, nor even of alienness. If you were to have that experience, it would not be the Lord, and it would not be ethics. You cannot therefore testify that whatever it is calls upon you is somebody. And such is precisely the ethical universe.[28]

Lyotard insists upon the absolute 'absence' of the addressor in the phrase of revelation or prescription – we must not even think the phrase itself the addressor. 'The occurrence is not the Lord. The pagans know this and laugh over this edifying confusion.'[29] The Church, of course, is not pagan and yet it knows that the phrase is not the Lord, or not always. The burning bush is not the Lord; that would be idolatry. But there is more than one sort of revelatory phrase. For the Church, the event of God is above all the phrase of Jesus Christ.

THE EVENT OF THE CHRIST-PHRASE

Jesus Christ is the occasion of many a phrase, a word spoken or an act done which positions the addressee to Jesus as his or her addressor. 'Put out into the deep water and let down your nets for a catch.'[30] But Jesus also says and does phrases that position the addressee in relation to an addressor who is and is not the man who speaks and acts towards them.

> One day, while he was teaching, Pharisees and teachers of the law were sitting near by (they had come from every village of Galilee and Judea and from Jerusalem); and the power of the Lord was with him to heal. Just then some men came, carrying a paralyzed man on a bed. They were trying to bring him in and lay him before Jesus; but finding no way to bring him in because of the crowd, they went up on the roof and let him down with his bed through the tiles into the middle of the crowd in front of Jesus. When he saw their faith, he said, 'Friend, your sins are forgiven you.' Then the scribes and the Pharisees began to question, 'Who is this who is speaking blasphemies? Who can forgive sins but God alone?'[31]

[28] Lyotard, *Differend*, pp. 115–16. [29] Lyotard, *Differend*, p. 116.
[30] Luke 5.4. [31] Luke 5.17–21 (Matthew 9.1–8; Mark 2.1–12).

Lyotard's account of story-telling among the Cashinahua people of the upper Amazon serves to illuminate this story about Jesus.[32] Each Cashinahua story-teller begins by saying that he is passing on a story that he has been told. The narrator was first a narratee. It is only at the end of the story that he gives his own name. But when one of the narratees tells the story again, the name of the previous narrator is forgotten. It is once more a story that was told to the narrator by an anonymous other.

Since some of the stories concern marriage moieties, the narrator is often also the referent of the story that positions him within the social structure. Thus the narrator often situates himself on 'the two forgotten poles of Western thought': the pole where 'one is the recipient of a narrative in which one is narrated', and the pole 'where one receives a narrative that has been narrated to you', the poles of referent and addressee. The one who speaks is one who has been 'spoken' and thus, 'through his name and through the story he tells, he claims to belong to the tradition'.[33]

The Cashinahua is obliged to retell the story he hears, as a 'relay that may not keep its charge but must pass it on'. It is an almost 'physical' fact that 'stories are animated with movement and that as they pass over you, you must pass the movement on'.[34] There is heteronomy in that the narrator is not the author of what he tells; but 'in point of fact, there never are authors'. The pole of the addressor is not privileged. Thus this heteronomy is not servitude but passivity, and this is the pragmatics of tradition (as also prayer): 'S/he who speaks can speak only inasmuch as s/he is spoken'.[35]

When Jesus returns from the desert he begins to teach in the synagogues, where he reads the Scriptures to the assembly. He passes on the word written by another; a word of which he

[32] Jean-François Lyotard and Jean-Loup Thébaud, *Just Gaming*, translated by Wlad Godzich, Theory and History of Literature 20 (Manchester: Manchester University Press, 1985) pp. 32–43.

[33] Lyotard and Thébaud, *Just Gaming*, p. 33.

[34] Lyotard and Thébaud, *Just Gaming*, p. 35.

[35] Lyotard and Thébaud, *Just Gaming*, p. 38.

is both the addressee and the referent. Finding himself narrated in the scroll of Isaiah, he is able to speak because he has been spoken.

When he came to Nazareth, where he had been brought up, he went to the synagogue on the sabbath day, as was his custom. He stood up to read, and the scroll of the prophet Isaiah was given to him. He unrolled the scroll and found the place where it was written: 'The Spirit of the Lord is upon me, because he has anointed me to bring good news to the poor. He has sent me to proclaim release to the captives and recovery of sight to the blind, to let the oppressed go free, to proclaim the year of the Lord's favour.' And he rolled up the scroll, gave it back to the attendant, and sat down. The eyes of all in the synagogue were fixed on him. Then he began to say to them, 'Today this Scripture has been fulfilled in your hearing.'[36]

The story of Jesus in the synagogue at Nazareth reminds us that the event of God is always connected with other events through the necessity of linking phrases. The event of God may come to us as if from nowhere – one day Jesus walks out of Nazareth to become the story of the world[37] – but at the same time it is always-already phrased just insofar as it is known at all, the referent of other phrases. The immediacy of God's event is always mediated: it is the shock of the familiar. Thus, while Jesus follows the logic of Cashinahua story-telling, where the pole of the addressee is privileged, he also bends it in the direction of what Lyotard considers peculiarly Hebraic: the privileging of the addressor pole.

The pragmatics of Cashinahua tradition allow one to speak insofar as one is spoken; but this cannot be said of Yahweh. 'One cannot say that he speaks inasmuch as he is spoken'.[38] In the phrase of divine address, of Yahweh to Moses, of God to his people, the place of the addressor is not available to the one who is addressed, since the request of God cannot come from the people. The one who is addressed 'must never pass over to

[36] Luke 4.16–30 (Matthew 13.53–8; Mark 6.1–6); Isaiah 61.1–2; 58.6.

[37] Mark 1.9.

[38] Lyotard and Thébaud, *Just Gaming*, p. 38.

the position of the one who speaks, that is, he must never assume the authority that the one who addressed him is supposed to have'.[39] This then is the impiety of Jesus in the story of the paralysed man, when he is portrayed as speaking with authority: he has improperly passed over to the position of 'the one who speaks'. Yet at the same time he remains the one who is addressed and spoken. He is entirely mobile within the phrase of divine address, positionable as addressor or addressee, referent or meaning, or some or all of them at once, or as the phrase itself, as that which gives the poles or instants to one another. Jesus is constituted by, and constitutive of, God's story.

Just insofar as the Spirit enables a person to recognise in the Son the very image of the Father, to hear and feel God in the word and presence of Jesus, then Jesus is the phrase that gives the Creator to the creature, the very occurrence of the Lord. Through the Spirit, Jesus becomes the phrase or word in which the Father is given to the believer and the believer to the Father.

The Christ-phrase, who is himself the appearance or occurrence of God, positions Father and believer as addressor and addressee, and vice versa. For Christ is both the Word of the Father to the Church, and the prayer of the Church to the Father.[40] It is in John's Gospel that the mobility of Jesus is most evident, as also his ability to constitute the phrase universe that unites the disciples to one another as friends of the Father in Christ. Christ is the phrase of peace that unites all, whose presence is the forgiveness of sins.

When it was evening . . . and the doors of the house where the disciples had met were locked for fear of the Jews, Jesus came and stood among them and said, 'Peace be with you.' After he said this, he showed them his hands and his side. Then the disciples rejoiced when they saw the Lord. Jesus said to them again, 'Peace be with you. As the Father has sent me, so I send you.' When he had said this, he breathed on them and said to them, 'Receive the Holy Spirit. If you

[39] Lyotard and Thébaud, *Just Gaming*, p. 39. [40] Matthew 6.9–13.

forgive the sins of any, they are forgiven; if you retain the sins of any, they are retained.'[41]

Christ does not simply forgive his disciples, but gives himself to them as forgiveness itself. He is the phrase that places the Church in both the addressee and addressor pole in the act of pardon: 'You are forgiven'. 'It is not so much that on Easter day he forgives the disciples who betrayed him and fled; rather, he is bestowed on them as an Easter gift, the act of forgiveness which has been given the form of the sacrament of pardon.'[42]

Jesus Christ is the event of God already spoken in the Scripture, who gives himself to be spoken in the power of the Spirit. In him the Church addresses the One by whom it is addressed in him. In him the Church itself becomes the phrase in which he is given to others and they to him. The Church is the tradition that passes on the Christ-phrase, which, infinitely repeated, is always unique whenever, by the Spirit, in the Son, the Father is given to the addressee and the addressee to the Father.

TELLING GOD'S STORY THREE WAYS

The Christian Bible tells the story of God. It is a many-layered narrative, complex in multiple ways, severally authored, which tells the story of God and of God's people. It is the story of God and the Hebrews, of God and the Christ of God, of God and the Church. In the Bible, the story of Jesus of Nazareth recapitulates or retells the story of Israel's encounter with and formation by the 'I am' to Moses, the 'It is the Lord who speaks' to the prophets. The story of Jesus – the narrative of

[41] John 20.19–23. One cannot read this passage, however, without noting its tribulations: the cost of Christ's peace, already paid – the wounding of his body – and to pay, the 'fear' that will render the Church in need of forgiveness. See above chapter 5.

[42] Hans Urs von Balthasar, *The Glory of the Lord: A Theological Aesthetics*, vol VII, translated by Brian McNeill C.R.V. (Edinburgh: T. and T. Clark, 1989), p. 152. Balthasar notes that 'everything to do with the sacraments is handed over without defences to human misuse'.

his journey from the wilderness to the house of his 'Father' – recapitulates, retells, the journey of God's chosen children from slavery to new life: the coming forth of God's servant Israel. The story of Christ is the retelling of God bringing forth God's people, from death to new life through parted waters.

This retelling and remembering of Israel by Jesus, of a people's history by one person's life, is not a representation but a presentation. This means that though it is a retelling it is also a new story, a second story, a story changed from the first, that changes the first. And this changing is true also when the story of Jesus is, in its turn repeated and retold by those who come after him. Stories are always told, and telling is always retelling, and retelling changes the story. Each telling is singular.

Christ's retelling of the Law and the Prophets opens the story out, sends it in a new unforeseen direction, gives it a new unforeseen meaning. Retelling is not a closing but an opening, and this opening – actually, concretely, historically – was and is an opening to the Church. The story of the Church is the third story, and it may have only just begun. Thus, though we can be telling the story of the Church – in our chronicles and histories, in our books, reports and memos, our prognostications, projections and proposals – we cannot 'tell it as it is'. That waits upon a future retelling. For the Church – which is the retelling of Christ's story – will, in its turn, be an opening out to another story, another retelling. And that retelling will truly 'tell it as it is'.

But here and now, in this place and time – in place and time – we have three stories only, of which the second retells the first and foretells the third; just as the first foretells the second and, through the second, the third; and the third retells the other two, first and second. The third story not only tells the other two, it alone makes possible their telling. If it were not told, if it were not now being told, the other stories would not and could not be told either. For the third story is that of the community which alone has an interest, a calling and a passion, to tell the other two stories together. In this sense the third story is the primal story, the originary tale.[43]

The Spirit is the Christ-bringer, the event or presentation that brings Christ to the world,[44] and to the Church in the breaking of the bread and the passing of the cup, and that will bring the Church, through the unfolding of its story, to the promised second meeting with its Lord at the end of time. The Spirit is the bringer of the Son to the people and of the people to the Son. Just so, the third story brings the story of Christ to the Church – in, by and with the Church – and thus to the world, and in that work brings the world to the Son. The Spirit narrates the Son, in that it is the Spirit who brings the Son to the world; the Spirit that tells of the coming of the Son, just as, and insofar as, and because, the Church – with and in the Spirit – narrates the story of the Son with the people.

Insofar as the Church tells the stories of Father and Son, one can say that the Spirit narrates Father and Son, and thus that Father and Son proceed as much from the Spirit as that the Spirit proceeds from one or both of them. There is a radical and mutual coinhering of the three stories or 'persons', the ordering of which is pragmatic upon their telling. Insofar as the Church tells the story of the Son giving the Spirit[45] – of the story of Jesus opening out into the story of the Church – one can speak of a processional indeterminacy.

One can tell the stories of Father, Son and Spirit in different directions, and thus speak of their radical dependence upon one another, of their coinhering and internarrativity, their mutual entailment and telling. There is a dynamic to trinitarian story-telling, an omni-directionality of narrative movement. It is when one tries to restrict this motion that the Christian doctrine of God becomes distorted; that, for example, the place of the Spirit in the overall story becomes

[43] One might say that Judaism also tells the first story of Israel but not the second of Jesus as the Christ. But the Church's first story is different from Judaism's, precisely because it is linked to the story of Jesus as the Christ. It is a mistake to think the Hebrew Bible the same as the Christian 'Old Testament'. They are different texts because the products of different readings; different linkages.

[44] Luke 1.35. [45] John 20.22.

problematic, or that it becomes difficult to see how the event of God can be other than a moment in the past, remembered in the present.

To begin to imagine how one can break down the fixed construct of procession in the Trinity so that one can speak of the procession of Father and Son from the Spirit as much as of the Spirit from Father and/or Son, is to begin to imagine a radical trinitarian theology, one that does not smuggle in a substantial monism under the primacy or basicality of the Father.

The ordering or *taxis* of the (immanent) Trinity is indeterminate because the stories of the (economic) Trinity can be told in different ways. One can tell of the procession of the Spirit from the Father ('the Counsellor, the Holy Spirit, who the Father will send . . . '),[46] and of the Spirit from the Son ('I will send him to you . . . '),[47] and of the Spirit from the Father and the Son;[48] but one can also tell of the procession of the Son from the Father ('As the Father has sent me'),[49] and of the Son from the Spirit ('And the Holy Spirit will come upon you . . . '),[50] as well as of the Son from the Father and the Spirit;[51] and one can also tell of the procession of (our knowledge and love of) the Father from the Spirit ('When the Spirit of truth comes, he will guide you into all the truth . . . '),[52] as well as of (our knowledge of and love of) the Father from the Son ('I have given them the words which thou gavest me . . . '),[53] and from the Spirit and the Son.[54] Indeed, it is not just our knowledge and love of the Father that comes from the Son and the Spirit, but the relation of Son and Spirit to the Father that constitutes the Father as such. As Janet Martin Soskice reminds us, 'Father' is a semantically dependent term. It is because there is first a daughter or son that there is a father. The 'Father is Father in virtue of the Son – because it is the child who "makes" someone a father. . . . In this telling of

[46] John 14.26.
[47] John 16.7. [48] John 14.26 and 16.7.
[49] John 20.21. [50] Luke 1.35
[51] John 20.21 and Luke 1.35. [52] John 16.13
[53] John 17.8. [54] John 16.13 and 17.8.

the economy the Father, too, "is born" – or better, "becomes Father" – with the Son, and in the Spirit'.[55] Thus it is not necessary to speak of an ordering below or subordination in the stories or persons of the Trinity.[56] Nor is it necessary to hold to or not hold to the *Filioque*. What is necessary is that we learn to move more freely, more adventurously, in the stories of God.

THREE STORIES OF ONE COMMUNITY

There are three stories, of which the third encompasses the other two by retelling them or relating them one to another. Yet the third story, which, if one likes, stages the others (as the historical and narratorial precondition of their possibility), follows on from them. Thus all three stories are inter-constitutive of one another. This is possible because they are the stories of a community which reads, tells, acts and performs them, and that is, in turn, constituted by them, just as they are by it. So it is not possible to think the community without the stories or they without it, or one story without the others.

There are three stories, and together they constitute the threefold story of God. They are the stories of God with God's people, the stories of Father, Son and Spirit. They are the stories of the economic or revealed Trinity. They are the reason for any talk of Trinity at all. It is the experience of God with God's people, as Father, Son and Spirit, that impels the trinitarian naming, and that naming is the only and sufficient reason for the threefold telling of God. It is, as Cappadocian theology might have it, the one action, the one work, the one relation, the one event – of God with the people, of God loving the people, of, quite simply, God creating the people – that the three stories narrate. It is in the differences of the stories, and

[55] Janet Martin Soskice, 'Trinity and "the feminine other"', *New Blackfriars*, 75 (1994), 2–17 (p. 11).

[56] Compare *The Forgotten Trinity I: The Report of the BCC Study Commission on Trinitarian Doctrine Today* (British Council of Churches, 1989), p. 33.

in the different names of God in those stories, that there is found the one and only reason for distinguishing Father, Son and Spirit in the one work of God's creation.

It is the one action of God and the stories about it that matter, and not the names of God within those stories. 'Father', 'Son' and 'Spirit' are hallowed by tradition, but by the same token they are rendered contingent, ambiguous and shifting in meaning. Tradition is the historical performance of the third story, and it is still being performed, even now. Nothing is stable, all is open: the Spirit moves and breathes where the Spirit will.

Some have argued that to change the Christian name of God – 'Father, Son and Spirit' – is to turn away from God. Thus Alvin Kimel writes that the 'triune God has named himself, and he likes his name . . . Father, Son and Holy Spirit is our deity's *proper name*.'[57] Thus to name the triune God 'Creator, Redeemer and Sustainer/Sanctifier' or 'Creator, Christ and Holy Spirit' or 'Abba, Servant and Paraclete' or 'Producer, Appearance and Peace', is to name God improperly.[58] But to name God in these ways is to name God in the story of God, to remember by their absence all of God's other names; and to remember, by this proliferation and profligacy of names, that naming is political and that God does not have a proper name. 'God' is not a proper name.[59] It, along with all the others, is but one of the names that Christians, for want of something better, have used and use to talk about, and talk to, that which they take to be the true subject of the stories they tell, perform and make. It is when one turns away from these stories that one turns away from God. And these

57 Alvin F. Kimel, 'The God who likes his name: Holy Trinity, feminism, and the language of faith', *Interpretation*, 45 (1991), 147–58 (pp. 147–9). On this matter see in the same issue of *Interpretation* the contrasting views of Geoffrey Wainwright ('The doctrine of the Trinity: where the Church stands or falls', 117–32) and Susan Brooks Thistelwaite ('On the Trinity', 159–71).

58 The naming of the triune mystery as 'Producer, Appearance and Peace' is from Nicholas Lash, *Believing Three Ways in One God: A Reading of the Apostles' Creed* (London: SCM Press, 1992), p. 35.

59 See Nicholas Lash, '"Son of God": reflections on a metaphor', in *Theology on the Way to Emmaus* (London: SCM Press, 1986), pp. 158–66.

are stories about the retelling, renaming and reimagining of God.

It is possible to understand the doctrine of the Trinity as the pattern that allows the Church to construe the story of God aright. Three-in-one is the pattern that enables the Church to see that three stories are one story without thereby ceasing to be three stories. Through the doctrine of the Trinity, the stories of Yahweh, Jesus and the Church can be dramatically read and enacted as the one story of God-with-us. The doctrine is the '"summary grammar" of the pedagogy of salvation' by which the Church comes to appropriately work, think and worship.[60]

The classic statement of the doctrine of the Trinity as three persons of one substance may be understood, following George Lindbeck, as the rule of the Church's reading and telling of God's story; the regulation of the Church's constantly renewed performance, in its sacramental and social life, of the story of God and of God's people.[61] One may give the rule as three persons of one substance or as the pattern of three stories of one community. This rule or pattern, it may be suggested, is what has traditionally gone under the designation of the essential or immanent Trinity, and it stands to the doctrine of the economic Trinity as stage direction to performance.

Thus the Church is the community that is called to stage the Trinity, to be the presentation of that which, as Rowan Williams puts it, 'the Church intends to make present, as authoritative point of judgement and the resource for action in hope, in its corporate action, that action which is specific to it as Church.'[62] That action which is the enactment of the three stories of God in and by the one community.

Every telling of a story is a telling of a story changed from that told before. Every telling is singular (the same and

[60] Nicholas Lash, 'Considering the Trinity', *Modern Theology*, 2 (1986), 183–96 (p. 194).

[61] George Lindbeck, *The Nature of Doctrine: Religion and Theology in a Postliberal Age* (London: SPCK, 1984), pp. 92–6.

[62] Rowan Williams, 'The literal sense of Scripture', *Modern Theology*, 7 (1991), 121–34 (p. 130).

another). The telling or performing of a story constitutes a situation, an event, which is always singular in the 'pragmatics of its occurrence'.[63] There is thus a weight and burden to the telling of the story, which is to be judged not so much in terms of descriptive fidelity as in terms of fidelity of performance, a fidelity to the singularity of the present moment.

In this chapter I have sought to suggest how it is possible to understand the Christian doctrine of God – the doctrine of the Trinity – as the means by which the Church positions itself within the stories it writes and tells and by which it is written and told. It is by its doctrine of God that the Church is able to perform its stories, stories which are themselves, told and in the telling, the continuing event of God, the 'In the name of the Father and of the Son and of the Holy Spirit' addressed by the people to the One whose loved and created people they are. It is a doctrine which governs not so much the writing of the Trinity as its performance.

[63] Readings, *Introducing Lyotard*, p. xxiii.

CHAPTER 7

Only love

Wittgenstein once wrote: 'Only love can believe the Resurrection'.

If I am to be REALLY saved what I need is faith. And faith is faith in what is needed by my heart, my soul, not by my speculative intelligence. For it is my soul with its passions, as it were with its flesh and blood, that has to be saved, not my abstract mind.[1]

Only the way of love leads the heart – flesh and blood – to salvation. Speculation is of no use. Yet speculation, the exercise of the abstract mind, has long been thought the only way to a true and certain knowledge of Christ and the promise of salvation in his name. This was the interest of Enlightenment rationality, which sought to validate, and later refute, Christian themes at the bar of positivist reason.[2] The intent was to render the reasonableness of the Christian story, and in this endeavour history played a large part. The critical historian insisted that before faith could get to work, the historical intelligence must reconstruct what really happened – at the first Easter as elsewhere. Only then could faith play its part.

Enlightenment objectivism still has force today.[3] The

[1] Ludwig Wittgenstein, *Culture and Value* (Oxford: Basil Blackwell, 1980), p. 33e.

[2] For a brief account see Claude Welch, *Protestant Thought in the Nineteenth Century*, vol. I, 1799–1870 (New Haven and London: Yale University Press, 1972), pp. 30–51.

[3] See Jon D. Levenson, *The Hebrew Bible, the Old Testament, and Historical Criticism: Jews and Christians in Biblical Studies* (Louisville, Kentucky: Westminster/John Knox Press, 1993) and Stanley Hauerwas, *Unleashing the Scripture: Freeing the Bible from Captivity to America* (Nashville, Tennessee: Abingdon Press, 1993).

reasonable person must establish the historicity of the resurrection as a deduction from the historical data. She must establish its plausibility as a sufficient cause for the Church's proclamation of the risen Christ. Hugo Meynell argues that Christianity stands or falls by the truth of certain historical propositions that can be tested by 'an objective investigation which does not presuppose a conclusion one way or the other'.

To put it rather brutally, for a 'Christianity' without historical truth-conditions, and hence without liability in principle to falsification by historical investigation, whether Jesus Christ is the redeemer of humankind is not an all-important question of fact, but a relatively trivial one of temperament and taste.[4]

Not only is this a rather brutal way of putting the question, it too easily avoids its difficulty. It assumes that the concept of historical fact is unproblematic, untainted by hermeneutics.[5] And indeed, a naive positivism may be serviceable if used of questions regarding what Jesus said, and even of some of the things he did and underwent. But it is of little use with regard to whether Jesus healed the sick or raised the dead, or himself returned to his disciples from the tomb. As we are reminded by Walter Kasper, these are matters that 'objective investigation' – which is far from neutral – cannot corroborate.

People today will consider something historically true and real, if it is demonstrated to be historically credible and at least basically capable of objective verification: *Verum quod factum*. More precisely,

[4] Hugo A. Meynell, 'Faith, objectivity, and historical falsifiability', in *Language, Meaning and God: Essays in Honour of Herbert McCabe OP*, edited by Brian Davies OP (London: Geoffrey Chapman, 1987), pp. 145–61 (p. 146).

[5] 'I do not think that the concept "fact" is theory-neutral. I do not think that the concept "probability" is theory-neutral . . . If I am asked to use the language of factuality, then I would say, yes, in those terms, I have to speak of an empty tomb. In those terms I have to speak of the literal resurrection. But I think those terms are not privileged, theory-neutral, trans-cultural, an ingredient in the structure of the human mind and of reality always and everywhere' (Hans Frei, *Theology and Narrative: Selected Essays*, edited by George Hunsinger and William C. Placher (New York and Oxford: Oxford University Press, 1993), p. 211).

historical phenomena are understood in context and by analogy with other events. Where this understanding of factual reality is absolute, there is no place for the reality of the resurrection, which cannot be explained by reference to context or by analogy with the rest of reality.[6]

Historical positivism recognises only mutually analogous events. An event without analogy cannot register, and the resurrection is such an event. 'It pierces our whole world of living and dying in a unique way so that, through this breakthrough, it may open a path for us into the everlasting life of God.'[7] If we are to find a way to the resurrection we must go otherwise than by historical rationality: we must trust to the gospel story.[8] For it is by incorporation into the story of God's incarnate love that the heart finds its way to saving faith in what the story narrates: the risen life of Jesus Christ.

The second half of this chapter explores what it means to be incorporated into the story of the risen Christ, offering a narrativist construal of soteriological doctrine, of redemption and salvation. The first half of the chapter, however, considers the Church's knowledge of the event from which its life flows – the resurrection of Jesus Christ – attending in the first instance to the form of the resurrection story. For story, resurrection and incorporation are all part of the one economy of salvation.[9]

[6] Walter Kasper, *Jesus the Christ*, translated by V. Green (London: Burns and Oates, 1976), p. 130.

[7] Hans Urs von Balthasar, *Mysterium Paschale*, translated by Aidan Nichols OP (Edinburgh: T. and T. Clark, 1990), p. 194. The dilemma for analogous history writing is nowhere better stated than in Frances Young's 'conundrum': 'If Jesus was an entirely normal human being, no evidence can be produced for the incarnation. If no evidence can be produced, there can be no basis on which to claim that an incarnation took place.' Frances Young, 'Can there be any evidence?', in *Incarnation and Myth: The Debate Continued*, edited by Michael Goulder (London: SCM Press, 1979), p. 62.

[8] That the Church can trust the gospel story was the burden of chapters 4 and 5 above.

[9] For an account of this ancient theme of the *salus carnis* in Irenaeus see Basil Studer, *Trinity and Incarnation: The Faith of the Early Church*, translated by Matthias

READING FOR THE FORM

The historical intelligence has little respect for the integrity of the biblical witness, for the cadence of its story. It treats the gospel narratives as testaments of faith that must be rewritten in order to produce a neutral non-prejudiced account, the original narratives having been dismembered, some parts discarded and the remaining reordered in a rational manner. The form of the gospel story is thus destroyed and another put in its place.

But it is only by reading for the form of the story that one can hope to come to belief in the resurrection. For then the narratives are no longer read as a collection of conflicting evidence waiting for a theological Miss Marple to investigate and reveal who did what, when and where. Narratives that would be otherwise dismissed as so many 'red herrings' are given their due place in the overall story. The narratives of the resurrection are no longer in need of harmonisation, either by a refusal to see the differences, or by a criticism that, seeing the differences, chooses to tell another story. Rather the differences are constitutive of the story they tell. Unlike the critical historian, the Church must read for the form: for the story of the narratives. Hans Urs von Balthasar suggests that the clue to this understanding is given in the gospel's fourfold form – which is perhaps a 'little divine humour, a little divine irony' at the expense of the historians and their reconstructions.

This would suggest that the unique and divine plasticity of the living, incarnate Word could not be witnessed to other than through this system of perspectives which, although it cannot be further synthesised, compensates for this by offering a stereoscopic vista. And the divine irony would further suggest that the main fruits to be gathered from the very unfruitfulness and failure of the scientific experiment would be the ever clearer exigency of returning to the

Westerhoff and edited by Andrew Louth (Edinburgh: T. and T. Clark, 1993), pp. 55–64.

one thing necessary. We must return to the primary contemplation of what is *really* said, really presented to us, really meant.[10]

Balthasar further reminds us that the form of the gospel story comes from the event of the resurrection, which formed the early Church's understanding of everything that led to and away from it. For the resurrection was the light by which everything was illumined, the centre around which there gradually gathered a collection of images – including 'resurrection' and 'restoration to life' – that serve to mark but not describe the mystery. 'The images surround an inaccessible mid-point which alone has the magnetic force to arrange around itself, in concentric fashion, the image-garland.'[11] These images, as also the narratives in which they function, do not form an 'objective unity', and therefore do not mislead us into supposing that we could grasp the nature of the event that is their centre.

It is because the resurrection event is what it is that the gospel narratives are not perspicuous descriptions. The resurrection bursts apart 'profane narration', confronting 'exegetes with problems never fully soluble'. It 'engenders a multiplicity of human attempts to express it',[12] transforming all available categories and forcing the Church to reimagine both past and future.

In the event of the resurrection all previous schemata come to fulfilment and suffer their breakdown at one and the same time. They have to be used in preaching, but the very fact of their cumulative employment shows that each is powerless to contribute more than a fragment to a totality of a transcendent kind. 'What the disciples proclaimed goes beyond the limits of the thinkable.'[13]

[10] Hans Urs von Balthasar, *The Glory of the Lord: A Theological Aesthetics*, 7 vols., edited by Joseph Fessio SJ and John Riches (Edinburgh: T. and T. Clark, 1982–1991), vol. 1: Seeing the Form, p. 32.

[11] Balthasar, *Mysterium Paschale*, p. 200.

[12] Balthasar, *Mysterium Paschale*, p. 191.

[13] Balthasar, *Mysterium Paschale*, p. 198; quoting G. Koch, *Die Auferstehung Jesu Christi* (Tübingen, 1965), p. 53.

SEEING AND SAYING THE MYSTERY

The philosopher Martin Heidegger (1889–1976) – according to Paul de Man (1909–1983) – thought the poet Friedrich Hölderlin (1770–1843) the one person who had seen and 'named the immediate presence of Being'.[14]

> The poet . . . has seen Being as it truly is. He finds himself in the absolute presence of Being, he has been struck by the Heraclitean bolt of lightning of truth, henceforth he will no longer name the deceitful mask that Being presents to the metaphysician, but its authentic face. 'But now day breaks! I waited and I saw it coming/ And what I saw, the Holy be my word.'[15]

What is for de Man and Heidegger a question of Being is perhaps for Hölderlin a question of God – supposing these to be different questions.[16] Thus for Hans Urs von Balthasar, what the poet 'risks his whole existence for, is the presence, indeed, the urgency of an infinite love in the mystery of the world's being.'[17] But whether 'Being' or 'God', it is here the question of how to say the presence of the mystery that both comes and withdraws in the present of the existent; and, when adapted, the question of saying the One whose presence in the death of Christ raises him to life.

[14] Paul de Man, *Blindness and Insight: Essays in the Rhetoric of Contemporary Criticism*, second edition (London: Methuen and Co. Ltd, 1983), p. 252. On de Man's reading of Heidegger and Hölderlin see Christopher Norris, *Paul de Man: Deconstruction and the Critique of Aesthetic Ideology* (London: Routledge, 1988), pp. 11–17; and Ortwin de Graef, *Serenity in Crisis: A Preface to Paul de Man, 1939–1960* (Lincoln and London: University of Nebraska Press, 1993), pp. 94–8. Here, I am not so much concerned with de Man's exegesis as with the opportunity it affords to articulate a triadic structure by which to understand the Church's knowledge of the ineffable mystery of God in the death and resurrection of Jesus Christ through narrative.

[15] de Man, *Blindness and Insight*, p. 251; adapted.

[16] See further below chapter 8.

[17] Hans Urs von Balthasar, 'Hölderlin', in *Glory of the Lord*, vol. v, pp. 298–338 (p. 311). On Balthasar's reading of Hölderlin see Martin Simon, 'Identity and analogy: Balthasar's Hölderlin and Hamann', in *The Analogy of Beauty: The Theology of Hans Urs von Balthasar*, edited by John Riches (Edinburgh: T. and T. Clark, 1986), pp. 77–104.

How are we to shore up our remembrance of authentic Being so that we can find our way back to it? This *Fund*, this find, it must be somewhere; if it had never revealed itself, how could we speak of its presence? But here is someone – Hölderlin – who tells us that he has seen it, and that, moreover, he can speak of it, name it, and describe it; he has visited Being, and Being has told him some things that he has collected and that he is bringing back to mankind . . . Hölderlin knows Being immediately and he says it immediately; the commentator need only know how to listen. The work is there, itself a parousia. Being speaks through Hölderlin's mouth as God did through the mouth of the seer Calchas in the *Iliad*.[18]

But here Heidegger must ignore the fact that for Hölderlin such a naming is impossible. *'Hölderlin says exactly the opposite of what Heidegger makes him say.'*[19] Yes, Hölderlin has 'seen' Being/God.

In the lightning of the late poetry the entire cosmic theophany, which in the early and middle period has its centre in the whispering aethereal spirit, becomes compressed into the Platonic-apocalyptic moment of discharge. It is a road leading from the immediacy of an inspiration with its pulse in Nature's rhythm (with which it must therefore always die and be reborn), passing through the endurance of divine distance 'when 'tis over, and the Day extinguished', even to the experience of God in this selfsame darkness, as lightning.[20]

[18] de Man, *Blindness and Insight*, p. 253.

[19] de Man, *Blindness and Insight*, pp. 254–5. For de Man this reversal is the deep reason – beyond nationalism – that justifies Heidegger's choice of Hölderlin as the person who has seen and said Being. For in reversing Hölderlin, Heidegger nevertheless manages to speak about the same thing as the poet, though in reverse – and this is a 'major achievement . . . in a dialogue of this sort' (p. 255). As a number of writers have shown, Heidegger's myth-making relies upon just such reversals and exclusions. See Jacques Derrida, *Of Spirit: Heidegger and the Question*, translated by Geoffrey Bennington and Rachel Bowlby (Chicago: University of Chicago Press, 1989) and John D. Caputo, *Demythologising Heidegger* (Bloomington and Indianapolis: Indiana University Press, 1993), pp. 169–85.

[20] Balthasar, *Glory of the Lord*, vol. v, p. 314. What has Hölderlin seen? For de Man, 'Hölderlin says that, guided by Nature, he has seen the Holy. He does not say that he has seen God, but indeed the essence of the divine, the Holy, which transcends the gods as Being transcends beings. We may well grant Heidegger that we are indeed dealing with what he calls Being. The poet, faithful disciple of Being, is privileged because he is called upon to see it in its wondrous all-presence' (*Blindness and Insight*, p. 258).

But the poet cannot say what he has seen. For Hölderlin the 'anguishing question' of poetry is how to say Being;[21] but it remains a question. That which Heidegger thinks the poet achieves is that which the poet desires, and for which he prays, but which he does not accomplish.

'And what I saw, the Holy be my word.' He does not say: the Holy *is* my word. The subjunctive is here really an optative; it indicates prayer, it marks desire, and these lines state the eternal poetic intention, but immediately state also that it can be no more than intention. It is not because he has seen Being that the poet is, therefore, capable of naming it; his word prays for the parousia, it does not establish it. It cannot establish it for as soon as the word is uttered, it destroys the immediate and discovers that instead of stating Being, it can only state mediation.[22]

This problem is central for the saying of the Christian mysteries, not least the resurrection. The critical historian also wishes to say the truth, name the mystery. But insofar as she succeeds, she fails. For if nothing else, the canonical narratives teach that what they tell cannot be said; only believed in love. They offer a set of perplexing narratives whose differences defeat any attempt to otherwise render, simply and surely, the event of Christ's rising. They tell of Christ's return to his disciples – among the trees of the garden, on the road to Emmaus, in the locked room, by the lake shore[23] – and before that of the empty tomb; but of its emptying they say nothing. Some see the risen Christ but do not believe; whilst others believe who have not seen. Some seeing is unseeing, and vice versa. What has happened here? We have the signifiers but not the signified.

De Man tells us that for Heidegger the immediate can come to expression only because it is finally identifiable with

[21] de Man, *Blindness and Insight*, p. 256.

[22] de Man, *Blindness and Insight*, pp. 258–9; adapted.

[23] Respectively: John 20.11–18; Luke 24.13–35; John 20.19–29 and 21.1–23.

mediation, as that in which mediation has its possibility. Heidegger, on this reading, identifies the immediate (Being) with that which intercedes (language).

That which was ever present in all things gathers all isolated presents in a single presence and intercedes to allow each thing to manifest itself. Immediate all-presence is the power that intercedes for all that must be manifested through intercession, that is for all mediate things. But the immediate, it can never be mediated; rigorously speaking, the immediate is the intercession, that is the mediate character of the mediate, because it permits mediation in its being.[24]

De Man finds Heidegger's argument 'contradictory'. While it is correct that the 'immediate contains the possibility of the mediation of the mediate because it permits it in its being', it is not correct to say that 'the immediate *is*, therefore, itself the mediating intercession'.[25] In other words, while Being permits mediation – because it permits that which mediates – it is not itself that mediation. Adapted to the resurrection, however, we must say that while the resurrection permits its mediation through the gospel narratives, it remains other than those narratives.

With Heidegger we must affirm the identification of the immediate, not with the mediate, but with mediation ('mediating intercession'). Thematising the matter with regard to the resurrection it is necessary to distinguish between the (immediate) object of belief – the resurrection of the Lord; the mediate form of that object – the gospel narratives; and the mediation of the object in the form – the Church's reading of Scripture. It is this threefold structure that permits the identification and distinction of object and mediate.

The gospel narratives do not give us the resurrection, they do not in themselves lay before us the reality of Christ's risen life. Yet there is a discourse, or better, a performance in which

[24] Heidegger quoted in de Man, *Blindness and Insight*, p. 260.

[25] de Man, *Blindness and Insight*, p. 260.

the risen life of the Lord is manifested, a performance in which that life is identified with its mediation. This is the practice of prayer in which the Church reads the Scripture. It is a discursive practice made possible by the Spirit given at Pentecost; a participation in the Son's prayer to the Father. The identification of the immediate with its mediation in the mediate is therefore trinitarian; an identification that contains within it the trinitarian distinctions.

The ineffable mystery of God's life in the death of Christ – so that Christ is risen and returned to his disciples – is mediated through the gospel narratives in the reading of the Church. When the faithful gather to hear and receive the Word, to tell again the story of God's redeeming life in the death of the Son, they come to faithful knowledge of Christ's risen life because that life is present to them in their prayerful gathering. Through the Spirit, Christ reads and prays with his Church, a co-reading that Christ himself establishes.[26] This is the way of love to knowledge of Christ's identity as the one who was dead but is now alive, now and for ever more.

As we have seen (in chapter 3 above), the gospel narratives render the identity of Jesus Christ as the one who enacted our redemption through obedience to God.[27] But the identity of Christ is incomplete without the story of his resurrection. 'He was what he did and underwent: the crucified human saviour.'[28] But he was also the one who was raised from the dead. '*The identity of the crucified Jesus and that of the risen Lord are one and the same in the accounts.*'[29] It is this aspect of the accounts – that the one who was dead is the one who is risen – that leads Hans Frei to develop an Anselmian 'argument' for the resurrection of Jesus.[30]

26 Luke 24.13–35. 27 Frei, *Theology and Narrative*, p. 51.

28 Frei, *Theology and Narrative*, p. 57. 29 Frei, *Theology and Narrative*, p. 58.

30 See further Kevin J. Vanhoozer, *Biblical Narrative in the Philosophy of Paul Ricoeur: A Study in Hermeneutics and Theology* (Cambridge: Cambridge University Press, 1990), pp. 163–4.

WHY DO YOU LOOK FOR THE LIVING AMONG THE DEAD?[31]

For Frei, the identity of Jesus as a 'singular, unsubstitutable human individual' comes to its 'sharpest focus in the death-and-resurrection sequence taken as one unbroken sequence.'[32] 'As a character in a story we know him far better here than in the earlier parts of the story.'[33] The resurrection story manifests Christ's identity more clearly than earlier parts of the story, in which it was possible to give different answers to Jesus' own question: 'Who do people say that I am?'[34] But in the story of the resurrection Jesus is manifested as 'who he is, the one who as the unsubstitutable human being, Jesus of Nazareth, is not a myth but the presence of God and saviour of men.'[35]

Whereas the narratives of the crucifixion focus on what Jesus did and was done to him, but leave his identity ambiguous ('Are you the king of the Jews?');[36] the resurrection narratives focus on his identity but leave ambiguous God's action in and for Jesus. 'Something does indeed take place in the resurrection, but it is not described and doubtless cannot be described . . . The foreground and the stress in the resurrection belong not to the action of God but to its confirmation of Jesus' identity. It is he who is present and none other when God is active. Jesus alone is manifested.'[37]

The form of the story holds together crucifixion and resurrection, ascribing both to the one individual, who is what he does and undergoes on the cross and in his return to the disciples as the presence of God. 'The two forms, in their dramatic transition, constitute a unity. In both one may say, "here he was most of all himself" and mean by this expression

[31] Luke 24.5. [32] Frei, *Theology and Narrative*, p. 59.
[33] Frei, *Theology and Narrative*, p. 60.
[34] Mark 8.27.
[35] Frei, *Theology and Narrative*, p. 74.
[36] Matthew 27.11; Mark 15.2; Luke 23.3 and John 19.33.
[37] Frei, *Theology and Narrative*, pp. 75–6.

not a mythological figure but the specific man named Jesus of Nazareth.'[38]

The story of the resurrection resolves ambiguity concerning the identity of Jesus. On the road to Emmaus Jesus himself retells the story of Israel so as to reveal the identity of God's Christ, recognised by the disciples in the breaking of the bread.[39] But now we must consider the identity that Luke's story itself serves to establish: Jesus as the person who was dead and *is* risen – the one whose non-resurrection is inconceivable. 'The Lord has risen indeed, and he has appeared to Simon!'[40]

In a sense the synoptic gospel writers are saying something like this: 'Our argument is that to grasp what *this* identity, Jesus of Nazareth, is, is to believe that, in fact, he has been raised from the dead. Someone may reply that in that case the most perfectly depicted character, the most nearly-life-like fictional identity ought also in fact to live a factual historical life. We answer that the argument holds good only in this one and absolutely unique case where the described identity is *totally* identical with his factual existence. He is the resurrection and the life; how can he be conceived as not resurrected?[41]

To understand the identity of Jesus as given in the gospel story is to understand that he is alive now, that indeed he is life itself: 'I am the resurrection and the life'.[42] 'To conceive of him as dead is not to conceive of him at all.'

He lives as the one who cannot not live, for whom to be what he is, is to be. But who or what he thus is, is unambiguously Jesus of Nazareth; and as Jesus he is the Son of man, the one whose history,

[38] Frei, *Theology and Narrative*, p. 76. Of the resurrection story Frei makes a point that he makes more generally of the gospel story, that it is not so much a mythological tale as a realistic narrative, for it is related of an unsubstitutable individual, a particular person enacting a particular life-story. Identifying the resurrected saviour figure with the particular individual Jesus demythologises the saviour myth, and opens the possibility that the story of Jesus is true in fact (Frei, *Theology and Narrative*, p. 75).

[39] Luke 24.13–35. [40] Luke 24.34.

[41] Frei, *Theology and Narrative*, p. 83. [42] John 11.25.

whose being as self-enactment in his unique circumstances it was to be delivered into the hands of sinful men, to be crucified, and to rise again . . . Who and what he is, what he did and underwent, and that he is, are all one and the same.[43]

If you know who Jesus is then you know that he is risen; if you don't know that he is risen you don't know who he is. That Jesus is risen from the dead is analytic of his identity in the gospel narratives. Therefore to understand his identity is to understand that he lives, and is now the presence of God to the Church. As with Anselm's identification of God as that-than-which-no-greater-can-be-thought, Frei's gospel identification of Jesus as he-who-cannot-not-live, is only an argument to the truth of the resurrection for faith. All it can mean for people without faith is that if they think Jesus was someone who died nearly two thousand years ago and that was the end of him, the end of his story, then they are not thinking of the singular individual identified in the gospel narratives. They are thinking of someone else, a character in another story. But this does not mean that to understand the identity of Jesus in the gospel story is to have faith in him; for faith is finding one's own story in his.[44]

The way of love to belief in the resurrection is threefold: Christ, narrative and faith folded upon one another – unfolded in the Church's performance of the story. Frei's Anselmian reflection serves to remind the Church that through the Spirit it comes to belief in the crucified and risen Christ who is with the Church through the Spirit, given in the Church's performance of his story. How Jesus comes to the Church in the eucharistic meal is the theme of the next chapter, but the rest of this chapter considers how incorporation into the Church's performance constitutes salvation as sharing in Christ's resurrection.

43 Frei, *Theology and Narrative*, p. 85.

44 See Kenneth Surin, *The Turnings of Darkness and Light: Essays in Philosophical and Systematic Theology* (Cambridge: Cambridge University Press, 1989), pp. 209–10.

ENFOLDING SIN

The story of Jesus is that of the risen saviour, the person whose life and death redeems humanity from slavery to sin. But how is this accomplished? How is the story of this man at the same time the story of human salvation? For on the face of it, his life and death have hardly accomplished what they are said to have done. Sin and death are everywhere apparent and peace is never more than a passing cessation of hostilities.

According to Michael Root, soteriology presumes the 'sufficient conditions' for narrative: 'two states and an event that transforms the first into the second'. The first state is that of sin, the second release from sin or salvation, and the transforming event that leads from one to the other is Jesus Christ. Soteriology is thus concerned to explain how the narrative transition from the first to the second state is achieved; in short, how 'Jesus saves'.[45]

A narrative soteriology suggests that salvation is not simply illustrated, but constituted by the story of Jesus. Salvation consists in establishing a *storied* relation between Jesus and those who are saved. They are included within his story, and it is this entering or enfolding in the story that constitutes salvation.[46] The task of soteriology is to elucidate this narrative enfolding.

Here we must recall again the idea that a person's identity has a narrative form, that a human 'self' is constituted by story. We have already encountered such an idea in discussing the work of Stephen Crites (chapter 3 above) and Jean-François Lyotard (chapter 6 above). It is also a theme in the work of Alasdair MacIntyre, for whom selfhood 'resides in the unity of a narrative which links birth to life to death as

[45] Michael Root, 'The narrative structure of soteriology', in *Why Narrative? Readings in Narrative Theology*, edited by Stanley Hauerwas and L. Gregory Jones (Grand Rapids, Michigan: William B. Eerdmans Publishing Company, 1989), pp. 263–78 (pp. 263–4). My discussion of salvation as enfoldment within the story of Jesus owes much to Root's essay, but my stress on the ecclesial constitution of the story is more closely in line with the theologies of Kenneth Surin and John Milbank.

[46] Root, 'Narrative structure', p. 266.

narrative beginning to middle to end.'[47] For MacIntyre, human actions are intelligible only in relation to intentions. 'To identify an occurrence as an action is in the paradigmatic instances to identify it under a type of description which enables us to see that occurrence as flowing intelligibly from a human agent's intentions, motives, passions and purposes.'[48] And a human agent's 'intentions, motives, passions and purposes', must in turn be situated within settings that render them intelligible, both to the agent and to others.[49] Such settings are various, ranging from discrete practices to institutions, but they will have histories.

> We place the agent's intentions . . . in causal and temporal order with reference to their role in his or her history; and we also place them with reference to their role in the history of the setting or settings to which they belong . . . Narrative history of a certain kind turns out to be the basic and essential genre for the characterization of human actions.[50]

MacIntyre suggests that human lives are, or are made of, enacted narratives. 'It is because we all live out narratives in our lives and because we understand our own lives in terms of the narratives that we live out that the form of narrative is appropriate for understanding the actions of others. Stories are lived before they are told – except in the case of fiction.'[51] Against those who would argue that human lives are narratives only in fiction,[52] MacIntyre insists that human life has intelligibility only insofar as we perceive ourselves to be actors

[47] Alasdair MacIntyre, *After Virtue: A Study in Moral Theory*, second edition (London: Duckworth, 1985), p. 205.

[48] MacIntyre, *After Virtue*, p. 209.

[49] MacIntyre, *After Virtue*, p. 206.

[50] MacIntyre, *After Virtue*, p. 208.

[51] MacIntyre, *After Virtue*, p. 212. MacIntyre quotes Barbara Hardy in support: 'we dream in narrative, day-dream in narrative, remember, anticipate, hope, despair, believe, doubt, plan, revise, criticize, construct, gossip, learn, hate and love by narrative'. 'Towards a poetics of fiction: an approach through narrative', *Novel*, 2 (1968), 5–14 (p. 5).

[52] See Louis O. Mink, 'History and fiction as modes of comprehension', *New Literary History*, 1 (1970), 541–58 (pp. 557–8).

in some narrative or other. We are never the sole authors of our narratives or start them at the beginning, for 'only in fantasy do we live what story we please . . . We enter upon a stage which we did not design and we find ourselves part of an action that was not of our making.'[53] But just insofar as we are actors in one or more narratives, our lives have some intelligibility; and just insofar as we author part if not all of our story, we experience freedom. Above all, it is the sense of an ending that gives meaning to our actions, and finally our lives.

> We live out our lives, both individually and in our relationships with each other, in the light of certain conceptions of a possible shared future, a future in which certain possibilities beckon us forward and others repel us, some seem already foreclosed and others perhaps inevitable. There is no present which is not informed by some image of some future and an image of the future which always presents itself in the form of a telos – or of a variety of ends or goals – towards which we are either moving or failing to move in the present.[54]

It is not just that narrative – the idea of a congruent and teleologically ordered sequence – gives meaning to human life, but that what it means to be a particular person, to have a particular identity, is to be the subject of a particular narrative. 'Personal identity is just that identity presupposed by the unity of the character which the unity of a narrative requires. Without such unity there would not be subjects of whom stories could be told.'[55] The unity of a human life is no more than the unity of the narrative enacted in that life.

MacIntyre continues his account of the narrative self in the direction of the narrative that makes for a life worth living, arguing that 'the good life for man is the life spent in seeking for the good life for man, and the virtues necessary for the seeking are those which will enable us to understand what more and what else the good life for man is.'[56] But we will not continue with him on his Aristotelian journey, since the Church believes that the 'what more and what else' for which

[53] MacIntyre, *After Virtue*, p. 213.
[54] MacIntyre, *After Virtue*, pp. 215–16.
[55] MacIntyre, *After Virtue*, p. 218.
[56] MacIntyre, *After Virtue*, p. 219.

we seek has already come to us in Jesus. The reason for going so far with MacIntyre is that the idea of selfhood as narrative, and finally as quest narrative, allows us to better understand salvation as the reordering of the subject's story by, and finally within, the story of Jesus Christ, who is the 'what more and what else' that constitutes the good for humankind.

A person's story is salvifically reordered by and within the story of Jesus just insofar as it comes to have a new *telos*, a new point and direction; or insofar as it becomes possible to think of it having a *telos*, an aim and an end which is other than extinction, for the first time. But what is this story, and how can one be said to enter it, such that it is more than an allegory of how to conduct one's life?

Here we must recall that Jesus' story is that of God's Christ who was dead but is risen. It is not just a story that culminates in the death, resurrection and ascension of Jesus, as narrated in the gospels. It is the story that continues in the history of the Church, in the life of the community to whom Christ returns always. Jesus' story is but the start of a story, which both retells his story and extends it in an indeterminate fashion, producing ever new, non-identical repetitions. For each Christian life aims to be the life of Jesus in its own circumstance. His life is the goal of the Church's life. So much is this the case, that John Milbank has suggested reading the gospels not as the story of Jesus, but as the story of the founding of 'a new kind of community, Israel-become-the-Church.'

> Jesus figures in this story simply as the founder, the beginning, the first of many. There is nothing that Jesus does that he will not enable the disciples to do: they will be able to cast out demons, heal the sick, raise the dead, forgive sins. And just as Jesus' proper source and place is not contained within this world, so also his followers are to be 'born again', and so somehow exceed their temporal origins – for if birth, like death, is not an event within life, but the opening of life, then a second birth in the midst of life must unite us, in our particular living identity, with that which opens out all life.[57]

[57] John Milbank, 'The name of Jesus: incarnation, atonement, ecclesiology', *Modern Theology*, 7 (1991), 311–33 (p. 317).

It is by entering the community of the Church that one enters the story of Jesus, and one does so through Baptism: immersion in the story. The imagery of Baptism is well known: the passage through water that is at one and the same time the death of the old and the birth of the new, recalling the passage of Israel from slavery to covenantal life through the parted waters of the sea, the passage of Jesus into his ministry through the waters of the Jordan, and finally his passage from death to life itself through deposition and entombment.[58] The baptismal water is a narrative transition that does not destroy the old story but reorders its trajectory toward a previously unforeseen end, a different unexpected *telos*. It is the new ending of the story – the promised life of the Kingdom – that reconstitutes the old story as one of sin, a story that is now seen to have had only a conditional goal, a meaning that could not satisfy, could not be the good of the person.

The Christian *telos* is paradoxical in that one moves towards it by following after. The promised life of the kingdom is already given in the person of Jesus, and it is in the practice of discipleship that the future arrives. Thus the story of Jesus is not only the beginning of the Church, but its conclusion: alpha and omega. He is both the beginning of a practice and its culmination.

> Not just the seed, but also the fully-grown tree, not just the foundation-stone but also the temple, not just the head, but also the body. Christ's full incarnate appearance lies always ahead of us – *if* we love the brethren, according to St John, *then* he will be manifested to us.[59] And in what is perhaps the original ending of Mark's gospel, the risen Christ is not recorded in his visibility, but as 'going before you to Galilee',[60] the place of the original gathering and going forth of the new community.[61]

[58] For the New Testament, Jesus is a 'new Moses, the founder of a new or renewed law and community' (Milbank, 'The name of Jesus', p. 318).

[59] John 14.18–23; 13.34.

[60] Mark 16.7.

[61] Milbank, 'The name of Jesus', p. 319.

Milbank insists that to think of Jesus as the founder of a new churchly practice is not to subordinate him to a general category, of which he is but one instance, albeit the first. 'On the contrary, the universal repeatability of Jesus is made possible by his specific historic occurrence, and this is never "dispensable" in specifying the conditions of our salvation because a genuine "foundation" is not the first instance of a general phenomenon, but rather is itself the "general", though specific, definition of that phenomenon.'[62]

The idea that the specific shape of Jesus' life is the true or good shape of every life is much the same as the idea that Jesus is the antitype of which each repetition is the type (see above chapter 2). But Milbank's stress on the 'repeatability' of Jesus allows us to better understand the idea that the story of Jesus is the story of each one of us, because it more forcibly reminds us that the story of Jesus is not complete without the story of the Church, and that therefore his story – his personhood or *persona*[63] – waits upon the eschaton for its complete narration. If Jesus is the 'source, goal and context of all our lives', we can come to know him fully only through knowledge of all our lives. 'To some extent, the observation of every human "person" follows this pattern, but only in the case of Jesus does an accurate rendering of his personhood involve an ultimate attention to everyone, in so far as their "truth" lies in Christ.'[64]

NARRATIVE WATERS

The idea of baptismal immersion as narrative enfolding is reminiscent of George Lindbeck's absorbent text: the baptised

62 Milbank, 'The name of Jesus', p. 324; adapted.

63 For Milbank, *persona*, 'personality' or 'personhood', is the 'total shape' of a person's actions and words: the story of a life in its historical context. Therefore, 'Jesus is "identical" with God, not in terms of an underlying "essence", or his general human "nature", but rather at the precise point of his irreplaceable specificity, or all that goes to make up his "personality", including his historical situation and his own response to it' (Milbank, 'The name of Jesus', p. 323). See further Bruce Marshall, *Christology in Conflict: The Identity of a Saviour in Rahner and Barth* (Oxford: Basil Blackwell, 1987), pp. 176–89.

64 Milbank, 'The name of Jesus', p. 325.

are absorbed into the waters of the biblical narrative (see chapter 2 above). But one should recall that it is better to think of absorbing the text than of being absorbed by it. This is because the text serves to give life, to refresh and invigorate, rather than to subsume and submerge its partakers. So we must stress that Baptism is entry into the story of Christ as the story of the Church; as the people who are learning to grow in the strength and shape of Christ, who are learning to live in the world as people who are not of the world, who are learning to speak a new language: the tongue of Pentecost.

The baptised come through the waters to a place established by the waters. In this place it is possible to live newly, to live toward a different end than elsewhere, to speak a different language than is spoken in other places. As Kenneth Surin stresses, Baptism is not something that simply changes one's identity by obliterating the old and installing the new. The old remains; it has made you what you are. But now it is enfolded within a new story, which by promise of a different future changes the past. What has been is no longer what has to be. Entering the Church is like starting to live in a new country, whose ways and idioms have to be learned.

> The Church is the gospel-shaped 'narrative space' where Christians learn to 'sacrifice' themselves, over and over again, to the community's narrative texts, to this 'new' language. This they do by consenting to be interrogated by these texts in such a way that they learn, slowly, laboriously and sometimes painfully, to live the way of Jesus. This interrogation – which is fundamental to the Church's 'pedagogy of discipleship' – may, depending on historical circumstances, have the consequence of actually decomposing, as opposed to reinforcing, certain already existing patterns of Christian 'identity'.[65]

The point of stressing the Christian life as one of learning how to live in a new country and speak a new language, is that it is never something accomplished, but always in process. The Church is always becoming Christ-like, always moving

[65] Surin, *Turnings of Darkness and Light*, pp. 218–19.

forward by following after. Salvation is the gift of a journey, or, as Stanley Hauerwas puts it, an adventure.[66] One has to be adventurous to advance toward the perfection of Christ, because his life is constituted in part by every life patterned upon his. Thus the Christian adventurer must also be guided by those in the Church whose lives are exemplary repetitions of Christ's: the saints.

The lives of the saints – hagiographies – are imperative narratives. Their addressees, as Edith Wyschogrod notes, are to be 'swept up' by their imperative force, their power of rekindling. 'The comprehension of a saint's life understood from within the sphere of hagiography is a *practice* through which the addressee is gathered into the narrative so as to extend and elaborate it with her/his own life.'[67] The saints themselves are already gathered into the story of Christ, which they seek to extend and elaborate, repeating his life in their own. 'A background belief of virtually all Christian hagiography is that saints live their lives in the light of Christ's life. *Imitatio Christi* is the apothegm that illuminates saintly contemplation and the command that guides saintly conduct.'[68]

Wyschogrod, however, argues that the one thing a saint cannot do is to imitate Christ in his divine perfection. The saint undertakes both to 'construct' a life upon that of Christ's, and to 'show' how impossible it is to 'bring the divine life into plenary presence'. But this is not an objection to the saintly task, for we need not suppose it to be quite as Wyschogrod suggests. If we stress the materiality of God's identification with Jesus, and Jesus' identification with his disciples, as sketched above, we must suppose the 'plenary

66 We must remember that the peace of Christ in his Church is not something achieved, except in memory and expectation, but is now being 'learned, negotiated, betrayed, inched forward, discerned and risked.' Rowan Williams, 'Saving time: thoughts on practice, patience and vision', *New Blackfriars*, 73 (1992), 319–26 (p. 321).

67 Edith Wyschogrod, *Saints and Postmodernism: Revisioning Moral Philosophy* (Chicago and London: University of Chicago Press, 1990), p. xxiii.

68 Wyschogrod, *Saints and Postmodernism*, p. 13.

presence' of Christ an eschatological accomplishment, which waits upon the life of the saints. Following Milbank, we may suggest that Wyschogrod is overly Platonic in her understanding of the saintly task. Christianity, Milbank reminds us, 'is not founded upon the vision of a transcendent original which we must imitate.'

> Instead it makes its affirmations about the real, and about 'meaning', through the constant *repetition* of a historically emergent practice which has no real point of origination, but only acquires identity and relative stability *through* this repetition. And what is repeated is not an insight, not an idea (which is properly *imitated*), but a formal becoming, a structured transformation. The narrative and metanarrative forms of the gospel are therefore indispensable, not because they record and point us to a vision which is still available in its eternal 'presence', but rather because they enshrine and constitute the event of a transformation which is to be non-identically repeated, and therefore still made to happen.[69]

It is only through saintly imitation, and through 'observing the likeness of Jesus in others', that we begin to gain a sense of 'Jesus's personality'.[70] The saints are the exemplars of a practice which, in each non-identical repetition, constitutes the story of Christ: God with us.[71]

For the Church, the 'what else and what more' of seeking the good is not the pursuit of a principle or value, but the repetition of a life which is, as John Milbank puts it, a 'structured transformation'. In Jesus we see the overcoming of coercive and selfish power through the refusal of violence, the practice of forgiveness and the transformation of suffering. It is this practice which the Church aims to embody, and insofar

69 Milbank, 'The name of Jesus', p. 319.

70 Milbank, 'The name of Jesus', p. 325.

71 By stressing saintly practice rather than the representation of a transcendental presence, we may better understand Stanley Hauerwas's recommendation of the novel – and the novels of Anthony Trollope in particular – as a form within which we may receive 'moral training'. See Stanley Hauerwas, 'Constancy and forgiveness: the novel as a school for virtue', in *Dispatches From the Front: Theological Engagements with the Secular* (Durham and London: Duke University Press, 1994), pp. 31–57.

as it does so, it is enfolded, incorporated, into the very life of the risen Christ.

The gospels . . . narrate Jesus's utter refusal of selfish power, and relate this to a transformation which combines human words with power over violence and death in the suffering of the body itself. If the suffering body becomes an actively suffering body, suffering for the sake of joy, and a greater joy for all, then it becomes the body that is united with other bodies. And united bodies are the resurrection – the making of words effective and life-giving, because no longer linked to selfish power, which means always the threat to kill, a power of death which in the long run spells the death of power.[72]

Salvation is thus no more and no less than entry into the narrative space of the Church; passage through baptismal waters into a new country. It is beginning to speak a new language in the company of those who are called to be friends by one who does not desert his friends even though they desert him.

[72] Milbank, 'The name of Jesus', p. 319.

Epilogue
In the middle of the story

I am the Alpha and the Omega, the beginning and the end. To the thirsty I will give water as a gift from the spring of the water of life.

Revelation 21.6

CHAPTER 8

Eating the Word

A group of friends gather for a meal, each bringing something to the table. They bring bread and wine. Their host brings himself. He has called them together, to share food and drink with one another. He tells them that in sharing the bread and drinking the cup they are sharing in him. He has given himself to them. He has given them his life.

> On a thorsday a soper y made
> With frendis and foys to make hem glad
> Of brede and wyne the sacrament
> Euyr to be oure testament . . . [1]

The Eucharist enfolds all the themes of narrativist theology. It is itself a narrative that enfolds the participants within the biblical story, not simply in each performance but in the cycle of performances throughout the Church's liturgical year. The biblical story is present not only in the readings of the lectionary, but in the very language of the liturgy which, through penitence and acclamation, comes to focus on the life, death and resurrection of Jesus Christ. The participants' absorption into the story is made possible through their absorption of the story in and through its ritual enactment.[2]

[1] A fifteenth-century poem quoted in Miri Rubin, *Corpus Christi: The Eucharist in Late Medieval Culture* (Cambridge: Cambridge University Press, 1991), pp. 307–8. It pictures Christ as the charter of our redemption. 'The Eucharist is God, and his offering, the charter [testament or gospel], is at once evidence of a sacrifice, and the sacrificed body itself' (p. 308).

[2] On the importance of ritual for narrativist theology see Ronald L. Grimes, 'Narrative and ritual criticism', in *Ritual Criticism: Case Studies in Its Practice, Essays*

They are not simply witnesses of the story, but characters within it. They do not simply recall the forgiveness of sins but ask and receive forgiveness; they do not repeat the praise of others but give praise themselves; they do not merely remember the night on which Jesus was betrayed but, mindful of their own daily betrayal, gather with the apostles at that night's table, themselves called by the one who in that darkness called his disciples to eat with him. Above all, they do not merely remember the giving of the bread and the passing of the cup, but, receiving the bread and passing the cup amongst themselves, they too share in that night's food.[3]

Toward the end of his book on *The Promise of Narrative Theology*, George Stroup discusses the Eucharist. He notes how it brings Church and Christ together in the performance of the scriptural story.

> It is the Christian narrative which mediates between the bread, the body of Christ, and Jesus Christ's spiritual presence. To 'remember' him is not simply to bring Jesus of Nazareth to mind but to 'actualise' those narratives in which he has his identity, to engage in that form of confession which fuses the narrative identity of the self to the narrative history of Jesus Christ.[4]

The Word of God is present in the word of Scripture and in the bread and wine of the eucharistic sacrament whenever a person is incorporated into the Christian narrative: 'the Word is present when the Spirit enables personal and communal identity to be fused to the narrative history of God's grace.'[5] As the bread is broken and dispersed among the people so they are brought together, united by the One who is

on Its Theory (Columbia, South Carolina: University of South Carolina Press, 1990), pp. 158–73. I am grateful to Samuel Wells for drawing my attention to this work.

3 See further Catherine Pickstock, 'The sacred as polis: language as synactic event', *Literature and Theology*, 8 (1994), 367–83 (p. 376).

4 George Stroup, *The Promise of Narrative Theology* (London: SCM Press, [1981] 1984), p. 254.

5 Stroup, *Promise of Narrative Theology*, p. 258.

dispersed among them.[6] In this last chapter I want to reflect on the objective nature of God's story through consideration of Christ's gift of himself in the narrative ritual of the eucharistic meal.

EATING NARRATIVES

What is given in the Eucharist? Without question, and perhaps almost without notice, the Eucharist gives first and quite simply, the story of a meal. At a certain time and in a certain place – 'On the night he was betrayed' – a group of friends gather for a meal. Not once upon a time, but at a certain time. Not anywhere or somewhere, but there in Jerusalem. The Eucharist narrates a story of particular events in the past. But it is this story of past events that commands the present narration: 'Do this in memory of me'. The Eucharist is not a pious memorial that merely recalls the past, for even before it begins to remember it is called into the present by the past. Its becoming is not of itself. It becomes what it is, always-already, from the past.

The Eucharist is story and meal, narrative and food. When the meal is over, the one who has gathered his friends together shows the depth of his love for them by taking bread, breaking it and giving it to them. He gives them wine, and he tells them the story that is about to unfold and is unfolding even as the Eucharist is being performed, it itself called into being by the story it narrates. He gives the story that the Eucharist, first and quite simply now gives. It is given by him for all.

The Eucharist – story and meal, praise and performance – is the gift of Christ, and Christ – the Body of Christ, which is

[6] See Pickstock on the rite of the synaxis in Pseudo-Dionysius' *Ecclesiastical Hierarchy* ('Sacred polis', p. 374). 'This, then, is what the hierarch reveals in the sacred rites, when he uncovers the veiled gifts, when he *makes a multiplicity of what had originally been one, when the distributed sacrament and those receiving it are made perfectly one,* when a perfect communion of all the participants is achieved.' Pseudo-Dionysius, *The Complete Works*, translated by Colm Luibheid (New York: Paulist Press, 1987), p. 222 (444c); emphasis added. See further Paul Rorem, *Pseudo-Dionysius: A Commentary on the Texts and an Introduction to Their Influence* (New York: Oxford University Press, 1993), pp. 99–104.

Christ-and-the-people-of-Christ-incorporated, inscribed in Christ's own story – is the gift of the Eucharist. In the eucharistic meal Christ gathers his friends together. For this is the nature of charity: to be with one another so as to love one another; to nourish and build up the one body of Christ.

THE IMPOSSIBLE GIFT

The Eucharist is the pure gift of God. It is the good gift, the gift beyond measure, the gift of the trinitarian charity. But Jacques Derrida teaches that the gift is impossible. First, a gift must be given without return. Second, all giving receives a restitution. Therefore the gift is impossible.

Jacques Derrida identifies the gift in relation to the law (*nomos*) of exchange, the economy or circle of giving and return. The gift is that which interrupts economy, because it is that which is not returned. It does not and must not circulate.[7]

> For there to be a gift, there must be no reciprocity, return, exchange, countergift, or debt. If the other *gives* me back or owes me or has to give me *back* what I *give* him or her, there will not have been a gift, whether this restitution is immediate or whether it is programmed by a complex calculation of a long-term deferral or différance.

Derrida asserts that this is the 'semantic precomprehension of the word "gift" in our language or in a few familiar languages'.[8]

The gift is *aneconomic* and thus impossible, and not simply

[7] Jacques Derrida, *Given Time: I Counterfeit Money*, translated by Peggy Kamuf (Chicago and London: University of Chicago Press, 1992), p. 7. Derrida's discourse is poised against Marcel Mauss's famous work of 1923–24, *The Gift: The Form and Reason for Exchange in Archaic Societies*, translated by W. D. Halls (London: Routledge, 1990) – for it 'speaks of everything but the gift' (Derrida, *Given Time*, p. 24).

[8] Derrida, *Given Time*, p. 12. As Aquinas notes, 'a gift, according to Aristotle, is literally a giving that can have no return, i.e. it is not given with repayment in mind and as such denotes a giving out of good will'. St Thomas Aquinas, *Summa Theologiæ*, vol. 7, translated by T. C. O'Brien (London: Blackfriars Eyre and Spottiswoode, 1976), 1a, 38, 2, responsio.

impossible but *the* impossible. It is, Derrida writes, the very figure of the impossible. 'It announces itself, gives itself to be thought as the impossible'.[9] Why is the gift impossible? Derrida argues that the conditions for the possibility of the gift are at the same time the conditions of its impossibility: 'these conditions of possibility define or produce the annulment, the annihilation, the destruction of the gift'.[10] The conditions of the gift are stated in the following axiom: 'In order for there to be gift, gift event, some "one" has to give some "thing" to someone other, without which "giving" would be meaningless'.[11] But the gift – the giving of some thing to someone – is impossible because there is no giving without return.

If there is to be a gift the donee must not make a return nor be indebted, and the donor must not expect a return or restitution. But this means that the donee must not recognise the gift as a gift. 'If he recognises it as gift, if the gift *appears to him as such*, if the present is present to him *as present*, this simple recognition suffices to annul the gift'.[12] This is because the recognition is already to give back a 'symbolic equivalent'. The donor, likewise, must not recognise the gift as a gift: 'otherwise he begins, at the threshold, as soon as he intends to give, to pay himself with a symbolic recognition, to praise himself, to approve of himself, to gratify himself, to congratulate himself, to give back to himself symbolically the value of what he thinks he has given or what he is preparing to give'.[13] This is the impossibility or double-bind of the gift. 'For there to be gift, it is necessary that the gift not even appear, that it not be perceived or received as gift'.[14]

It would seem that if there is to be a gift it must be forgotten. But it cannot be forgotten by the conscious mind alone. It must also be forgotten by the unconscious, it must not remain there or elsewhere as repressed. For that would be to keep the gift by exchanging places, by displacing. The gift is

[9] Derrida, *Given Time*, p. 7.
[10] Derrida, *Given Time*, p. 12.
[11] Derrida, *Given Time*, p. 11.
[12] Derrida, *Given Time*, p. 13.
[13] Derrida, *Given Time*, p. 14.
[14] Derrida, *Given Time*, p. 16.

recognised in the unconscious and thus annulled. If there is to be a gift there has to be an absolute forgetting; nothing must be left behind. Derrida says that this absolute forgetting, this forgetting of forgetting, which is at the same time not nothing, cannot be understood in philosophical, psychological or psychoanalytic categories. Rather, it is on the basis 'of what takes shape in the name *gift*' that we can hope to think about absolute forgetting.[15] Thus the gift becomes the condition of forgetting, as its establishment – the forgetting condition. Gift and forgetting are 'each in the condition of the other', forgetting in the condition of the gift and the gift in the condition of forgetting.[16]

Derrida, taking his way by Heidegger, likens the logic of the gift to that of Being and Time. Being is not but there is Being; Time is not but there is Time.

> Heidegger recalls that in itself time is nothing temporal, since it is nothing, since it is not a thing (*kein Ding*). The temporality of time is not temporal, no more than proximity is proximate or treeness is woody. He also recalls that Being is not being (being-present/present-being), since it is not something (*kein Ding*), and that therefore one cannot say either 'time is' or 'being is'.[17]

In being-present and in present-time, Being and Time withdraw; there is a forgetting of Being and Time. The gift, if there is a gift, also withdraws, forgotten in the very moment of giving.

The logic of the impossible gift comes into play as soon as there is a subject, as soon as there is a donor and a donee, a giver and a recipient. So one must conclude that 'if there is gift, it cannot take place between two subjects exchanging objects, things or symbols'.[18] The question of the gift, therefore, has to be placed before that of the subject, just as the question of Being is placed before it is determined as substantial being.

Is it then possible that in the Eucharist Christ is given to us

15 Derrida, *Given Time*, p. 17.
16 Derrida, *Given Time*, p. 18.
17 Derrida, *Given Time*, p. 20.
18 Derrida, *Given Time*, p. 24.

as unconditional charity, as gift? Is it possible that Christ escapes the law of exchange, the circle of return? Instead of a gift, are we not rather given an obligation, a contract and a covenant? Or is the Eucharist the proper name of the gift, of the impossible? So that all gifts, if there be any, are types of this gift?[19]

I now propose to approach these questions by way of the question of how we may best articulate – at the level of doctrinal grammar – the giving of the eucharistic gift. This is the question of transubstantiation. It is a question because transubstantiation is the name, not of an explanation, but of a rigorous recollection of the eucharistic mystery. St Thomas begins his account of the change of bread and wine into the body and blood of Christ by reminding us that 'we could never know by our senses that the real body of Christ and his blood are in this sacrament, but only by our faith which is based on the authority of God.'[20] The doctrine of transubstantiation adds nothing to, but only articulates, the eucharistic mystery of faith. The argument to be considered is that transubstantiation is the best articulation we have.

TRANSUBSTANTIATION AND ITS TRANSCRIPTIONS

St Thomas Aquinas teaches that in the Eucharist we are fed spiritual food under the species of bread and wine, the proper matter of the sacrament.[21] It is a spiritual food because it contains Christ crucified, bodily himself. Christ comes to us in this sacrament out of friendship, for as Aristotle teaches, friends want to live together. The Eucharist is the sign of supreme charity.[22]

[19] John Milbank, in a profound article published too late for proper digestion here, also takes up Derrida's problematising of the gift and seeks a theological response in the idea of Christian agape as 'purified gift-exchange', as 'delay and non-identical repetition', purged of all 'archaic agonistic components'. See John Milbank, 'Can a gift be given? Prolegomena to a future trinitarian metaphysic', *Modern Theology*, 11 (1995), 119–61 (p. 131).

[20] St Thomas Aquinas, *Summa Theologiæ*, vol. 58, translated by William Barden (London: Eyre and Spottiswoode, 1965), 3a, 75, 1, responsio.

[21] Aquinas, *Summa*, 3a, 74.

[22] Aquinas, *Summa*, 3a, 75, 1, responsio.

Christ is in the sacrament because the substance of the bread is changed into that of the body, and the substance of the wine into that of the blood. The change is supernatural and effected by God alone. It is 'not a formal change, but a substantial one. It does not belong to the natural kinds of change, and it can be called by a name proper to itself – "transubstantiation".'[23]

What are we to make of such a doctrine as transubstantiation, with its ancient ideas of 'matter' and 'form', 'substance' and 'accident'? Must we not, with Richard Dawkins, find it 'daft'?[24] Perhaps it is, in the sense that what Aquinas does with the concepts he borrows from Aristotle makes little sense within Aristotelian ontology.[25] But perhaps this is not a problem, for we can think transubstantial logic its own thing.

A more serious charge against transubstantiation is that it 'fixes and freezes' the person of Christ in an 'available, permanent, handy, and delimited thing'. Transubstantiation – as Jean-Luc Marion notes – is then 'the imposture of an idolatry that imagines itself to honour "God" when it heaps praises on his pathetic "canned" substitute (the reservation of the Eucharist), exhibited as an attraction (display of the Holy Sacrament), brandished like a banner (processions), and so on.'[26] God becomes a very real presence, but the presence of a mute thing, placed at the disposal of the community.

23 Aquinas, *Summa*, 3a, 75, 4, responsio.

24 Richard Dawkins likens religion to a computer virus ('Is God a computer virus?' *New Statesman and Society*, 18 December 1992/1 January 1993, 42–5). Successful viruses are hard to detect, but there are typical symptoms: conviction without evidence or reason; feeling virtuous about this; thinking mystery a good thing. Catholics suffer from a particularly strong form of the virus, for they believe the 'Mystery of the Transubstantiation'. 'Any wimp in religion could believe that bread symbolically represents the body of Christ, but it takes a real, red-blooded Catholic to believe something as daft as the transubstantiation' (p. 44).

25 See G. Egner (P. J. Fitzpatrick), 'Some thoughts on the eucharistic presence', in Herbert McCabe, *God Matters* (London: Geoffrey Chapman, 1987), pp. 130–45. See further P. J. Fitzpatrick, *In Breaking of Bread: The Eucharist and Ritual* (Cambridge: Cambridge University Press, 1993).

26 Jean-Luc Marion, *God Without Being: Hors Texte*, translated by Thomas A. Carlson, foreword by David Tracy (Chicago: University of Chicago Press, 1991), p. 164.

In view of such criticism, it is not surprising to find transubstantiation rendered in other than Aristotelian idiom. Thus we are offered transignification and transfinalization, and told that in such transcriptions, 'substance, being, essence, meaning, significance and end' can be 'completely identical'.[27] They remain transubstantial because they seek to articulate Catholic faith in the eucharistic presence of Christ. They seek – as Herbert McCabe puts it – to avoid, on the one hand, a merely metaphorical or symbolic understanding of the Eucharist, and, on the other hand, a physicalist understanding of the Eucharist which supposes some disguised chemical change in the bread and wine.

An accessible re-writing of transubstantiation is offered by Gareth Moore in his short essay, 'Transubstantiation for beginners' (1986). He suggests that for the believer, the consecrated bread and wine are understood no longer according to their appearance but according to their context. It is context which constitutes the eucharistic change. He gives the example of a five pound note. Apart from the institution of money it is just a piece of brightly coloured paper. But given the institution of money and the forms of life in which a five pound note functions, it is no longer just a piece of paper. There is also a difference, a substantial difference, between a genuine and a forged five pound note. One is issued by authority, the other not. Institution and use makes the five pound note what it is.

In the same way, a piece of bread becomes something other than just a piece of bread by being taken up and used in a certain way in the life of the Church. A consecrated host differs from a perhaps identical piece of bread by being embedded within a certain institution and its way of life. To understand it we must look not only at it, but around it.[28]

27 Karl Rahner and Herbert Vorgrimler, *Concise Theological Dictionary*, second edition (London: Burns and Oates, 1983), p. 510.

28 Gareth Moore, 'Transubstantiation for beginners', *New Blackfriars*, 67 (1986), 530–7 (p. 536). That Moore finds an analogy for transubstantiation in the order of monetary exchange cannot be considered accidental for a discussion that seeks to problematise ideas of 'gift' and 'exchange'. See further David Moss, 'Costly giving:

To believe in paper money is to live in a money economy; to believe in transubstantiation is to live as part of the Church, 'to live the life of the Church centred around the Eucharist'.[29]

However attractive – because comprehensible – Moore's re-writing of transubstantiation as transignification, it is not immune from criticism. Jean-Luc Marion offers a powerful critique of such re-writing in his essay 'The Present and the Gift'.[30] He does so in favour, not of wimpish symbolism, but of real, red-blooded transubstantialism.

KEEPING DISTANCE

Jean-Luc Marion teaches that what matters with regard to particular accounts of the eucharistic mystery is whether or not they put the eucharistic presence at the disposal of the community or the community at the disposal of Christ.

> [If] it is still Christ, the priest *in persona Christi*, who gives to the community the new meanings and goals of the bread and wine, precisely because the community does not produce them, does not have them at its disposal, or perform them; then this gift will be welcomed as such by a community that, receiving it, will find itself nourished and brought together by it.[31]

But if it is the community that gives the 'new meanings and goals of the bread and wine', then the bread and wine will be less the mediation of God's presence in the community, than the community's awareness of itself in its search for God's presence. For then, even as it receives the bread and wine, it will still be seeking and finding only its own collective consciousness.[32] It would seem that Moore's account – as far as it goes – is in danger of doing this: making God's presence

on Jean-Luc Marion's theology of gift', *New Blackfriars*, 74 (1993), 393–9. 'What is at stake for Marion . . . is the very possibility of our being delivered from the economic exchange of debt and account into "an entirely other exchange", characterised by "the play of donation, abandon and pardon"' (p. 394).

29 Moore, 'Transubstantiation for beginners', p. 537.

30 Marion, *God Without Being*, pp. 161–82.

31 Marion, *God Without Being*, p. 165.

32 Marion, *God Without Being*, pp. 165–6.

dependent on the institution and performance of the community.

Marion suggests that in such renderings of the eucharistic mystery, it is not so much that the presence of Christ is relocated from the bread and wine to the community, as that Christ's presence ceases to be distinct from the collective consciousness. Christ's presence endures for as long as the community is present. Presence becomes dependent on present consciousness. Once that consciousness has disappeared, the community dispersed, there is nothing left to constitute and maintain presence. The consecrated bread can be thrown out or burnt. With the community gone, divine presence is relegated to the past.[33]

As Marion develops this theme, eucharistic presence is 'measured by what the attention of the human community presently accords to it.'[34] He describes it as a perfect inversion of perpetual adoration. Rather than the eucharistic presence ceaselessly provoking our attention, it is our attention that provokes and governs the eucharistic presence.[35] And because our attention is intermittent, presence is interim.

It is thus that Marion turns the tables on those who would find in transubstantiation a reification of eucharistic presence, a form of idolatry putting God at the disposal of the community. Eucharistic theologies that seek to understand the divine presence in terms of the community's will, attention or consciousness, are places where idolatry 'knows its triumph'.[36]

This is where Marion thinks the theology of transubstantiation can help. First, in order to appreciate that the eucharistic present is not determined by ourselves, we must so distinguish it from ourselves that we can admit its distance from us. It is Christ who determines our union with him, his presence with us. Marion argues that 'the theology of

[33] Marion, *God Without Being*, p. 167.
[34] Marion, *God Without Being*, p. 167.
[35] Marion, *God Without Being*, pp. 167–8. On the liturgical need for the 'deprioritisation of the psyche' see Pickstock, 'Sacred polis', p. 373.
[36] Marion, *God Without Being*, p. 168.

transubstantiation alone offers the possibility of distance, since it strictly separates my consciousness from Him who summons it. In the distance thus arranged, the Other summons, by his absolutely concrete sacramental body, my attention and my prayer.'[37]

Transubstantiation has the virtue of keeping the distance that marks out the Other from ourselves. 'In becoming conscious of the thing where eucharistic presence is embodied, the believing community does not become conscious of itself, but of another, of the Other par excellence.'[38] Even if transubstantiation risks a material idolatry, it avoids the supreme spiritual idolatry of supposing Christ's presence our self-consciousness. The very thing for which Hegel chided Catholicism – that 'the spirit of all truth is in actuality set in rigid opposition to the self-conscious spirit'[39] – marks out an escape from this most subtle of idolatries.

> What the consecrated host imposes, or rather permits, is the irreducible exteriority of the present that Christ makes us of himself in this thing that to him becomes sacramental body. That this exteriority, far from forbidding intimacy, renders it possible in sparing it from foundering in idolatry, can be misunderstood only by those who do not want to open themselves to distance.[40]

It is a matter of choosing between the idol and distance, between ourselves and the transcendent God.

CHANGING LANGUAGES

Herbert McCabe also turns to language for his re-written transubstantialism, but avoids Marion's criticism by insisting that the change of language – with which he replaces the change of substance – is given not by, but to the community. The eucharistic gift is thus understood as the gift of a new language, a new society and a new body: the body of Christ.

[37] Marion, *God Without Being*, p. 177.
[38] Marion, *God Without Being*, p. 168.
[39] Marion, *God Without Being*, p. 169.
[40] Marion, *God Without Being*, p. 169.

For McCabe, the risen body of Christ is present in the Eucharist in the mode of language, in the signs we use. 'Our language has become his body.'[41] Or, we might say, his language has become our body. McCabe understands language as an extension of the human body. Language allows us to do far more in the world than we could if we only had our bodily parts and senses, our sight and hearing, our teeth and hands. Language allows us to realise a social, communicated world as our habitat.

The human body extends itself into language, into social structures, into all the various and complex means of living together, communicating together what men have created, but all of them are rooted in the body; there is no human communication which is not fundamentally bodily communication.[42]

Language changes, usually slowly and without notice, but sometimes suddenly and dangerously, and when it does, the bodies whose extensions it is, change also. McCabe is interested in radical change, social revolution. The world after revolution cannot be described in pre-revolutionary language, for revolution is a complete change of language and world. At best, the revolutionary can picture the world that comes after in parables.[43] New worlds come only through revolution, through death and resurrection. A new world is thus a new language, a new communication; and it is this – a new world, language and communication – that are given in the Eucharist. Christ comes to us as a new medium of communication.[44] He gives us nothing other than himself and his language: body and word. He offers us his friendship.[45]

In the first century of our era, the gift of Christ's body and word were returned with death. But as the gift of God it was not destroyed. Once given it is not taken back. On the other side of death, on the other side of the revolution, the body of Christ is more alive, more bodily, than before. He is 'available

[41] McCabe, *God Matters*, p. 118.
[42] McCabe, *God Matters*, p. 121.
[43] McCabe, *God Matters*, p. 122.
[44] McCabe, *God Matters*, p. 123.
[45] McCabe, *God Matters*, p. 124.

in his bodiliness more than he was, he is now able to be present to all men and not just to a few in Palestine.'[46] The body of the risen Christ, that comes to us in the Eucharist, comes to us from our promised future; it is post-revolutionary, more bodily.

Thus re-written, the doctrine of transubstantiation teaches that the bread and wine undergo a revolutionary change, changing not into something else, but more radically into food and drink; for 'Christ has a better right to appear as food and drink than bread and wine have.'[47] This is because food and drink signify the sharing of a common world, of bodily communication. McCabe holds that apart from sexual union, there is no more primitive and fundamental form of bodily communication than the sharing of food. The common meal is a symbol of unity because it is rooted in the life of the body. Food is a language in which we communicate and come together. Thus Christ is the true bread because in him we come truly together; he is more truly food than food itself.

When people gather for the Eucharist, they gather for a meal that is at the same time the language of their bodily communication; and this language-meal is not their own, but comes to them from beyond the site of their gathering, from beyond and after the revolution. It is a language they can barely speak; but it is the language in which they can most truly communicate; be most bodily, most alive. McCabe thus articulates the eucharistic change as a change of language. In the Eucharist, 'the language itself is transformed and becomes the medium of the future, the language itself becomes the presence, the bodily presence of Christ.'[48] This account is transubstantial because, while the 'accidents' of pre-revolutionary language remain, its 'substance' is post-revolutionary. The signs are the same, but their meanings have changed; they are barely comprehensible.

It is time to start a return to the question of the impossible

[46] McCabe, *God Matters*, p. 125.
[47] McCabe, *God Matters*, p. 127.
[48] McCabe, *God Matters*, p. 128. See Pickstock, 'Sacred polis', p. 377.

gift; but I shall do so by way of Marion's own transcription of transubstantiation. In it he seeks to refuse metaphysics, and above all, the metaphysics of time as this has been constituted from Aristotle to Hegel. This is in keeping with his larger project to think God other than by way of Being, as prior to Being, as pre-ontological: God without Being.[49]

As we have seen, Derrida suggests that the gift as such can be thought only prior to the subject, prior to the relation of giver and given that annuls the gift in the very moment it is given. But for Marion the gift comes first, prior to being, subject and relation.[50] Thus it is, and remains, pure gift. It is not given between some ones; rather some ones, all ones, are given. Nor are they given some thing; they are simply given. Love's gift of being is more commonly known by way of the doctrine of creation. Thus creation is another name for gift; another name for Eucharist.

PRESENT TIME

Jean-Luc Marion argues that the idolatry of eucharistic consciousness is dependent upon a certain conception of time. It views time as the present moment which determines past and future. If there is presence it is now, valid only 'as long as the present of consciousness measures it and imparts the present to it starting from the consciousness of the present.'[51]

This is the ordinary conception of time, and it constitutes the 'function, stake, and characteristic' of metaphysics as a whole, from Aristotle to Hegel.[52] The present moment, the here and now, assures consciousness of that which is, in the present moment. The here and now constitutes the past as that which ends when the present begins, and the future as

[49] Much of Milbank's article, 'Can a gift be given?', is concerned to contest Marion's theology of charity beyond ontology, arguing for '*another* ontology, perhaps precisely an ontology of the gift, but all the same an ontology' (p. 137).

[50] In this it is like the phrase that gives addressor to addressee rather than being given by one to the other. See above chapter 6.

[51] Marion, *God Without Being*, p. 170.

[52] Marion, *God Without Being*, p. 170.

that which begins when the present ends. Past and future are negatively determined; both nonpresent and nontime. Therefore they do not and cannot give an assurance of being to consciousness; that assurance is only conferred by the present. It is only in the here and now that there can be eucharistic presence. Thus a theology that would reduce eucharistic presence to the present moment of collective consciousness in the here and now, turns out to be more metaphysical than the transubstantiation it would criticise. 'Idolatry finds its metaphysical completion in the very enterprise that claimed to criticize an apparently metaphysical eucharistic theology.'[53]

Marion seeks to think eucharistic presence without yielding to the three forms of idolatry he identifies: the material idolatry of the transubstantial thing, the spiritual idolatry of collective consciousness, and the temporal idolatry of the ordinary conception of time.

> Can the eucharistic presence of Christ as consecrated bread and wine determine, starting from itself and itself alone, the conditions of its reality, the dimensions of its temporality and the dispositions of its approach? Does eucharistic presence suffice for its own comprehension?[54]

The eucharistic gift is not determined by the ordinary conception of time; it is not determined as the presence of the present moment, of the here and now. Rather the present is determined, is given, by the eucharistic gift. It is the present of the gift. 'Eucharistic presence must be understood starting most certainly from the present, but the present must be understood first as a gift that is given.'[55] Time must be understood according to the order of the gift; it must be understood as that which is given, rather than as that which gives. Time must be understood as gift: as creation.

Presence is to be understood starting from the gift. It is the gift which constitutes presence in the present. The

[52] Marion, *God Without Being*, p. 171.

[54] Marion, *God Without Being*, p. 171.

[55] Marion, *God Without Being*, p. 171.

eucharistic gift includes the fundamental terms of the temporality of the gift.[56] According to the order of the gift, the eucharistic present is temporalized not from the here and now, but from the past, the future and finally the present. From the past it is temporalized as memorial; from the future as eschatological announcement, and from the present as 'dailyness and viaticum'.[57] This is not the metaphysical concept of time, which understands the whole from the present; rather it is a gifted concept of time, which understands the present from the whole. It follows, according to Marion, that eucharistic presence is to be understood 'less in the way of an available permanence than as a new sort of advent.'[58]

The eucharistic present is temporalized from the past as memorial, but not in the sense of remembering what is no longer, of calling to mind a nonpresence. That would be to think the past from the here and now. 'It is a question of making an appeal, in the name of a past event, to God, in order that he recall an engagement (a covenant) that determines the instant presently given to the believing community.'[59] Thus the past event is understood as the pledge of the present moment: the advent of the Messiah. In the Eucharist the people do not recall to mind the death, resurrection and ascension of Christ, as if they might have forgotten this, but rather remember before God that this event has not ceased to determine their day and future. 'The past determines the reality of the present – better, the present is understood as a today to which alone the memorial, as an actual pledge, gives meaning and reality.'[60]

Once we understand the temporalization of the present from the past we also understand its temporalization from the future. For the memorial is the pledge of an advent completed from the future. It is not simply a waiting, but an asking and a hastening of Christ's return. Already the future determines

[56] Marion, *God Without Being*, p. 172.
[57] Marion, *God Without Being*, p. 172.
[58] Marion, *God Without Being*, p. 172.
[59] Marion, *God Without Being*, p. 172.
[60] Marion, *God Without Being*, p. 173.

the present moment as its anticipation. 'The Eucharist anticipates what we will be, will see, will love: *figura nostra*, the figure of what will be, but above all ourselves, facing the gift that we cannot yet welcome, so, in the strict sense, that we cannot yet figure it. In this way, "sometimes the future lives in us without our knowing it".'[61] Marion's quotation from Proust will remind us of McCabe's unknown language, and of the gift that is the forgetting condition.

Past and future are not the nonpresence of the ordinary conception of time, but the very determinants of the eucharistic present. What then of this present that they make possible? 'Each instant of the present must befall us as a gift: the day, the hour, the instant, are imparted by charity.'[62] The present day is never our possession. Marion invokes the figure of manna. Each day is given and gathered as was the manna in the wilderness. The Christian day, like Christian bread, is given daily and daily requested of the Father.

The eucharistic present is given by Christ: a present that is always anterior to itself because always-already given in the memorial; and always in anticipation of itself because always-already called to announce its completion from the future.[63] And in this gift of the present is the presence of the one from whom it comes. What we may call eucharistic time – the eucharistic present as moment and gift, temporalized from the past and the future, from the memorial and the *epiktasis* – is the paradigm of every present moment, of every time as gift. 'The temporal present during which the eucharistic present endures resembles it: as a glory haloes an iconic apparition, time is made a present gift to let us receive in it the eucharistically given present.'[64]

The present of the eucharistic presence comes to us, confused by us, under the form of the here and now. This is because our charity does not have enough lucidity to see

61 Marion, *God Without Being*, p. 174, quoting M. Proust, *A la recherche du temps perdu*, Pléiade, vol. 2 (Paris, 1954), p. 639.

62 Marion, *God Without Being*, p. 175.

63 Marion, *God Without Being*, p. 176. See Pickstock, 'Sacred polis', pp. 379–81.

64 Marion, *God Without Being*, p. 175.

the present moment as a present gift.[65] We are incorrigibly, spontaneously idolatrous; we want to take possession of the day.

Jean-Luc Marion seeks to save transubstantiation from metaphysics for what may be loosely called a postmodern theology, by transcribing it from the idiom of ontology into that of temporality; not the temporality of metaphysics itself – the order of the here and now – but a properly Christian temporality that becomes the paradigm of every present moment.[66] It is the temporality of the Christian story.

In and through the present moment of the here and now there is given to us the good grace; a moment that is given, always-already, from the past in which it is pledged and from the future it anticipates and in which it is completed. The present moment is narrativized from the past and the future; the beginning and the end. And in this given moment we receive the presence of Christ in the bread and wine he hands to us.

THE GIFT OF RETURN

Aquinas discusses gift as the personal and proper name of the Holy Spirit. It would seem that gift is not the personal name of the Spirit because it is the name of God's essence in relation to creation.[67] To this, Aquinas answers that a gift is given from someone to another, handed over and thus possessed, first by the donor – who has the gift to give – and then by the recipient – who is given the gift to have.

The gift of God is possessed either as essence, when the gift is identical with the giver; or as created thing, when the gift is different from the divine donor; or, thirdly, when the gift is related by origin to the giver. The Son belongs to the Father by origin, as does the Spirit to Father and Son. 'As one who belongs to the giver through origin, then, the Gift of God

[65] Marion, *God Without Being*, pp. 175–6.

[66] Marion, *God Without Being*, p. 176. [67] Aquinas, *Summa Theologiæ*, 1a, 38, 1.

[Spirit] is distinct personally from the giver [Father and Son] and is a personal name.'[68]

> The gift is the very 'being-given', or givenness of God: God as 'donation' . . . God's giving never leaves God's hands, in which are held all things as 'being-given' . . . God's 'gift', like God's 'utterance', names an eternal relationship of origin.[69]

Aquinas also teaches that gift is the proper name of the Spirit, as denoting the relationship of origin to Father and Son. However, outside of Aquinas's theology of the trinitarian relations – within a more mobile trinitarianism – we may surely name the Son as gift also.[70] As Aquinas notes: 'There is Isaiah, *A Son is given to us*. To be gift, then, fits the Son as much as it does the Holy Spirit.'[71] Christ is also given; and here as well, giver and gift are one.

In this giving of Christ we are given to one another also, insofar as we are incorporated into the body of Christ, written into his story, called on to the stage to perform his drama. Gift and given, Christ and the donees who receive him, are one. To receive the gift of God is to be incorporated into the triune life, into the eternity of donation, of giving and receiving back again. Indeed, the unity of the body of Christ is the unity of giver, gift and given – of teller, story and listener; of playwright, play and player; of host, meal and guest – and the unity of the Body is the presence given in the present of the Eucharist.[72]

In this way, perhaps, we can begin to say how the impossible logic of the gift is overcome in the gift that is simply the giving

68 Aquinas, *Summa Theologiæ*, 1a, 38, 1, responsio.

69 Nicholas Lash, *Believing Three Ways in One God: A Reading of the Apostles' Creed* (London: SCM Press, 1992), pp. 92 and 105. God's 'utterance' is of course the Word or Son. See further Jean-Luc Marion, 'Metaphysics and phenomenology: a relief for theology', translated by Thomas A. Carlson, *Critical Inquiry*, 20 (1994), 572–91 (pp. 587–9).

70 See above chapter 6.

71 Aquinas, *Summa Theologiæ*, 1a, 38, 2.

72 See further John D. Zizioulas, *Being as Communion: Studies in Personhood and the Church*, Contemporary Greek Thinkers 4 (Crestwood, New York: St Vladimir's Seminary Press, 1993).

of God. For this giving exceeds the ontological conditions and limits of the 'impossible gift'. All the terms of the gift – donor, donation and donee – are collapsed into the one event that is finally the Body of Christ. God gives only himself. When God gives, nothing passes from God to someone else; rather God draws near. Nor is God given to someone else, for the 'someone else' is the being of the gift. 'It is a gift to no-one, but rather establishes creatures as themselves gifts'.[73] This is not to conceive God's giving as a 'pure gesture', giving only giving, without content.[74] For always what is given must be understood from Christ, and thus from the Body of Christ. The 'Body' is the being of the gift.

Here it seems that we must allow for an element of exchange or return in the divine donation. Yes – as John Milbank after Marion notes – it is right to say that no return can be made to God, 'since there is nothing extra to God that *could* return to him. God gives 'to' no-one, but creates all *ex nihilo*, causes all by his grace, exemplary purity of gift, whose absolute gratuity and spontaneity removes it from all taint of exchange.'[75] Here, however, Milbank points us to the seeming paradox of 'absolute gratuity with absolute exchange'.[76] For what is given absolutely is an absolute return, for return to God is the being and beat of the human heart. We are made for God. And this is our possibility as free creatures – who are always-already forgetting our giftedness – because of Jesus Christ, who is the perfect return of God's gift. In him, 'infinite return is realised as perfect return, God's return of himself to himself, and it is disclosed to us that the divine created gift, which realises an inexorable return, is itself grounded in an intra-divine love which is relation and exchange as much as it is gift.'[77]

Thus we must recognise what Milbank calls the 'exchangist

72 Milbank, 'Can a gift be given?', p. 135.

74 Milbank makes this criticism of Marion; 'Can a gift be given?', pp. 133–4.

75 Milbank, 'Can a gift be given?', p. 134.

76 Milbank, 'Can a gift be given?', p. 135.

77 Milbank, 'Can a gift be given?', pp. 135–6.

character of the divine gift'.[78] But in also recognising the inexorability of God's gift – its character as grace such that its reception and return are inevitable and are themselves given by God – it becomes difficult to maintain the distinction between exchange and gift necessary to Derrida's problematic (the spatial passage of donation from donor to donee). For what is given is the return or exchange, if 'exchange' has meaning here.

The gift of return is given in the death of Christ on the cross – 'a man making an infinite and complete return to God' – which as sinners we refuse, but as members of the Body, accept.[79] It is this gift we receive in the Eucharist; for which there can be no return other than to return to the God by whom and for whom we are given absolutely.

JOHN EATS THE BOOK

For Pierre Bersuire (c. 1290–1362), Christ is a sort of book inscribed on human flesh, and eating the body of Christ is like eating a sort of book.

> Christ is a sort of book written into the skin of the virgin . . . That book was spoken in the disposition of the Father, written in the conception of the mother, exposited in the clarification of the nativity, corrected in the passion, erased in the flagellation, punctuated in the imprint of the wounds, adorned in the crucifixion above the pulpit, illuminated in the outpouring of blood, bound in the resurrection, and examined in the ascension.[80]

In the book of Revelation John is given a book to eat. It is sweet in his mouth, but bitter in his belly. It is the body-book of Christ, as the medieval commentator Hugh of St Cher tells us: 'Indeed this book is the life of Christ . . . the sacraments

[78] Milbank, 'Can a gift be given?', p. 136.
[79] Milbank, 'Can a gift be given?', p. 136.
[80] Pierre Bersuire, *Repertorium morale*; quoted in Jesse M. Gellrich, *The Idea of the Book in the Middle Ages: Language Theory, Mythology, and Fiction* (Ithaca: Cornell University Press, 1985), p. 17.

and mysteries of the Church'.[81] In one fourteenth-century manuscript illustration of the scene (see cover), the eucharistic significance of John's eating is suggested by the postures of the angel and the visionary. As John lifts the book to his mouth, the angel gently supports John's right elbow while steadying the book with his right hand, as if offering the host or assisting with the chalice. 'It is the familiar gesture of taking the Eucharist, through which the "Word made flesh" becomes "bread" ... and the *logos* of Christ's life is truly ingested.'[82]

The image of John eating the book – which is both Christ's risen body in the bread of the Eucharist and the divine *logos* in the word of Scripture – is a figure for narrativist theology. To live within this scriptural image is to consume the Word of God in the community of the Church; becoming part of the story as the story becomes part of oneself. It is to find oneself beneath the sheltering wings of God's charity, a recipient of the gift that is "return", enfolded within the eternal giving of the triune God. As the angel assists John in eating the book, their forearms constitute a symbol of the trinitarian life, a triangular shape at the centre of the picture, which joins the heavenly and the human worlds. John's right arm rises through the middle to place a third hand on the book of life, the charter of redemption, whose performance is resurrection. It is a symbol hardly visible, yet secretly present in this scene of God's infinite compassion: the giving of the story for the nurturing of the world.

81 Quoted in Gellrich, *Idea of the Book*, p. 22. See also Rubin, *Corpus Christi*, p. 307. Rubin discusses the medieval idea of the charter of Christ, the document of redemption written on the flesh of the crucified (pp. 306–8). Lesley Smith notes that for mendicant commentators eating the book develops 'a sense more specific to preachers: it signifies exposition or preaching; but this can be truly accomplished only if the book has been enfolded in the heart and retained in the memory.' See Lesley Smith, 'The theology of the twelfth- and thirteenth-century Bible', in *The Early Medieval Bible: Its Production, Decoration and Use*, edited by Richard Gameson (Cambridge: Cambridge University Press, 1994), pp. 223–32 (p. 229).

82 Gellrich, *Idea of the Book*, p. 22; slightly adapted.

Bibliography

Alter, Robert. *The Art of Biblical Narrative*. London and Sydney: George Allen and Unwin, 1981.

Alter, Robert and Frank Kermode (eds.) *The Literary Guide to the Bible*. London: Collins, 1987.

Anderson, Pamela Sue. *Ricoeur and Kant: Philosophy of the Will*. AAR Studies in Religion vol. 66. Atlanta, GA: Scholars Press, 1993.

Aquinas, St Thomas. *Summa Theologiæ*. General editor Thomas Gilby OP. 61 vols. London: Blackfriars Eyre and Spottiswoode, 1964–81.

Aristotle, *On the Art of Poetry*. In *Classical Literary Criticism*. Translated by T. S. Dorsch. Harmondsworth: Penguin Books, 1965. 31–75.

Auerbach, Erich. *Mimesis: The Representation of Reality in Western Literature*. Translated by Willard R. Trask. Princeton, New Jersey: Princeton University Press, 1953.

Scenes from the Drama of European Literature. Theory and History of Literature vol. 9. Manchester: Manchester University Press, 1984.

Augustine, St. *Confessions*. Translated by R. S. Pine-Coffin. Harmondsworth: Penguin Books, 1961.

On Christian Doctrine. A Select Library of the Nicene and Post-Nicene Fathers. Edited by Philip Schaff, vol. 2. Grand Rapids, Michigan: William B. Eerdmans Publishing Company, [1886] 1977.

The Trinity. The Works of Saint Augustine vol. 5. Translated by Edmund Hill OP. Brooklyn, New York: New City Press, 1991.

Bal, Mieke. *Narratology: Introduction to the Theory of Narrative*. Translated by C. von Boheemen. Toronto: University of Toronto Press, 1985.

Balthasar, Hans Urs von. *The Glory of the Lord: A Theological Aesthetics*, 7 vols. Edited by Joseph Fessio SJ and John Riches. Edinburgh: T. and T. Clark, 1982–1991.

Mysterium Paschale. Translated by Aidan Nichols OP. Edinburgh: T. and T. Clark, 1990.

Barth, Karl. *Protestant Thought: From Rousseau to Ritschl*. Translated by Brian Cozens. Revised by H. H. Hartwell. New York: Harper Brothers, 1959.

Benjamin, Andrew and Christopher Norris. *What is Deconstruction?* London: Academy Editions, 1988.

Bennington, Geoffrey. *Lyotard: Writing the Event*. Manchester: Manchester University Press, 1988.

Berlin, Adele. *Poetics and Interpretation of Biblical Narrative*. Sheffield: Almond Press, 1983.

Berlin, Isaiah. *The Magus of the North: J. G. Hamann and the Origins of Modern Irrationalism*. London: John Murray, 1993.

Bloom, Harold *et al.* (eds.) *Deconstruction and Criticism*. London: Routledge and Kegan Paul, 1979.

Booth, Wayne C. *The Rhetoric of Fiction*. Chicago: University of Chicago Press, 1961.

Boyle, Nicholas. 'Understanding Thatcherism'. *New Blackfriars* 69 (1988): 307–24.

Bradley, A. C. *Oxford Lectures on Poetry*. London: Macmillan, 1950.

Brockelman, Paul. *The Inside Story: A Narrative Approach to Religious Understanding and Truth*. Albany, New York: State University of New York Press, 1992.

Bruns, Gerald L. *Hermeneutics Ancient and Modern*. New Haven and London: Yale University Press, 1992.

Burnham, Frederic B. (ed.). *Postmodern Theology: Christian Faith in a Pluralist World*. San Francisco: Harper Collins, 1989.

Byrne, Peter. *Natural Religion and the Nature of Religion: The Legacy of Deism*. London and New York: Routledge, 1989.

Cameron, Averil. *Christianity and the Rhetoric of Empire: The Development of Christian Discourse*. Berkeley: University of California Press, 1991.

Caputo, John D. *Demythologising Heidegger*. Bloomington and Indianapolis: Indiana University Press, 1993.

Connelly, Joseph (ed.). *Hymns of the Roman Liturgy*. Westminster, Maryland: Newman Press, 1957.

Corner, Mark. Review of *The Nature of Doctrine* by George Lindbeck. *Modern Theology* 3 (1986): 110–13.

Cowper, William. *The Poems of William Cowper*. Edited by J. C. Bailey. London: Methuen and Company.

Crites, Stephen. 'The narrative quality of experience'. In Hauerwas, Stanley and L. Gregory Jones (eds.) *Why Narrative? Readings in Narrative Theology*. Grand Rapids, Michigan: William B. Eerdmans Publishing Company, 1989. 65–88.

Crossan, John Dominic. *The Historical Jesus: The Life of a Mediterranean Jewish Peasant*. Edinburgh: T. and T. Clark, 1991.

Culpepper, R. Alan. *Anatomy of the Fourth Gospel: A Study in Literary Design*. Philadelphia: Fortress Press, 1983.

Cupitt, Don. *Taking Leave of God*. London: SCM Press, 1980.

The Long-Legged Fly: A Theology of Language and Desire. London: SCM Press, 1987.

Creation Out of Nothing. London: SCM Press, 1990.

What is a Story? London: SCM Press, 1991.

The Time Being. London: SCM Press, 1992.

'Unsystematic ethics and politics'. In Berry, Phillipa and Andrew Wernick (eds.) *Shadow of Spirit: Postmodernism and Religion*. London: Routledge, 1992. 149–55.

After All: Religion Without Alienation. London: SCM Press, 1994.

Curtis, Philip. *A Hawk Among Sparrows: A Biography of Austin Farrer*. London: SPCK, 1985.

Curtius, Ernst Robert. *European Literature and the Latin Middle Ages*. Translated by Willard R. Trask. London: Routledge and Kegan Paul, 1953.

Dawkins, Richard. 'Is God a computer virus?' *New Statesman and Society* 18 December 1992/1 January 1993: 42–5.

D'Costa, Gavin. 'Revelation and revelations: discerning God in other religions'. *Modern Theology* 10 (1994): 165–83.

Deconinck-Brossard, Françoise. 'England and France in the eighteenth century'. In Prickett, Stephen (ed.) *Reading the Text: Biblical Criticism and Literary Theory*. Oxford: Basil Blackwell, 1991. 136–81.

Derrida, Jacques. *Of Grammatology*. Translated by Gayatri Chakravorty Spivak. Baltimore and London: Johns Hopkins University Press, [1967] 1976.

Limited Inc. Translated by Samuel Weber and Jeffrey Mehlman. Evanston, Illinois: Northwestern University Press, 1988.

Of Spirit: Heidegger and the Question. Translated by Geoffrey Bennington and Rachel Bowlby. Chicago: University of Chicago Press, 1989.

Given Time: 1. Counterfeit Money. Translated by Peggy Kamuf. Chicago and London: The University of Chicago Press, 1992.

DiNoia, J. A. OP. *The Diversity of Religions: A Christian Perspective*. Washington, DC: Catholic University of America Press, 1992.

Eagleton, Terry. *The Ideology of the Aesthetic*. Oxford: Basil Blackwell, 1990.

'Discourse and discos: theory in the space between culture and capitalism'. *Times Literary Supplement* 15 July 1994: 3–4.

Eco, Umberto. *Semiotics and the Philosophy of Language*. London: Macmillan, 1984.

Evans, G. R. *The Language and Logic of the Bible: The Earlier Middle Ages*. Cambridge: Cambridge University Press, 1984.

Falck, Colin. *Myth, Truth and Literature: Towards a True Post-Modernism*. Cambridge: Cambridge University Press, 1989.

Farrer, Austin. *The Glass of Vision*. Westminster: Dacre Press, 1948.

The Rebirth of Images: The Making of St John's Apocalypse. Westminster: Dacre Press, 1949.

'On dispensing with Q'. In Nineham, D. E. (ed.) *Studies in the Gospels*. Oxford: Basil Blackwell, 1955. 55–88.

Interpretation and Belief. Edited by Charles C. Conti. London: SPCK, 1976.

Ferreira, M. Jamie. *Doubt and Religious Commitment: The Role of the Will in Newman's Thought*. Oxford: Clarendon Press, 1980.

Fish, Stanley. *Doing What Comes Naturally: Change, Rhetoric, and the Practice of Theory in Literary and Legal Studies*. Oxford: Clarendon Press, 1989.

Fitzpatrick, P. J. [Egner, G.] 'Some thoughts on the eucharistic presence'. In McCabe, Herbert. *God Matters*. London: Geoffrey Chapman, 1987. 130–45.

In Breaking of Bread: The Eucharist and Ritual. Cambridge: Cambridge University Press, 1993.

Ford, David. *Barth and God's Story: Biblical Narrative and the Theological Method of Karl Barth in the 'Church Dogmatics'*. Studies in the Intercultural History of Christianity vol. 27. Frankfurt am Main and Berne: Verlag Peter Lang, 1981.

The Forgotten Trinity 1: The Report of the BCC Study Commission on Trinitarian Doctrine Today. British Council of Churches, 1989.

Fowl, Stephen E. and L. Gregory Jones. *Reading in Communion: Scripture and Ethics in Christian Life*. Biblical Foundations in Theology. London: SPCK, 1991.

Fox, Robin Lane. *The Unauthorized Version: Truth and Fiction in the Bible*. London: Viking, 1991.

Frei, Hans W. *The Eclipse of Biblical Narrative: A Study in Eighteenth and Nineteenth Century Hermeneutics*. New Haven and London: Yale University Press, 1974.

The Identity of Jesus Christ: The Hermeneutical Bases of Dogmatic Theology. Philadelphia: Fortress Press, 1975.

Types of Christian Theology. Edited by George Hunsinger and William C. Placher. New Haven: Yale University Press, 1992.

Theology and Narrative: Selected Essays. Edited by George Hunsinger and William C. Placher. New York and Oxford: Oxford University Press, 1993.

Frye, Northrop. *The Great Code: The Bible and Literature*. London: Routledge, 1982.

Fukuyama, Francis. *The End of History and the Last Man*. London: Hamish Hamilton, 1992.

Funk, Robert W. *The Poetics of Biblical Narrative*. Sonoma, California: Polebridge Press, 1988.

Gabel, John B. and Charles B. Wheeler. *The Bible as Literature: An Introduction*. New York and Oxford: Oxford University Press, 1986.

Gadamer, Hans-Georg. *Truth and Method*. London: Sheed and Ward, 1975.

Geertz, Clifford. *The Interpretation of Cultures: Selected Essays*. New York: Basic Books, 1973.

Gellrich, Jesse M. *The Idea of the Book in the Middle Ages: Language Theory, Mythology, and Fiction*. Ithaca and London: Cornell University Press, 1985.

Genette, Gérard. *Narrative Discourse*. Translated by Jane E. Levin. Oxford: Basil Blackwell, 1980.

Gilby OP, Thomas. 'The senses of Scripture'. Appendix 12 in St Thomas Aquinas, *Summa Theologiæ*, vol. 1. Edited by Thomas Gilby OP. London: Blackfriars Eyre and Spottiswoode, 1964. 140–41.

Gnuse, Robert. *The Authority of the Bible: Theories of Inspiration, Revelation and the Canon of Scripture*. New York and Mahwah: Paulist Press, 1985.

de Graef, Ortwin. *Serenity in Crisis: A Preface to Paul de Man, 1939–1960*. Lincoln and London: University of Nebraska Press, 1993.

Green, Garret (ed.). *Scriptural Authority and Narrative Interpretation: Essays on the Occasion of the Sixty-Fifth Birthday of Hans W. Frei*. Philadelphia: Fortress Press, 1987.

Grimes, Ronald L. *Ritual Criticism: Case Studies in Its Practice, Essays on Its Theory*. Columbia, South Carolina: University of South Carolina Press, 1990.

Gustafson, James M. 'The sectarian temptation: reflections on theology, the Church, and the university'. *Proceedings of the Catholic Theological Society* 40 (1985): 83–94.

Gutierrez, Gustavo. *A Theology of Liberation*. London: SCM Press, 1983.

Hardy, Barbara. 'Towards a poetics of fiction: an approach through narrative'. *Novel* 2 (1968): 5–14.

Hart, Kevin. *The Trespass of the Sign: Deconstruction, Theology and Philosophy*. Cambridge: Cambridge University Press, 1989.

Hauerwas, Stanley. *A Community of Character*. Notre Dame, Indiana: University of Notre Dame Press, 1981.

The Peaceable Kingdom: A Primer in Christian Ethics. London: SCM Press, [1983] 1984.

'The church as God's new language'. In Green, Garrett (ed.) *Scriptural Authority and Narrative Interpretation*. Philadelphia: Fortress Press, 1987. 179–98.

Unleashing the Scripture: Freeing the Bible from Captivity to America. Nashville, Tennessee: Abingdon Press, 1993.

Dispatches from the Front: Theological Engagements with the Secular. Durham and London: Duke University Press, 1994.

Hauerwas, Stanley and L. Gregory Jones (eds.) *Why Narrative? Readings in Narrative Theology*. Grand Rapids, Michigan: William B. Eerdmans Publishing Company, 1989.

Hegel, G. W. F. *Lectures on Fine Art*, 2 vols. Translated by T. M. Knox. Oxford: Clarendon Press, 1975.

Hegel on Tragedy. Edited by Anne and Henry Paolucci. Westport, Connecticut: Greenwood Press, [1962] 1978.

Hick, John. *An Interpretation of Religion: Human Responses to the Transcendent*. London: Macmillan, 1989.

Hugh of St Victor. *The Didascalicon of Hugh of St Victor: A Medieval Guide to the Arts*. Translated with an introduction by Jerome Taylor. Records of Western Civilization. New York: Columbia University Press, [1961] 1991.

Hunsinger, George. *How to Read Karl Barth: The Shape of His Theology*. New York and Oxford: Oxford University Press, 1991.

'Afterword: Hans Frei as theologian'. In Frei, Hans. *Theology and Narrative: Selected Essays*. New York: Oxford University Press, 1933. 235–70.

Irvine, Martin. *The Making of Textual Culture: 'Grammatica' and Literary Theory, 350–1100*. Cambridge Studies in Medieval Literature vol. 19. Cambridge: Cambridge University Press, 1994.

Jameson, Fredric. 'Postmodernism and consumer society'. In Hal Foster (ed.) *Postmodern Culture*. London: Pluto Press, 1985. 111–25.

Postmodernism, or the Cultural Logic of Late Capitalism. London: Verso, 1991.

Jencks, Charles. 'The rise of post-modern architecture'. *Architectural Association Quarterly* 7/4 (1975): 3–14.

Language of Post-Modern Architecture. New York: Rizzoli, 1977.

The Post-Modern Reader. London and New York: Academy Editions and St Martin's Press, 1992.

Jenson, Robert W. 'The Christian Doctrine of God'. In Wainwright, Geoffrey (ed.) *Keeping the Faith: Essays to Mark the Centenary of Lux Mundi*. London: SPCK, 1989. 25–53.

'The Hauerwas project'. *Modern Theology* 8 (1992): 285–95.

John Paul II. *Centesimus Annus*. London: CTS Publications, 1991.

John of Salisbury. *The Metalogicon of John of Salisbury*. Translated by Daniel D. McGarry. Berkeley: University of California Press, 1955.

Josipovici, Gabriel. *The Book of God: A Response to the Bible*. New Haven and London: Yale University Press, 1988.

Jüngel, Eberhard. *God as the Mystery of the World: On the Foundation of the Theology of the Crucified One in the Dispute Between Theism and Atheism*. Translated by Darrell L. Guder. Grand Rapids, Michigan: William B. Eerdmans Publishing Company, 1983. 299–314.

Kasper, Walter. *Jesus the Christ*. Translated by V. Green. London: Burns and Oates, 1976.

Kelber, Werner H. *Mark's Story of Jesus*. Philadelphia: Fortress Press, 1979.

Kelsey, David H. *The Uses of Scripture in Recent Theology*. Philadelphia: Fortress Press, 1975.

Kermode, Frank. *The Genesis of Secrecy: On the Interpretation of Narrative*. Cambridge, Massachusetts and London: Harvard University Press, 1979.

Kerr, Fergus. 'Frei's types'. *New Blackfriars* 75 (1994): 184–93.

Kimel, Alvin F. 'The God who likes his name: Holy Trinity, feminism, and the language of faith'. *Interpretation* 45 (1991): 147–58.

Kingsbury, Jack Dean. *Matthew as Story*, second edition. Philadelphia: Fortress Press, 1988.

Kort, Wesley A. *Story, Text and Scripture: Literary Interests in Biblical Narrative*. University Park and London: The Pennsylvania State University Press, 1988.

Lash, Nicholas. *Newman on Development*. London: Sheed and Ward, 1975.

Theology on the Way to Emmaus. London: SCM Press, 1986.

'Considering the Trinity'. *Modern Theology* 2 (1986): 183–96.

'When did the theologians lose interest in theology?' In Marshall, Bruce D. (ed.) *Theology and Dialogue: Essays in Conversation with George Lindbeck*. Notre Dame, Indiana: University of Notre Dame Press, 1990. 131–47.

Believing Three Ways in One God: A Reading of the Apostles' Creed. London: SCM Press, 1992.

'Not exactly politics or power?' *Modern Theology* 8 (1992): 353–64.

'The end of history?' *Concilium* (1994): 6/47–56.

Le Corbusier. *Towards a New Architecture*. Translated by Frederick Etchells. London: The Architectural Press, 1927.

Levenson, Jon D. *The Hebrew Bible, the Old Testament, and Historical Criticism: Jews and Christians in Biblical Studies*. Louisville, Kentucky: Westminster/John Knox Press, 1993.

Lindbeck, George. *The Nature of Doctrine: Religion and Theology in a Postliberal Age*. London: SPCK, 1984.

'The story-shaped Church: critical exegesis and theological interpretation'. In Green, Garret (ed.) *Scriptural Authority and Narrative Interpretation*. Philadelphia: Fortress Press, 1987. 161–78.

'Scripture, consensus, and community'. In Richard John Neuhaus (ed.) *Biblical Interpretation in Crisis: The Ratzinger Conference on Bible and Church*. Grand Rapids, Michigan: Eerdmans, 1989. 74–101.

'Response to Bruce Marshall'. *The Thomist* 53 (1989): 403–6.

Loewe, Raphael. 'The "plain" meaning of Scripture in early Jewish exegesis'. *Papers of the Institute of Jewish Studies in London* 1 (1964): 140–85.

Lonergan, Bernard. *Method in Theology*. London: Darton, Longman and Todd, 1972.

The Way to Nicea: The Dialectical Development of Trinitarian Theology. Translated by Conn O'Donovan. London: Darton, Longman and Todd, 1976.

Loughlin, Gerard. 'On telling the story of Jesus'. *Theology* 87 (1984): 323–29.

'Myths, signs and significations'. *Theology* 89 (1986): 268–75.

'Noumenon and phenomena'. *Religious Studies* 23 (1987): 493–508.

'See-saying/say-seeing'. *Theology* 91 (1988): 201–9.

'Making it plain: Austin Farrer and the inspiration of scripture'. In Loades, Ann and Michael McLain (eds.) *Hermeneutics, the Bible and Literary Criticism*. London: Macmillan, 1992. 96–112.

'Christianity at the end of the story or the return of the master-narrative'. *Modern Theology* 8 (1992): 365–84.

'Writing the Trinity'. *Theology* 97 (1994): 82–9.

'Using scripture: community and letterality'. In Davies, Jon, Graham Harvey and Wilfred G. E. Watson (eds.) *Words Remembered, Texts Renewed: Essays in Honour of John F. A. Sawyer*. Sheffield: Sheffield Academic Press, 1995. 321–39.

Lowe, Walter. *Theology and Difference: The Wound of Reason*. Bloomington and Indianapolis: Indiana University Press, 1993.

Lukács, Georg. *The Theory of the Novel: A Historico-Philosophical Essay on the Forms of Great Epic Literature*. Translated by Anna Bostock. London: Merlin Press, 1971.

Lyotard, Jean-François. *The Postmodern Condition: A Report on Knowledge*. Translated by Geoff Bennington and Brian Massumi. Foreword by Frederic Jameson. Theory and History of Literature vol. 10. Manchester: Manchester University Press, 1984.

The Differend: Phrases in Dispute. Translated by Georges Van Den Abbeele. Manchester: Manchester University Press, [1983] 1988.

The Lyotard Reader. Edited by Andrew Benjamin. Oxford: Basil Blackwell, 1989.

Heidegger and 'the Jews'. Translated by Andreas Michel and Mark S. Roberts. Minneapolis: University of Minnesota Press, 1990.

The Postmodern Explained to Children: Correspondence 1982–1985. Translated by Julian Pefanis and Morgan Thomas. London: Turnaround, 1992.

Lyotard, Jean-François and Jean-Loup Thébaud. *Just Gaming*. Translated by Wlad Godzich. Theory and History of Literature vol. 20. Manchester: Manchester University Press, 1985.

MacIntyre, Alasdair. *After Virtue: A Study in Moral Theory*, second edition. London: Duckworth, 1985.

MacKinnon, Donald. *The Problem of Metaphysics*. Cambridge: Cambridge University Press, 1974.

Malbon, Elizabeth Struthers. 'Narrative criticism: how does the story mean?' In Capel, Janice and Stephen D. Moore. *Mark and Method: New Approaches in Biblical Studies*. Minneapolis: Fortress Press, 1992. 23–49.

Man, Paul de. *Blindness and Insight: Essays in the Rhetoric of Contemporary Criticism*, second edition. London: Methuen and Co. Ltd, 1983.

Mandel, Ernst. *Late Capitalism*. London: Verso, 1978.

Marion, Jean-Luc. *God Without Being: Hors Texte*. Translated by Thomas A. Carlson. Chicago: University of Chicago Press, 1991.

'Metaphysics and phenomenology: a relief for theology'. Translated by Thomas A. Carlson. *Critical Inquiry* 20 (1994): 572–91.

Markham, Ian S. *Plurality and Christian Ethics*. New Studies in Christian Ethics. Cambridge: Cambridge University Press, 1994.

Marshall, Bruce D. *Christology in Conflict: The Identity of a Saviour in Rahner and Barth*. Oxford: Basil Blackwell, 1987.

'Aquinas as postliberal theologian'. *The Thomist* 53 (1989): 353–402.

'Absorbing the world: Christianity and the universe of truths'. In Marshall, Bruce D. (ed.) *Theology and Dialogue*. Notre Dame, Indiana: Notre Dame University Press, 1990. 69–102.

Marshall, Bruce D. (ed.). *Theology and Dialogue: Essays in Conversation with George Lindbeck*. Notre Dame, Indiana: University of Notre Dame Press, 1990.

Mauss, Marcel. *The Gift: The Form and Reason for Exchange in Archaic Societies*. Translated by W. D. Halls. London: Routledge, [1923–24] 1990.

McCabe, Herbert OP. *God Matters*. London: Geoffrey Chapman, 1987.

McPartlan, Paul. *The Eucharist Makes the Church: Henri de Lubac and John Zizioulas in Dialogue*. Edinburgh: T. and T. Clark, 1993.

Meynell, Hugo A. 'Faith, objectivity, and historical falsifiability'. In Davies, Brian OP (ed.) *Language, Meaning and God: Essays in Honour of Herbert McCabe OP*. London: Geoffrey Chapman, 1987. 145–161.

Michalson, Gordon E. Jr. 'The response to Lindbeck'. *Modern Theology* 4 (1988): 107–20.

Middleton, Deborah F. 'The story of Mary: Luke's version'. *New Blackfriars* 70 (1989): 555–64.

Milbank, John. *Theology and Social Theory: Beyond Secular Reason*. Oxford: Basil Blackwell, 1990.

'"Postmodern critical Augustinianism": a short summa in forty-two responses to unasked questions'. *Modern Theology* 7 (1991): 225–37.

'The name of Jesus: incarnation, atonement, ecclesiology'. *Modern Theology* 7 (1991): 311–33.

'Can a gift be given? Prolegomena to a future trinitarian metaphysic'. *Modern Theology* 11 (1995): 119–61.

Mink, Louis O. 'History and fiction as modes of comprehension'. *New Literary History* 1 (1970): 541–58.

Moberly, Walter. '"Old Testament" and "New Testament": the propriety of the terms for Christian theology'. *Theology* 95 (1992): 26–32.

Moore OP, Gareth. 'Transubstantiation for beginners'. *New Blackfriars* 67 (1986): 530–537.

Moore, Stephen D. *Literary Criticism and the Gospels: The Theoretical Challenge*. New Haven and London: Yale University Press, 1989.

Moss, David. 'Costly giving: on Jean-Luc Marion's theology of gift'. *New Blackfriars* 74 (1993): 393–9.

Nancy, Jean-Luc. *The Inoperative Community*. Edited by Peter Connor. Theory and History of Literature vol. 76. Minneapolis and Oxford: University of Minnesota Press, 1991.

Neurath, Otto. *Empiricism and Sociology*. Edited by M. Neurath and R. S. Cohen. Dordrecht: D. Reidel Publishing Company, 1973.

Newman, John Henry. *On the Inspiration of Scripture*. Edited with an introduction by J. Derek Holmes and Robert Murray SJ. London: Geoffrey Chapman, 1967.

Letters and Diaries of John Henry Newman, vol. 25. Edited by C. S. Dessain and Thomas Gornall SJ. Oxford: Clarendon Press, 1973.

An Essay in Aid of a Grammar of Assent. Introduced by Nicholas Lash. Notre Dame, Indiana: University of Notre Dame Press, [1870] 1979.

Norris, Christopher. *Paul de Man: Deconstruction and the Critique of Aesthetic Ideology*. London: Routledge, 1988.

Norton, David. *A History of the Bible as Literature*, 2 vols. Cambridge: Cambridge University Press, 1993.

Novak, Michael. *The Spirit of Democratic Capitalism*. London: IEA Health and Welfare Unit, [1982] 1991.

O'Neill, Colman E. 'The rule theory of doctrine and propositional truth'. *The Thomist* 49 (1985): 417–42.

Patrides, C. A. *The Grand Design of God: The Literary Form of the Christian View of History*. London: Routledge and Kegan Paul, 1972.

Phillips, D. Z. *Faith and Philosophical Enquiry*. London: Routledge and Kegan Paul, 1970.

'Lindbeck's audience'. *Modern Theology* 4 (1988): 133–154.

Faith After Foundationalism. London: Routledge, 1988.

Pickstock, Catherine. 'The sacred as polis: language as synactic event'. *Literature and Theology* 8 (1994): 367–83.

Plato. *The Republic*. Translated by Desmond Lee. Revised second edition. Harmondsworth: Penguin Books, 1987.

Poland, Lynn M. *Literary Criticism and Biblical Hermeneutics: A Critique of Formalist Approaches*. AAR Academy Series vol. 48. Chico, CA: Scholars Press, 1985.

Powell, Mark Allan. *What is Narrative Criticism? A New Approach to the Bible*. London: SPCK, [1990] 1993.

'Toward a narrative-critical understanding of Mark'. *Interpretation* 47 (1993): 341–46.

Pseudo-Dionysius. *The Complete Works*. Translated by Colm Luibheid. New York: Paulist Press, 1987.

Rahner, Karl and Herbert Vorgrimler. *Concise Theological Dictionary*, second edition. London: Burns and Oates, 1983.

Readings, Bill. *Introducing Lyotard: Art and Politics*. London: Routledge, 1991.

Reeves, Marjorie. 'The Bible and literary authorship in the middle ages'. In Prickett, Stephen (ed.) *Reading the Text: Biblical Criticism and Literary Theory*. Oxford: Basil Blackwell, 1991. 12–63.

Reventlow, Henning Graf. *The Authority of the Bible and the Rise of the Modern World*. Translated by John Bowden. London: SCM Press, [1980] 1984.

Rhoads, David and Donald Michie. *Mark as Story: An Introduction to the Narrative of a Gospel*. Philadelphia: Fortress Press, 1982.

Ricoeur, Paul. *Freedom and Nature: The Voluntary and the Involuntary*. Evanston: Northwestern University Press, [1950] 1966.

Hermeneutics and the Human Sciences: Essays on Language, Action and Interpretation. Edited and translated by John B. Thompson. Cambridge: Cambridge University Press, 1981.

'On interpretation'. In Montefiore, Alan (ed.) *Philosophy in France Today*. Cambridge: Cambridge University Press, 1983. 175–97.

Time and Narrative, 3 vols. Translated by Kathleen McLaughlin/ Blamey and David Pellauer. Chicago and London: The University of Chicago Press, 1984–1988.

'Life in quest of narrative'. In David Wood (ed.) *Paul Ricoeur: Narrative and Interpretation*. Warwick Studies in Philosophy and Literature. London and New York: Routledge, 1991. 20–33.

Robinson, John A. T. *Honest to God*. London: SCM Press, 1963.

Root, Michael. 'The narrative structure of soteriology'. *Modern Theology* 2 (1986): 145–58. Reprinted in Hauerwas, Stanley and L. Gregory Jones (eds.) *Why Narrative? Readings in Narrative Theology*. Grand Rapids, Michigan: William B. Eerdmans Publishing Company, 1989. 263–78.

Rorem, Paul. *Pseudo-Dionysius: A Commentary on the Texts and an Introduction to Their Influence*. New York: Oxford University Press, 1993.

Rose, Gillian. *The Broken Middle: Out of Our Ancient Society*. Oxford: Basil Blackwell, 1992.

Rose, Margaret A. *Parody: Ancient, Modern, and Post-Modern*. Literature, Culture, Theory vol. 5. Cambridge: Cambridge University Press, 1993.

Rubin, Miri. *Corpus Christi: The Eucharist in Late Medieval Culture*. Cambridge: Cambridge University Press, 1991.

Salmon, Rachel and Gerda Elata-Alster. 'Retracing a writerly text: in the footsteps of a midrashic sequence on the creation of the male and female'. In Loades, Ann and Michael McLain (eds.) *Hermeneutics, the Bible and Literary Criticism*. London: Macmillan, 1992. 177–97.

Sanders, E. P. *The Historical Figure of Jesus*. London: Allen Lane/Penguin Press, 1993.

Sawyer, John F. A. 'Combating prejudices about the Bible and Judaism'. *Theology* 94 (1991): 269–78.

Schneidau, Herbert N. *Sacred Discontent: The Bible and Western Tradition*. Baton Rouge: Louisiana State University Press, 1976.

Scholes, Robert and Robert Kellog. *The Nature of Narrative*. New York: Oxford University Press, 1966.

Schwartz, Regina M. (ed.). *The Book and the Text: The Bible and Literary Theory*. Oxford: Basil Blackwell, 1989.

Schweitzer, Albert. *The Quest of the Historical Jesus: A Critical Study of Its Progress from Reimarus to Wrede*. New York: Macmillan, [1906] 1968.

Sewell, Richard. *The Vision of Tragedy*. New Haven: Yale University Press, 1959.

Simon, Martin. 'Identity and analogy: Balthasar's Hölderlin and Hamann'. In Riches, John (ed.) *The Analogy of Beauty: The Theology of Hans Urs von Balthasar*. Edinburgh: T. and T. Clark, 1986. 77–104.

Simon, Ulrich. *Pity and Terror: Christianity and Tragedy*. London: Macmillan, 1989.

Smalley, Beryl. *The Study of the Bible in the Middle Ages*. Oxford: Clarendon Press, 1941.

Smith, Lesley. 'The theology of the twelfth- and thirteenth-century Bible'. In Gameson, Richard (ed.) *The Early Medieval Bible: Its Production, Decoration and Use*. Cambridge: Cambridge University Press, 1994. 223–32.

Smith, Ronald Gregor. *J. G. Hamann 1730–1788: A Study in Christian Existence*. London: Collins, 1960.

Soskice, Janet Martin. 'Trinity and "the feminine other"'. *New Blackfriars* 75 (1994): 2–17.

Spinoza, Benedict de. *The Chief Works of Benedict de Spinoza*, 2 vols. Translated by R. H. M. Elwes. New York: Dover Publications, 1951.

Spong, John Shelby. *Born of a Woman: A Bishop Rethinks the Birth of Jesus*. San Francisco: Harper Collins, 1992.

Steiner, George. *The Death of Tragedy*. London: Faber and Faber, 1961.

'A note on absolute tragedy'. *Literature and Theology* 4 (1990): 147–56.

Sternberg, Meir. *The Poetics of Biblical Narrative: Ideological Literature and the Drama of Reading*. Bloomington, Indiana: Indiana University Press, 1985.

Strauss. D. F. *The Life of Jesus Critically Examined*. London: SCM Press, [1835] 1973.
Stroup, George W. *The Promise of Narrative Theology*. London: SCM Press, [1981] 1984.
Studer, Basil. *Trinity and Incarnation: The Faith of the Early Church*. Translated by Matthias Westerhoff. Edited by Andrew Louth. Edinburgh: T. and T. Clark, 1993.
Surin, Kenneth. *The Turnings of Darkness and Light: Essays in Philosophical and Systematic Theology*. Cambridge: Cambridge University Press, 1989.
Sutherland, Stewart R. 'Christianity and tragedy'. *Literature and Theology* 4 (1990): 157–68.
Tannehill, Robert C. *The Narrative Unity of Luke-Acts: A Literary Interpretation*. Philadelphia: Fortress Press, 1986.
Tanner, Kathryn E. 'Theology and the plain sense'. In Green, Garret (ed.) *Scriptural Authority and Narrative Interpretation*. Philadelphia: Fortress Press, 1987. 59–78.
Taylor, Mark C. *Journeys to Selfhood: Hegel and Kierkegaard*. Berkeley: University of California Press, 1980.
Deconstructing Theology. Atlanta, Georgia: Scholars Press, 1982.
Erring: A Postmodern A/Theology. Chicago: University of Chicago Press, 1984.
Altarity. Chicago: University of Chicago Press, 1987.
Disfiguring: Art, Architecture, Religion. Chicago: University of Chicago Press, 1992.
Nots. Chicago: Chicago University Press, 1993.
Taylor, Mark C. and Esa Saarinen. *Imagologies: Media Philosophy*. London: Routledge, 1994.
Thiemann, Ronald F. *Revelation and Theology: The Gospel as Narrated Promise*. Notre Dame, Indiana: University of Notre Dame Press, 1984.
Thistelwaite, Susan Brooks. 'On the Trinity'. *Interpretation* 45 (1991): 159–71.
Tilley, Terrence F. 'Incommensurability, intratextuality, and fideism'. *Modern Theology* 5 (1989): 87–117.
Tracy, David. 'Lindbeck's new program for theology: a reflection'. *The Thomist* 49 (1985): 460–72.
Trible, Phyllis. *Texts of Terror: Literary–Feminist Readings of Biblical Narratives*. Overtures to Biblical Theology vol. 13. Philadelphia: Fortress Press, 1984.
Tulloch, John. 'Dr Newman's *Grammar of Assent*'. *The Edinburgh Review* 132 (October 1870): 382–414.
Vanhoozer, Kevin J. *Biblical Narrative in the Philosophy of Paul Ricoeur:*

A Study in Hermeneutics and Theology. Cambridge: Cambridge University Press, 1990.

'Philosophical antecedents to Ricoeur's *Time and Narrative*'. In Wood, David (ed.) *Paul Ricoeur: Narrative and Interpretation*. Warwick Studies in Philosophy and Literature. London and New York: Routledge, 1991. 34–54.

Wainwright, Geoffrey. 'The doctrine of the Trinity: where the Church stands or falls'. *Interpretation* 45 (1991): 117–32.

Wallace, Mark I. *The Second Naiveté: Barth, Ricoeur, and the New Yale Theology*. Studies in American Biblical Hermeneutics vol. 6. Macon, Georgia: Mercer University Press, 1990.

Ward, Graham. 'Barth and postmodernism'. *New Blackfriars* 74 (1993): 550–6.

Watson, Francis. 'Is revelation an "event"?' *Modern Theology* 10 (1994): 383–99.

Welch, Claude. *Protestant Thought in the Nineteenth Century*, 2 vols. New Haven and London: Yale University Press, 1972.

White, Graham. 'Karl Barth's theological realism'. *Neue Zeitschrift für Systematische Theologie und Religionsphilosophie* 26 (1984): 54–70.

White, Hayden. *Metahistory: The Historical Imagination in Nineteenth-Century Europe*. Baltimore: Johns Hopkins University Press, 1973.

Tropics of Discourse: Essays in Cultural Criticism. Baltimore: John Hopkins University Press, 1978.

'The metaphysics of narrativity: time and symbol in Ricoeur's philosophy of history'. In Wood, David (ed.) *On Paul Ricoeur: Narrative and Interpretation*. London and New York: Routledge, 1991. 140–59.

Wiesel, Elie. *The Gates of the Forest*. Translated by Frances Frenaye. New York: Holt, Rinehart and Winston, 1966.

Wiles, Maurice. *The Remaking of Christian Doctrine*. London: SCM Press, 1974.

'Scriptural authority and theological construction: the limitations of narrative interpretation'. In Green, Garrett (ed.) *Scriptural Authority and Narrative Interpretation*. Philadelphia: Fortress Press, 1987. 42–58.

Williams, Rowan D. 'Language, reality and desire in Augustine's *De Doctrina*'. *Literature and Theology* 3 (1989): 138–50.

'Postmodern theology and the judgement of the world'. In Burnham, Frederic B. (ed.) *Postmodern Theology*. San Francisco: Harper Collins, 1989. 92–112.

'The literal sense of Scripture'. *Modern Theology* 7 (1991): 121–34.

'Saving time: thoughts on practice, patience and vision'. *New Blackfriars* 73 (1992): 319–26.

Open to Judgement: Sermons and Addresses. London: Darton, Longman and Todd, 1994.

Wittgenstein, Ludwig. *On Certainty*. Edited by G. E. M. Anscombe and G. E. von Wright. Translated by G. E. M. Anscombe. Oxford: Basil Blackwell, [1967] 1981.

Culture and Value. Translated by P. Winch. Oxford: Basil Blackwell, [1977] 1980.

Wood, Charles M. *The Formation of Christian Understanding: An Essay in Theological Hermeneutics*. Philadelphia: Westminster Press, 1981.

Wright, T. R. *Theology and Literature*. Oxford: Basil Blackwell, 1987.

Wyschogrod, Edith. *Saints and Postmodernism: Revisioning Moral Philosophy*. Chicago and London: University of Chicago Press, 1990.

Young, Frances. 'Can there be any evidence?' In Goulder, Michael (ed.) *Incarnation and Myth: The Debate Continued*. London: SCM Press, 1979. 62.

The Art of Performance: Towards a Theology of Holy Scripture. London: Darton, Longman and Todd 1992.

Zizioulas, John D. *Being as Communion: Studies in Personhood and the Church*. Contemporary Greek Thinkers vol. 4. Crestwood, New York: St Vladimir's Seminary Press, 1993.

Index